A STAR BOOK

AL CAPONE

The Biography of a Self-Made Man

By

FRED D. PASLEY

GARDEN CITY PUBLISHING COMPANY

GARDEN CITY, NEW YORK

INJURED INNOCENCE (?)

"*What you got on me, chief?*" is Al's usual question
when he is suspected of some crime. The answer
so far has been "*Nothing.*" He is here seen with
Commissioner of Detectives, John Srege.

AL CAPONE

THE BIOGRAPHY OF A SELF-MADE MAN

PART ONE

IN the barber-shop of the twenty and one shaving-mugs, Amato Gasperri, proprietor, was inking black crosses opposite the names of John Scalise and Albert Anselmi.

"Such nize boys," he was saying, wagging his head sadly.

They had just been taken for a ride, along with Joseph Guinta—the dancing torpedo with the chilled-steel eyes, who sought to rule Chicago's Unione Sicilione and its $10,000,000 a year alky-cooking guild, biggest subsidiary of the city's $60,000,000-a-year illicit liquor industry.

Old patrons of Amato, these, like those others whose names in gilt Spencerian script embellished the cups in the wall rack fronting his chair. His shop was their rendezvous in happier days. Fast friends, then, cronies; some waiters, some bartenders, some street cleaners, some owners of vegetable stores, ice-cream parlors, or confectioneries. Amato has lost nineteen of his best cash customers. Nineteen crosses. Nineteen such nize boys killing each other—taking each other for rides.

He can't understand. As he stood there in his white starched jacket and apron, dolorously engaged in his pen ritual, the simple-minded little baldheaded barber was a pathetic figure, bewildered at the sudden and dubious celebrity thrust upon him by the freakish twist of the fortunes of bootleg war.

"Yes," darting a fearsome glance about, and lowering his voice, "only two left—Johnny Torrio and Al Capone."

He reached for Torrio's cup.

"I marked a cross for Johnny once, but rubbed it off. You remember. Everybody thought he was as good as dead."

He meant the time Torrio stopped four shotgun slugs and a revolver bullet in the jaw as he and Mrs. Torrio motored up to the curb of their South Side home.

Such nize boys.

"Al and Johnny would drop in for a game of pinochle or to talk about the ponies or what grand opera they were going to next," he was saying.

Generally, it would be Verdi. The discriminating Capone was partial to both *Rigoletto* and *Il Trovatore*, but *Aïda* was his favorite, and in its opulent score there was nothing comparable to the tenor aria, sung by Rhadames when he returns victorious from the wars to declare his love for the captive princess.

This reminded Amato that James Colosimo likewise had a passion for grand opera; Big Jim, whose shaving-mug tops the rack of the twenty and one; who was wont to reminisce of his immigrant beginnings, when often he didn't have the price of a flop; who started as water boy for a railroad section-gang, became a city white-wing, and rose to be a millionaire cabaret owner; friend of Amelita Galli-Curci, Luisa Tetrazzini, George M. Cohan, Cleofonte Campanini, and Caruso.

Since the March morning in 1920 when Big Jim slumped to the floor of his café with a bullet in the brain, more than five hundred men have died in gangster slayings. Out of the carnage, in 1927, Capone emerged supreme and unchallenged as Chicago's bootleg boss—the John D. Rockefeller of some twenty thousand anti-Volstead filling-stations—controlling the sources of supply from Canada and the Florida east coast and the operations of local wildcat breweries and distilleries; frequently referred to as the municipal cabinet member without portfolio—commissioner of lawlessness. New York City has a monument to civic virtue. Capone is Chicago's monument to civic thirst.

To the upright drys he was anathema, to the downright wets a public benefactor, to the politicians Santa Claus.

Coming to Chicago in 1920 an impecunious hoodlum, in 1929 he was estimated by attachés of the internal revenue service to be worth $20,000,000. This seems unbelievable, which is characteristic. Most of the facts of the Capone saga—itself reading like a movie scenario of Creasy's *Fifteen Decisive Battles*—seem unbelievable.

As Manhattan has its roaring Forties, so Chicago, southward of the Loop and the Rialto, has its sinful, ginful Twenties. It is here, in the pinochle period of 1920, in Amato's three-chair barber-shop, not far from

Wabash Avenue and around the corner from the Colosimo café and the evil Four Deuces, that the biographer of Capone picks up the red thread of his career.

Not then the seigneur of a magnificent estate on Palm Island, Miami Beach, Florida, and jolly Falstaffian host at swimming-parties in its marble bathing-pool.

Not then the Loop first-nighter, attended by eighteen tuxedoed gentlemen in waiting—a bodyguard outnumbering that of the President of the United States— quick of eye and quicker on the draw; posted strategically about the house; rising as one man as he goes to indulge in the entr'acte cigarette.

Not then riding in state along the fashionable Lake Shore Drive, the Boul' Mich', or Sheridan Road, in a specially built limousine of armor-plated top and body, with double panes of bullet-proof glass; preceded by a scout flivver and followed by a touring car of expert sharpshooters.

Not then the suave patron of the turf clubhouse and the dog-track's private box; impeccably tailored; diamond solitaires in tie-pin and ring; rose in buttonhole; binoculars slung over shoulder.

Not then the Big Shot, occupying two floors of a downtown hotel as G. H. Q., issuing orders to the police, rebuking a judge over the telephone.

The unknown Capone of 1920, making a lowly début into the Chicago underworld at the behest of Johnny Torrio, was ostensibly just one of the bourgeoisie; loud of dress, free of profanity; no paunch then; stout-muscled, hard-knuckled; a vulgar person; a tough baby from Five Points, New York City; bouncer and

boss of the Four Deuces; Torrio's all-round handy
man.

Unheralded his coming, and considerable time was
to elapse before the unsuspecting public and authorities were to be made aware of his presence and its
epochal significance. For Capone was to revolutionize
crime and corruption by putting both on an efficiency
basis, and to instill into a reorganized gangland firm
business methods of procedure. He had served with the
A.E.F. overseas in the World War and the instilling
was to be with machine guns.

A pleasant enough fellow to meet—socially—in a
speakeasy—if the proprietor were buying Capone
beer; a fervent handshaker, with an agreeable, well-
nigh ingratiating smile, baring a gleaming expanse of
dental ivory; a facile conversationalist; fluent as to
topics of the turf, the ring, the stage, the gridiron, and
the baseball field; what the police reporters call "a
right guy"; generous—lavishly so, if the heart that
beat beneath the automatic harnessed athwart the left
armpit were touched.

"God help us when he gets sore, though!" sighed
a professional man who has had intimate dealings with
him. "He is as temperamental as a grand opera star,
childishly emotional."

Height, about five feet, eight inches; weight, around
190 pounds; thirty-two years old—far beyond the
life expectancy of the Chicago gangster. Ponderous of
movement till engaged in action, then as agile as a
panther.

He is Neapolitan by birth and Neanderthal by instinct. A sob sister, seeing him scowl, would reach into

the cannery for "Gorilla Man"—the flat nose; the thick, pendulous lips; the big bullet head, squatting, rather than sitting, on the lumpy neck; the scar on the left cheek, along the protuberant jawbone; and the great shaggy black eyebrows—hairy battlements, once seen, not forgotten, lending the harsh, swart visage a terrifying aspect.

An amazing figure, this newcomer from Five Points. Here was Cicero, a flourishing industrial suburb, thirty minutes west of the Loop by the elevated; population, 70,000; thrifty, home-owning people. He was to take Cicero, bag and baggage, as Grant took Vicksburg, and convert it to his purposes—only the capture was to be effected at the polling-booth with gun and blackjack. He was to install his own mayor and chief of police; Capone dog-tracks and Capone gambling dens were to run wide open, and Capone resorts were to flaunt their ribaldry across the way from the hundred churches of Berwyn, Riverside, Oak Park, and River Forest.

In Chicago, while his machine gunners roved the streets, assassinating upstart bootleg rivals as well as saloonkeepers who refused to buy Capone beer, he was to be immune from all prosecution—thumbing his nose at four chiefs of police as each had his crowded hour and issued his fulminations. He was to get really serious with one, Michael Hughes, when Hughes in 1927 announced that he had "chased Capone out of Cicero, and for that matter out of further business dealings in Cook County."

"I'm getting sick of fellows like Hughes using me to attract glory to themselves," said Al. "I never met

Hughes in my life, nor have I ever even received a telephone call from him. Chase me out of Cook County? Well, he hasn't done it and he won't do it."

He didn't.

Capone outgrew Torrio as Torrio had outgrown Colosimo. The stories of the three interlink into a continuous narrative of politics and the underworld. Colosimo's ends at the threshold of the Volstead era —or when bootlegging was still in process of development as a major industry in the city that votes five to one wet. But he founded the system and organization, which Torrio and Capone expanded and improved upon.

Colosimo, the Italian immigrant of the nineties, quitting his job as section-gang water boy to push a broom in the First Ward, met up with the picturesque aldermen, Michael Hinky Dink Kenna, and John the Bathhouse Coughlin. Hinky Dink ran the Workingman's Exchange, where for five cents one could purchase a schooner of beer the size and shape of a goldfish bowl. The Bathhouse wrote poetry and wore flaming vests.

They appreciated Colosimo because of his vote-swinging ability. Popular from the start with his fellow white-wings, he had immediately organized them into a social and athletic club, which delivered as a unit at election time. The alderman conferred upon him a precinct captaincy and certain privileges appertaining to the old levee district, which was located within the boundaries of the ward and bisected by the night-life whoopee spots of Twenty-second Street.

The street-sweeper became, successively, pool-room

proprietor, saloon-keeper, partner in sundry red-light enterprises, and finally, Big Jim of Colosimo's Café, 2128 South Wabash Avenue; while the precinct captain burgeoned into a ward boss, with patronage, flashy clothes, diamond-studded watch, diamond fob, diamond rings and stick-pin, and diamond-set garters.

With prosperity there befell him what all too frequently befalls the Italian or Sicilian who amasses wealth—persecution by the American Mafia; letters threatening, first, kidnaping for ransom, then torture and death. He concluded that he needed a bodyguard, and going to New York City, he retained Torrio.

After his arrival in 1910 the persecution ceased. The case of three blackhanders is typical of what happened. They had made repeated demands on Colosimo, which he had ignored. One day they walked into the café and told him if $25,000 were not forthcoming on the morrow he would be killed. He conferred with Torrio, and said he would meet them the next afternoon at 4:30 o'clock under a railroad viaduct in Archer Avenue. It was a rendezvous with death for them, for instead of Colosimo there were four men with sawed-off shotguns volleying slugs at point-blank range.

Torrio lived by the gun. It was his trade. He was one of the elder fuglemen of the Five Points gang, from which, in 1912, Charles Becker, the police lieutenant, recruited Gyp the Blood and Lefty Louie, among others, to kill Herman Rosenthal, the gambler, who was about to expose Becker for grafting.

The Five Pointers are smart fellows—cosmopolites of crime. He who rises to leadership with them is no ordinary ruffian, and Torrio rated a vice presidency. He had executive ability, business sagacity, and a practical imagination. He was skilled in the duplicity of politics. He was proficient in the civilities—smooth of tongue and adroit of manner. He had a plausible front. And he was young—only twenty-nine and ambitious.

Colosimo, fat and prosperous and nearing forty, was smugly content with things as they were, satisfied to operate within the Twenty-second Street district. Torrio looked far beyond the confines of the First Ward to the latent opportunities throughout metropolitan Chicago. He saw a vice-monopoly of an entire county—and acted promptly.

Torrio towns sprang up, the first one being Burnham, eighteen miles southeast of the Loop, convenient to the 100,000 workers in the steel mills and oil refineries of Gary, Whiting, Calumet City, Hammond, East Chicago, and South Chicago. Dance halls, cribs, and gambling dens ran day and night, with Patton, the famous boy mayor, in charge.

The automobile was supplanting the horse and buggy. The pleasure-bent motorist was a source of revenue not to be overlooked. Torrio roadhouses appeared alongside the concrete highways, catering to all tastes. The click of the slot machine, the whirr of the roulette wheel, the entertainer's song, the electric piano, and the jazz orchestra made the night clamorous at many a prairie crossroads.

With the advent of prohibition and the closing of the 15,000 legalized oases in Chicago and vicinity, Torrio was confronted with the thirst-quenching problem. He had leased a couple of breweries to supply the needs of his own resorts, but the outside demand speedily became so great and the prices offered so high that he found he could make more money selling at wholesale than at retail.

It opened his eyes to the possibilities of the beer and booze traffic. While no man in 1919 could have foreseen the fabulous profits of later years, Torrio readily visioned enough to capture his imagination. He realized that it was the opportunity of a lifetime.

Hundreds of small-fry bootleggers had leaped into the new get-rich-quick field. It was like a gold rush. These must be eliminated. Torrio, studying the situation, was convinced that the only way to exploit it— at least, to his financial satisfaction—was to acquire absolute control of the traffic. There must be no competition. There might be consolidations—ententes—but there must be no independent rivals.

In the meantime Colosimo had died, in a murder mystery never solved. A lone assassin, secreting himself in the check-room of the café, in the morning hours when it was empty save for the help, had shot him and slipped away. His funeral was impressive for the number of State legislators, judges, and city and county officials attending. Torrio was a pallbearer, as also were Anthony D'Andrea and Diamond Joe Esposito, Democratic and Republican committeemen from the old Nineteenth Ward, who were to die by the sawed-off shotgun.

The policy Torrio had formulated aiming at a monopoly of the illicit liquor traffic was based on ruthlessness. The dictum that in the whole of the 932 square miles of Cook County there was not room for a rival in the bootleg trade could be enforced only with the gun. Torrio, of course, knew that. The colossal effrontery of his attitude probably never occurred to him. He simply saw another business opportunity—a big one— and proposed to take advantage of it. The reader must bear in mind always the point of view of Torrio and his kind. They had but one code—that of the gun: Might made right.

Torrio, now thirty-nine, with a multiplicity of interests, had, at Colosimo's death, succeeded to the underworld leadership. The direction of so many nefarious activities left him little time to undertake the execution of his new business venture. There would have to be much preliminary work, primarily concerned with organization. The criminal element, heretofore operating in Chicago as individuals or as independent groups, would have to be unified, brought under centralized control, disciplined, trained to obey orders. To lick this ragtag into shape would be a man-sized job. Torrio needed a combination of hard-boiled army drill sergeant and field general.

His unhesitating choice was the twenty-three-year-old Five Pointer, whom his mates called Al; who had quit school in the fourth grade to help his parents in the struggle for existence in the slums; who had learned to prowl the streets and alleys with the sharp wits of those who begin as mischievous gamins, pillaging vegetable carts, and end as wharf rats, looting trucks and warehouses. He had soon commanded respect by reason of his fighting ability and fast thinking. He had joined the Five Pointers, to be rewarded with a lieutenancy. He was a demon in action, whether with fists or gat. The New York City police had already questioned him in two murders—bum raps, of course. Torrio, who had been watching his progress from the start, considered him the only likely candidate for the job—somewhat wild yet, but having all the stuff necessary to put it over. Torrio's judgment was certainly vindicated.

In 1920, Torrio's income, net, was $100,000 a year. He declared Capone in on a fourth of this, with the understanding that he was to share a half in the proceeds of the bootleg industry. To a man engaged in a legitimate line of endeavor, $25,000 a year may seem a tidy sum. It was not so for Capone. He was most often broke and borrowing from his employer. He is an inveterate gambler and prodigal spender. He admits today, though, that the happiest part of his Chicago career was the period of impecunious anonymity when he could play pinochle in Amato's barber-shop or eat ravioli in Diamond Joe Esposito's Bella Napoli café without having to face the front door with pistol cocked; when he didn't have to wear a steel-plated vest; when there were no enemies to offer as high as $50,000 for his death—when he could sleep nights. Capone is one who will tell you, in no moralizing way, that crime doesn't pay. And if you ask why he doesn't retire, he will answer, "Once in, there is no out."

The scene of the Capone début was a four-story, red brick structure, housing 57 varieties of divertissement and skullduggery. On the ground floor were the Torrio general offices and a saloon and café. The second and third floors were devoted to gambling, and the fourth to the demimonde. The place derived its name from its street number, 2222 South Wabash Avenue. It was just south of Twenty-second Street. No slumming parties ever visited the Four Deuces. It was too tough. Twelve murders had been committed there—and never solved.

Capone's first maneuver was a striking exhibition of the odd cunning of the criminal mind. He established a business alibi for himself. He had cards printed, reading:

ALPHONSE CAPONE

Second Hand Furniture Dealer 2220 South Wabash Avenue

Then, in a corner room of the Four Deuces building opening on the street, he assembled his stock. It consisted of a glass showcase, filled with tooled leather novelties and bric-a-brac; a square piano, three golden-oak tables; a fernery; an aquarium; a rocking chair; a few small rugs; and a shelf of books, among which was a family Bible.

Our new fellow townsman, as has been indicated, was rather doggish—churlish—disputatious—inclined to belligerency. He was, in a word, crude; a diamond in the rough. The urbane Torrio applied himself to polishing him off. He instructed him in the social graces and in the art of dissembling to conceal one's thoughts. He taught him the commercial value of the bland smile and the ready handshake.

The polishing-off process was slow. Occasionally

the pupil would roister. Illustrative of this, is an interesting episode—interesting because it marks Capone's initial bow to the authorities, his first appearance on any Chicago police blotter, or in the public prints, and because it shows his comparative obscurity as late as August of 1922, when the episode occurred.

Newspapers considered it so unimportant that but one used it—inside, as filler. Capone's first name was unknown and his last misspelled. The item is here reproduced from the original City News Bureau copy, verbatim:

Alfred Caponi, 25 years old, living at the notorious Four Deuces, a disorderly house at 2222 South Wabash avenue, will appear in the South Clark street court today to answer to a charge of assault with an automobile. Early this morning his automobile crashed into a Town taxicab, driven by Fred Krause, 741 Drake avenue, at North Wabash avenue and East Randolph street, injuring the driver. Three men and a woman, who were with Caponi, fled before the arrival of the police.

Caponi is said to have been driving east in Randolph street at a high rate of speed. The taxicab was parked at the curb.

Following the accident, Caponi alighted and flourishing a revolver, displayed a special deputy sheriff's badge and threatened to shoot Krause.

Patrick Bargall, 6510 South Claremont avenue, motorman of a southbound street car, stopped his car and advised Caponi to put the weapon in his pocket, and the latter then threatened him, according to witnesses.

In the meantime, the Central police had been notified and they hurried to the scene, arresting Caponi. Krause was given first aid treatment by an ambulance physician.

AL CAPONE

The City News Bureau did not state accurately the case against Capone. Besides assault with an automobile, he was charged with driving while intoxicated and with carrying concealed weapons. Any of these three is a serious offense. For the last one, in Philadelphia, in May of 1929, he was sentenced to serve a year in prison.

Facing all three in Chicago, in August of 1922, he enjoyed complete immunity from prosecution. He did not even appear in court. The case never came to trial. The charges were mysteriously dropped, expunged from the record. The fix was in. The political hookup was functioning. And the hoodlum from Five Points was carrying the symbol of authority of Cook County's highest law-enforcing agency. . . . "Following the accident, Caponi alighted, and, flourishing a revolver, displayed a special deputy sheriff's badge." . . .

The hookup. The story begins and ends with it. The red thread of the Capone career is strung on it. Back of the machine and sawed-off shotgun crews; nerving the arm of the assassin and the thug; riding at the wheel of every death car; exploiting crime and its spoils—the hookup.

In 1922, when Capone was flaunting his special deputy sheriff's badge, Peter M. Hoffman, coroner, was the Republican party's nominee for sheriff, in a desperately contested campaign. The Democrats mopped up the county, the office of sheriff being one of the few the Republicans managed to save. Incidentally, in that same election a proposition to liberalize the Volstead Act to allow light wines and beer carried the city and county by a vote of five to one. Hoffman, a wet, succeeded Charles W. Peters, another Republican.

Federal Judge James H. Wilkerson, in October of 1925, sent Hoffman to jail for thirty days and fined him $2,500 for hospitality to Terry Druggan and Frankie Lake, beer barons and hijackers and Capone allies, while they were Hoffman's guests on a Federal court sentence. In the hearing before Judge Wilkerson, witnesses quoted Morris Eller, sanitary district trustee and boss of the Bloody Twentieth Ward, as saying, "Treat the boys right." The sheriff had let them motor about the city at will and live for the greater part of the time in a $12,000-a-year apartment in Millionaire's Row, on the Lake Shore Drive. The jail term ended Hoffman's vote-seeking career, but not his tenure of a job. Anton J. Cermak, a Democrat, president of the board of Cook County commissioners, put him on his payroll as assistant chief forester of the forest preserves at $10,000 a year, which was $40 more than Hoffman got as sheriff.

Capone at the Four Deuces and around Amato's pinochle table, in 1920, '21 and '22, was meeting an assorted company. Some were common loafers, some were fellows who still made a pretense of earning an honest livelihood; but mostly they were men of sinister pursuits, who shunned the sunlight to skulk in the underworld jungle. They were soon to emerge into the open to play stellar rôles in the drama of the gangs.

They were such characters as even Chicago, inured to labor sluggers and pistol-toters of the kidney of Peter and Dutch Gentlemen, Mossy Enright, and Big Tim Murphy, did not suspect existed. They were a new species. Viewed in retrospect by one who knew them, at the distance of only a few years, they seem as unreal as those figures that creep across the imagination in the grotesqueries of a troubled dream.

Lined up at the long mahogany bar of the Four Deuces at hours when the city slept, one might encounter:

The six brothers of the itching trigger-fingers—the Gennas, whose name sounds like a rattler's hiss, but who differed from the rattler in that instead of warning, they lulled their victims with unctuous guile.

Sam Samoots Amatuna, the sartorial pastel, of the pale brow and tapering fingers, of whom it was said, "He wore silk gloves on his soul"; whose jet-black eyes burned like those of a mad poet when he crooned mammy songs; who was so delicately adept at putting garlic on bullets, so that even if they did not hit a vital spot, infection would develop.

John Scalise and Albert Anselmi—only two, but bracketed in gangland's lexicon as the Homicide Squad —Capone's ace gunners.

Vincent the Schemer Drucci, the cop-hater, who began as a telephone-coinbox thief, and came to be celebrated in the Capone saga as the Shootin' Fool.

Samuel J. Nails Morton, who won the French *Croix de Guerre* in the World War; the Man on Horseback.

Dion O'Banion, the soft-spoken, smiling florist; the gladhanding assassin; bloodthirstiest angel face that ever trod the Chicago badlands; described by former Chief of Police Morgan A. Collins as "Chicago's arch criminal, who has killed or seen to the killing of at least twenty-five men."

23

Earl Hymie Weiss, Little Hymie, always fingering his rosary; ex-burglar and safe-cracker; election terrorist; gunman preëminent; smartest of them all; who refined murder to a technique—a trade for skilled mechanics only. It was Weiss who gave to the world the ceremonial known to the talkie and the press as "taking him for a ride."

Bertsche, the internationally fingerprinted confidence man, familiar with the cuisine of French, German, and English prisons; his pal, Skidmore, the pot-bellied ex-saloonkeeper.

Louis Alterie, the blustering cowboy from Colorado, who drew from the hip and twirled two guns, but who, when the shooting got going good, was to find Chicago too wild, and exit for his ranch.

Maxie Eisen, the Simon Legree, so-called, of the pushcart peddlers; dean of the racketeers; a Uriah Heep of hypocrisy.

The West Side O'Donnells—Klondike and Myles—who feared nobody; whose stir-daffy machine gunner, James Fur Sammons, was to forget and spray a drum of bullets the wrong way, or right at the O'Donnells.

"A good killer," mused Klondike, "but unreliable; we'll have to bump him off."

Occasionally, Polack Joe Saltis would waddle into the Four Deuces; again, one of the South Side O'Donnells—no relation of the West Side O'Donnells. They numbered four—the brothers Ed, Steve, Walter, and Tommy. Ed, the oldest, nicknamed Spike, was their leader; a devout church member, never missing Sunday mass at St. Peter's, always scrupulous to donate $10 or $20 to keep the votive candles burning.

These were the luminaries—a cross-section of the melting-pot, Italian, Sicilian, Irishman, Pole, Jew—who were to stimulate business for three classes: lawyers, undertakers, and florists. The lawyers were to profit by quantity production of habeas-corpus writs; the undertakers by intense rivalry in funeral pomp and insistence on ever more elegant and higher-priced caskets; and the florists by an insatiable demand for profuseness in floral pieces.

Truly, it was an assorted company that Capone met at the Four Deuces. Many—very many—of the ties there formed were to prove lasting. They were to last into eternity, and after every inquest, as the friends of the deceased assembled for the obsequies, there was to be the basket of flowers with the remembrancer, "From Al."

Poor old Joe Howard didn't get any. Naturally. But what the hell? They gave him a swell shooting party a half-block from the Four Deuces, at Heinie Jacobs' saloon, 2300 South Wabash Avenue, and the Big Shots joined in. Yes, sir, the Big Shots themselves finally took notice of Joe. What more could he ask? A guy can't have all the breaks.

They laid Joe out on a slab in the morgue. No silk-hatted, frock-coated mortician for him. No bronze casket. A pine box. No granite shaft. A wooden marker. Joe is pushing up the daisies in a far corner of the potter's field.

Joe was a bum, a nondescript; what is generally described as an "underworld character"; relic of a bygone day, when a fellow who packed a pair of brass knucks was a hard egg, and a Smith & Wesson was a deadly arsenal. Joe was highly regarded then. He had been fairly successful as a burglar and safe-blower and his rusty gat boasted three notches, but—"he never did any killings among gangland's members because he didn't have the guts."

That probably explained why Joe was persona non grata at the Four Deuces—no social standing whatsoever with the Torrio set, tolerated as one beneath contempt. So Joe hung around Heinie's place, where the customers were of a milder sort and where he was assured an appreciative audience when the Bourbon inspired him to wax eloquent about Joe Howard—which was often.

This new get-rich-quick racket of hijacking and booze running that everybody was talking about fascinated Joe. The more he thought of it, the better it looked. Sure, a gent had to be tough to get away with it, but that only made it all the better. Joe was tough. He would tell the world.

Loading up his gat, he started in. By way of variety, he attempted to rob the Old Rose Distillery warehouse at 447 North Clark Street. Sergeant Irwin Holberg of the East Chicago Avenue station arrived as the last of ten barrels was being hoisted aboard a truck in the alley. He literally had the goods on Joe, but the case dragged along for months and finally was dismissed.

Joe had his hookup, too.

Warehouse-looting proving not so profitable, Joe decided to go in for hijacking exclusively. Luck was with him. He pulled off two good jobs in one night. The next evening, over the three fingers of Bourbon in Heinie's place, he was gabbing to the boys what a cinch it was.

AL CAPONE

It was the day after that that the Big Shots finally took notice of him. He was parked at the cigar case in front of Heinie's bar. George Bilton, an automobile mechanic, and David Runelsbeck, an aged carpenter, both rooming in the neighborhood, had stopped for a friendly drink and a smoke. Heinie was sitting behind the cigar case. It was six o'clock of a quiet afternoon in May. Joe, as usual, was talking. The rest were listening.

The swinging doors flapped. Two men entered. Runelsbeck's version of what happened, as told to Michael Hughes, then chief of detectives, was:

" 'Hello, Al,' cried Joe, putting out his hand. The man he spoke to stuck out his hand, but it held a revolver, and he fired six times. Joe keeled over dead, still grinning."

Nobody now remembers Joe. He was forgotten in the underworld almost as soon as he was gone, but the killing had a peculiar significance: Joe, the nondescript, had horned in on the Capone-Torrio business venture; his death was notice that they were prepared to enforce the dictum of no rivals, regardless, in the bootleg industry.

Thirty minutes after Howard's slaying, a general order was flashed to all police stations to arrest Capone. Chief Hughes, as soon as he had concluded his interrogation of Runelsbeck and other witnesses, said:

"I am certain it was Capone, and I know just how it was done. Howard and the other three were at the cigar counter. In came Capone and another man. One reached over and took hold of Howard's coat, drawing Howard to him. Then he put a gun against Howard's cheek and pulled the trigger. Five more bullets followed the first one, all effective."

A morning newspaper published a picture of Al with the caption:

"Tony (Scarface) Capone, also known as Al Brown, who killed Joe Howard by firing six shots into his body in the saloon of Heinie Jacobs, at 2300 South Wabash Avenue, in a renewal of the beer war."

That was May 8th.

The inquest was May 9th.

Overnight, the witnesses were stricken with an ailment that has since become epidemic in such cases—loss of memory. Heinie Jacobs was certain, now that he thought it over, that he had been called to a rear room to answer a telephone just before the shooting. No, he didn't hear or see anything. Runelsbeck, visibly frightened, was positive that he couldn't identify Capone if brought face to face with him. Bilton was missing.

Captain James McMahon of the Cottage Grove Avenue station thereupon booked Jacobs and Runelsbeck on charges of being accessories after the fact, explaining that the action was merely technical. He suspected, he stated, that they were concealing the identity of the slayer.

The inquest was continued until May 22d. The police wanted to find Capone. He had disappeared the night of the shooting. They did not find him and on May 22d the inquest was continued indefinitely.

It was more than a month after Joe got his that Al walked into the Cottage Grove station, June 11th, and remarked to Captain McMahon:

"I hear the police are looking for me. What for?"

The Captain hustled him down to the Criminal Courts Building, where he met a youthful assistant State attorney named William H. McSwiggin. Told he was wanted for the killing of Howard, Al spoke as follows:

"Who, me? Why, I'm a respectable business man. I'm a second-hand furniture dealer. I'm no gangster. I don't know this fellow Torrio. I haven't anything to do with the Four Deuces. Anyway, I was out of town the day Howard was bumped off. You had better do your talking to my lawyer."

But the assistant State attorney announced that he had a case against him and would move for an indictment. He was new on the job and doubtless sincere, but nothing happened. The interesting fact now is that McSwiggin should interview Capone on his first serious murder rap (serious, that is, from the point of view of unwelcome publicity). For within a year and ten months young McSwiggin and the gangsters, James J. Doherty and Thomas Duffy, were to be mowed down by machine-gun fire in front of a Cicero saloon and Capone was to be hunted as a boss killer.

The much-continued Joe Howard inquest—whose total cost to the taxpayers was $4,000, considerably in excess of Joe's value as a social asset—was finally terminated July 22d. Captain McMahon was present with his witnesses. Runelsbeck again testified that Joe said, "Hello, Al," to the murderer. The captain presented the police case against Capone. And here is the verdict, copied from the official records:

We, the jury, find that Joe Howard came to his death on the premises at 2300 South Wabash Avenue, from hemorrhage and shock due to bullet wounds in the head, face and neck; said bullets being fired from a revolver or revolvers in the hand or hands of one or more unknown, white male persons, in the vestibule of said saloon on said premises. . . . We recommend that Henry Jacobs and David Runelsbeck be discharged from police custody and further recommend that the unknown persons be apprehended and held to the grand jury upon a charge of murder until discharged by due process of law.

Joe's estate was inventoried, the legal description being: "1 pair cuff buttons; cash, $17."

The unknown persons were never apprehended and neither was Capone again bothered.

If Joe Howard was friendless and obscure, Jerry O'Connor, George Spot Bucher, and Georgia Meeghan were not. They were henchmen of the South Side O'Donnells, whose hookup was fully as powerful as that of Torrio.

For instance, Spike, their leader and oldest brother, was elsewhere when the Volstead gold rush started. He was sorting hemp in Joliet Penitentiary, having been sent down for complicity in the $12,000 daylight holdup of the Stockyards Trust and Savings Bank. The following appealed to Governor Len Small, either by letter or in person, in his behalf, according to the published report of the Chicago Crime Commission:

State Senators James C. O'Brien, Edward J. Hughes, Patrick J. Sullivan, Robert W. Schultze, P. H. Carroll, and Frank J. Ryan; State Representatives Thomas J. O'Grady, James P. Boyle, George S. Moran, John F.

Healy, and Michael Maher; Judge George Kersten of the criminal court of Cook County.

The governor paroled him to Senator Ryan, and then and there sociability at the Four Deuces ceased for the O'Donnells. They tucked up their sleeves and waded in to dispute the field with Capone and Torrio out Bubbly Creek way, in Kerry Patch.

O'Connor, himself a former Joliet lifer, paroled, and Meeghan and Bucher were the O'Donnells' beer drummers. Their methods of overcoming sales resistance—in common use in the early days of haphazard competition —were simple and direct. Entering a saloon or speakeasy, their revolvers dangling in belt holsters, they would accost the proprietor:

"Who you buying from?"

They knew his answer before he spoke, Spike having listed each place in the territory he regarded as his bailiwick. The drummers approached only those who had not given him their patronage.

"Well," they would continue, after receiving the answer, "how about going along with us?"

If he begged time to consider the proposition he was granted a stay of twenty-four hours, at the expiration of which, if the sales resistance still proved stubborn, they reinforced their arguments with fists or revolver butts. In the majority of cases this procedure was effective.

An exception was Jacob Geis. He was satisfied with Capone-Torrio beer and that ended it. A dour fellow and a berserk fighter, he had not only failed to respond to all persuasion; he had actually bounced the drummers out on their ears when they attempted coercive measures.

Geis and his bartender, Nicholas Gorysko, were serving six customers in his neighborhood saloon at 2154 West 51st Street early in the evening of September 7, 1923, when in walked Steve, Walter, and Tommy O'Donnell, with O'Connor, Meeghan, and Bucher.

"We're giving you one more chance," was Steve's greeting. "What say?"

"Nothing doing," said Geis.

They yanked him across the bar and beat him unmercifully. Gorysko, protesting, was knocked unconscious. Later, when the two were removed to the German Deaconess' Hospital, Geis was found to have a fractured skull. He was in a critical condition for weeks, physicians expecting him to die. His sturdy constitution pulled him through.

The embattled O'Donnells that night were out to show the recalcitrant trade what was best for it. They stormed five places where their rivals' beer was being sold and in each staged a slugfest. The police learned of it when one proprietor, Frank Kveton of 2300 West 21st Street, telephoned in a complaint.

Calling it a day after leaving Kveton's, the O'Donnells and their drummers repaired to Joseph Klepka's saloon at 5358 South Lincoln Street, a sort of headquarters, to meet Spike and partake of refreshments. They were grouped at the end of the bar, enjoying beer and sandwiches, when the front door swung wide to admit four men, headed by Daniel McFall, then a deputy sheriff. Six witnesses—residents of the neighborhood playing cards in a rear room—told what happened.

"Stick up your hands or I'll blow you to hell," shouted McFall, and a bullet from his .38 whistled over Spike's head.

The O'Donnells scattered for the front and side doors. As they did a fifth man appeared—"short and stocky, wearing a gray raincoat and carrying a double-barreled sawed-off shotgun." At a signal from McFall he withdrew, and McFall and the others pursued the O'Donnells to the street, where the real shooting occurred. It lasted only three minutes, but when it was over Jerry O'Connor lay dead on the sidewalk—shot through the heart.

Ten days later, September 17th, Meeghan and Bucher, driving south on Laflin Street in their roadster, halted at Garfield Boulevard for traffic, and from a green touring car that slipped alongside came a fusillade of revolver bullets and sawed-off shotgun slugs to end their careers as beer drummers.

The late William E. Dever, six months in office as mayor, was inexpressibly shocked at the double killing. He revoked the licenses of two thousand soft drink parlors, summoned Chief of Police Morgan A. Collins and Chief of Detectives Hughes to his office, and assumed personal charge of the situation. He issued a statement that is highly interesting—that has a definite historical value—in the light of subsequent events:

Until the murderers of Jerry O'Connor and the murderers of these two men have been apprehended and punished, and the illegal traffic for control of which they battle has been suppressed, the dignity of the law and the average man's respect for it is imperiled, and every officer of the law and every enforcing agency should lay aside other duties and join in the common cause—a restoration of law and order.

The police will follow this case to a finish as they do all others. This guerrilla war between hijackers, rum runners and illicit beer peddlers can and will be crushed.

I am just as sure that this miserable traffic with its toll of human life and morals can be stamped out as I am that I am mayor, and I am not going to flinch for a minute.

It was a brave utterance, by a brave and gallant man, uncompromisingly honest and sincere—but it was also a futile utterance. The situation he faced that night was the rising of the gangs. In the official records, Jerry O'Connor's death is indexed as the first killing of the bootleg war.

As well might Mayor Dever have tried to quell the whirlwind. Given a trustworthy police department— which he did not have, as was disclosed later by his own testimony—he could, perhaps, have combated the gangster element, per se. Given the United States Marines, he would have been powerless against the forces that lay behind that element. He could not combat public complacency—and public demand.

There were to be nine more killings similar to that of O'Connor in the fall of 1923; 16 in 1924; 46 in 1925, and 64 in 1926, Mr. Dever's last year in office. In this total of 135 gang murders, only six men were to be brought to trial, and of the six all were to be acquitted save one—Sam Vinci, who chose the occasion of a coroner's inquest to dispatch John Minatti with a .45 caliber automatic. His excuse was that John had killed his brother, Mike, and he thought the jury was going to free him. He was sent to Joliet Penitentiary for twenty-five years.

An immediate result of Mayor Dever's activity in the O'Connor-Meeghan-Bucher cases was the suspension of Captain Thomas Wolfe of the New City police station, in which district the three killings occurred. He had been too willing to release McFall, Chief Collins believed.

Capone was questioned. He was a second-hand furniture dealer, he said. The O'Donnells were fetched in to scrutinize him, and upheld the ethics by shaking their heads. The only enlightenment the authorities received was that Capone had acquired a permit to wear a gun. It had been issued by a justice of the peace of Cicero, Joseph Mischka.

Torrio was sought. He had disappeared. His attorney said he had gone to a wake. He could produce him if necessary. His attorney was Michael L. Igoe, protégé of the late George E. Brennan, boss of the Democratic party in Cook County and Illinois, State Representative, and minority leader in the House at Springfield; a commissioner of Chicago's South Parks Board; in 1920 an unsuccessful candidate for State's attorney on a platform that "crime must be voted out; criminals must be speedily prosecuted; the home must be safeguarded"; and again in 1924. He was defeated both times by Robert E. Crowe, Republican.

Daniel McFall was finally indicted for the O'Connor murder. He went to trial in January of 1924 and won a speedy acquittal. The bullet that pierced O'Connor's heart was a .32 caliber. The defense established that

McFall, who admitted that he was in Klepka's saloon, was carrying a .38 caliber gun. McFall and two others were indicted for the Meeghan-Bucher murder, but with the collapse of the O'Connor case, the State's attorney's office had the charges nolle prossed and the accused men were discharged from custody without going to trial.

The three casualties did not deter old Spike. He persisted with his syndicate. Apparently he did not know when he was licked. Morris Keane, a beer runner for him, was the fourth victim. His body was recovered in a lonely road, near the Sag Canal. Then Phillip Corrigan was picked off his beer truck. The mystery of it all baffled and infuriated Spike. During one of the numerous sessions at the detective bureau, he exploded with:

"I can whip this bird Capone with bare fists any time he wants to step out in the open and fight like a man."

His brother, Walter, and Henry C. Hassmiller, a gunman just imported by the O'Donnells, were next— shot to death in a roadhouse in Evergreen Park, a suburb south of Chicago. This second double killing decided Spike. He retired temporarily, and Kerry Patch returned to tranquillity and uninterrupted enjoyment of its Capone-Torrio beer.

The central fact in the rising of the gangs was the Torrio ambition for a monopoly of the illicit liquor traffic. It was the focal point in the reign of outlawry, and a debauching influence in politics. As Capone pushed it nearer to realization, and talk of the big money went the rounds, there was a general stampede of criminals to his camp. In the fall of 1923, when Mayor Dever's attention was directed to the situation, he had at his beck no fewer than seven hundred men, probably as vicious an aggregation as was ever assembled outside the walls of a penal institution. Twenty per cent of these were aliens and thirty per cent paroled convicts. Governor Small's board of pardons and paroles loosed nine hundred and fifty of the latter within a period of two years and ten months.

By the summer of 1924, the big money was so plentiful that a word had been coined to reduce the conversational overhead. The word was "grand," abbreviated to "gran'." A gran' was $1,000, and was the basic medium of exchange. There was, to be sure, the C—$100—but in the vocabulary of the new gentry, the gran' overshadowed all else.

"He offered a G man [government agent] ten gran' to forget it."

"I laid a gran' on the nose in the fifth race at Pimlico."

The Volstead gold rush was at its peak.

Affairs were such with the two former Five Pointers that Torrio was seeing Paris and other European capitals. He had purchased for his mother, a peasant woman, a seaside estate in Italy—where her retinue of servants numbered fifteen—and an automobile with a liveried chauffeur.

The impecunious hoodlum of 1920, who had thought $25,000 a year a fairly snug salary, was now disbursing, in the booze traffic alone, $25,000 a week in payrolls.

Cicero had been taken. The guns had barked April

1st, election day. There had been sluggings and kidnapings. Voters had been dragooned and intimidated. Gangster cars had raced through the streets, shooting it out with police squads, and terrorizing hundreds of citizens into staying at home. Capone's brother, Frank, had been killed in one battle.

This Cicero exploit and the antecedent circumstances constitute a prize chapter of the unbelievable Capone saga. Ed Konvalinka was a soda-jerker. He was cheery and obliging, displaying at his fountain tasks an alacrity and a dexterity pleasing to behold, and serving his clientele with a nicety of deference gratifying to individual self-esteem. Folks took quite a shine to Ed. He conversed entertainingly and informingly, being a close student of the daily press and reflecting well upon what he read. The soda fountain developed into something of an informal forum, a neighborhood town pump, with Ed as oracle.

There was more to Ed than met the eye. He was calculating cause and effect. He was ambitious politically. The soda fountain provided opportunity to cultivate friendships. The capital stock of a politician is goodwill. Ed figured each additional friendship as another investment in the Konvalinka future. Soon he was a precinct captain, then a leader in ward activities. Finally Governor Small heard favorably of him, and he was named Republican committeeman from Cicero.

Beyond that there can be only surmise now as to the destiny of the Konvalinka future in the course of ordinary events. For at that juncture it entered the realm of the extraordinary. Konvalinka had marked the rise of the Capone-Torrio combine in Chicago.

An idea was born, dazzling in its possibilities for the greater aggrandizement of the Republican committeeman from Cicero.

He divulged it to his friend, Edward Vogel, who approved it enthusiastically and approached Louis La Cava, a Capone field agent. La Cava arranged a conference between Konvalinka and Capone. The idea was to have a Konvalinka ticket. The candidates had already been selected by Konvalinka, Vogel, and La Cava. They were Joseph Klenha, for mayor; Frank Houchek, town clerk; T. J. Buckley, town collector; and Edward J. Carmody, town attorney. The proposition to Capone was that should he accomplish the ticket's election he could establish himself in Cicero and be immune from molestation by the authorities. That, Capone did on April 1st. The soda-jerker became a Main Street Warwick and the second-hand furniture dealer a feudal baron.

His fief was a typical American community— thirty minutes west of the Loop; population, 70,000; with Rotary, Kiwanis, and Lions clubs; Chamber of Commerce; prosperous banks and industries; a high school that rates as one of the finest educational plants in the Middle West; sewing circles; a ministers' association; sixty-eight per cent of its citizens owning their own homes.

Overnight, Cicero seceded from the Volstead United States and went wilder West, and wilder wet, than Chicago.

"Cash game inside; step in," droned cappers for the Ship, into the ears of passengers alighting from elevated trains at the terminal station. It was right next door—a composite of Monte Carlo gambling palace and Barbary Coast dance hall—craps, poker, stush, and faro—and, from midnight till dawn, a ritzy cabaret. The experienced Billy Mondi was the proprietor.

There was the Hawthorne Smoke Shop, run by Frankie Pope, the millionaire newsboy, where the handbook play aggregated $50,000 a day.

There was Lauterback's—a saloon in front, with whiskey seventy-five cents the shot; beer thirty-five cents the stein; wine thirty cents the glass; and in the rear, catering to men and women, the roulette wheels. The game here was said to be the biggest in the country, as much as $100,000 in chips being frequently stacked on the tables.

There were the Capone dog-tracks and the Capone Castle, as ballyhooers on the rubberneck buses described it to sightseers—Cicero's largest hotel, which Capone had commandeered as headquarters.

There were one hundred sixty-one bars running wide open day and night. Yes, there were Federal raids and Federal injunctions, but when the tumult and the shouting died, the "Business as Usual" signs were hung out. The injunctions were regarded as scraps of paper and the raids as hokum. A saloonkeeper explained it thus:

"When the cops and the prohibition agents come here after hours all the time to get drunk, why, of course, they go along with us. They always tip us off to the raids. An injunction means nothing. When the owner of a place is caught by one he opens up somewhere else under another name."

In Stickney, adjoining Cicero on the south, were the brothels, the form of vice in which Torrio specialized, and which he had originally introduced to Chicago in his Burnham venture. Five hundred Jezebels flocked to Stickney. There were houses with as many as sixty women, exceeding in size and number of inmates any establishment in Chicago in the days when Big Jim Colosimo cracked the whip for Hinky Dink and Bathhouse John in the old First Ward levee district.

A Capone-Torrio agent was posted in each gambling den, saloon, and brothel. So thoroughly organized was the combine and so autocratic were its methods that the proprietors had to pay the salaries of the agents, whose jobs were to see that the places received protection and that the combine got its split. This varied from twenty-five to fifty per cent of the gross receipts. By midsummer of 1924 Capone and Torrio were each pocketing $100,000 a week. The figures are those of government investigators.

They ruled by the gun. Eddie Tancl, saloonkeeper, that hard-bitten ex-pug of the cauliflower ears and pancake nose, refused to truckle to the combine. It could levy no tribute on him, and neither would he buy its beer. He was notified that he would have to go along or get out of town.

"Try and put me out," he snarled. "I was in Cicero long before youse guys came."

He was carried out in a coffin. The killers, Myles O'Donnell and James J. Doherty, knew they had been in a fight. Eddie Tancl stood toe to toe with them, trading shot for shot, and when at last he toppled, he hurled

41

his emptied gun in O'Donnell's face and gasped at his waiter, Leo Klimas:

"Kill the rat! He got me."

Klimas, himself sore wounded, leaped furiously upon O'Donnell, but a bullet from Doherty's gun finished him.

O'Donnell and Doherty and the law? Arrested, indicted, acquitted. Prosecutor, Assistant State's Attorney William H. McSwiggin. And the combine got the concession for the Tancl place.

The taking of Cicero set the stage for the real drama of the gangs—often called the Bootleg Battle of the Marne—in which the yeomanry of the Four Deuces swept into action, some with Capone, some against him, some for themselves, some for the devil take the hindmost. The Four Deuces was a house divided.

Until then the going had been easy for the combine— skirmishing, so to speak. The O'Donnells had kicked up the only sizable fuss, and they had been subdued with little effort. Not Capone's guns but the wily Torrio's diplomacy had kept the other gangs in check. He had enlisted on his side the badlands' cock o' the walk, Dion O'Banion, in 1924 the most powerful figure in the Chicago underworld.

Ever since the inception of the booze-monopoly project, Torrio had assiduously courted favor with him. In the taking of Cicero, O'Banion had lent his cohorts and artillery, his share of the spoils being the beer concession and a third interest in the Hawthorne Smoke Shop.

Capone, Torrio, and O'Banion at that time were known as the Big Three. There were, of course, many lesser gang chieftains, operating almost entirely within the boundary limits of their respective wards. It should be explained that the gangster element derives its strength originally from those wards where the population is heterogeneous or largely foreign-born, and either ignorant of, or indifferent to, its citizenship obligations. The gangster serves as the right arm of the corrupt politician at elections. He delivers the vote. In exchange he receives immunity from the law in so far as the politician can secure it. In the event that he commits a crime and the evidence is so overwhelmingly conclusive that he cannot escape prosecution, and if witnesses cannot be suborned, nor the jury fixed, and a conviction results—then a parole is forthcoming within a reasonable period, as in the case of Spike O'Donnell.

O'Banion's borough was the Forty-second and Forty-third wards, comprising the Gold Coast, where the town homes and coöperative apartments of the city's wealth and fashion overlook Lake Michigan. Westward, as the river is approached, the neighborhood deteriorates—rooming houses, small stores, with living quarters above, factories, tenements, and shacks. It is in this section, by means of floaters, repeaters, bribes, and ballot-box stuffing, that elections in the Gold Coast wards have frequently been decided. There is an old wheeze, "Who'll carry the Forty-second and Forty-third?" And the answer, "O'Banion, in his pistol pockets."

Reared in poverty, a plasterer's son, O'Banion at ten was hustling papers in the Loop, and learning things from the roustabouts of Circulation Alley. Before he was graduated from knee breeches he was one of the incorrigibles of the Market Street gang. His first job was as waiter in the McGovern brothers' saloon-café, a notorious place in North Clark Street, whose attachés practiced jackrolling as a diversion. O'Banion tried it, but didn't care for it. He decided to go in for burglary and safe-cracking. Now, to illustrate how effectively his political hookup was functioning even at the beginning of his career, and likewise, how a criminal is coddled in Chicago, we cite from the records:

March, 1921: Indictment No. 23893; charge, burglary; stricken off with leave to reinstate.

May, 1921: Indictment No. 24752; charge, burglary; stricken off with leave to reinstate.

May, 1921: Indictment No. 24755; charge, having burglar tools; stricken off with leave to reinstate.

July, 1922: Indictment No. 28982; charge, robbery; bond, $10,000, furnished by J. Braunlip and Titus A . Haffa [alderman of the Forty-third Ward]; nolle prossed.

Although Chief of Police Collins credited O'Banion with twenty-five notches, he was never brought to trial for murder. In 1921 Detective Sergeant John J. Ryan actually caught him in the act of cracking a safe in the Postal Telegraph Building, but he won an acquittal with the jury.

A mile beyond the Loop, at 738 North State Street, in a two-story brick building with a plate-glass front, was the shop of O'Banion, the florist—opposite the Holy Name Cathedral, where, as a boy, he had served as acolyte to Father O'Brien.

AL CAPONE

Here, in the daylight hours, he puttered amongst his flowers, shears or sprinkler in hand, an apron girting his mid-section. The passerby saw a man of medium height, broad-shouldered, narrow-hipped, lean-fleshed, an athlete in build, his small and graceful hands occupied in arranging the wares in vases or terra-cotta pots for the window display or the racks against the walls. He had an unerring sense of decorative values in color grouping and varieties. He could twist a sheaf of roses into a wreath or chaplet so deftly and gently as not to let fall a single petal.

In specially constructed pouches of his tailored clothes he carried three revolvers—one in the right front trousers pocket; one under the left armpit of the coat, and one in the left outside coat pocket. He was Chicago's only three-gun man, and ambidextrous.

His round Irish face wore an habitual grin. His fathomless blue eyes, wide and unblinking, stared at all comers with a candor fixed and impenetrable. His right leg was four inches shorter than his left, due to a street-car accident in his paper-hustling days, and this caused him to move with an odd rolling lurch. This and his trick of canting his head as he talked produced on most visitors an impression of infinite slyness, reminiscent of *Le jongleur de Notre Dame.*

He was a bundle of inexplicabilities—his innate love of flowers; his characteristic of killing without compunction; his hatred of alcohol as anything but a commodity—a stranger to beer and whiskey throughout his life; his passionless savagery; his "sunny brutality," a psychologist phrased it. To his way of thinking humanity was divided into two classes—"right guys" and

45

"wrong guys." Civilized existence, with its restraints and taboos, oppressed him. He went through the world like a man in a crowded street-car seeking elbow-room.

"We're big business without high hats," he told Earl Hymie Weiss, after an unusually profitable hijacking expedition.

A gargoyle peered out of the shutters of his mind.

O'Banion, the florist, quit the scene every evening at 6 o'clock and O'Banion, the bootlegger, appeared. The night hours were better for beer and booze running. O'Banion, the bootlegger, now and again, was too villainous even for Torrio.

A couple of West Side policemen had intercepted a truckload of beer and demanded a bribe of $300 to release it. The gangsters in charge telephoned to O'Banion. The wire to his florist shop had been tapped and the conversation was recorded for Chief Collins' files.

"Three hundred dollars!" said O'Banion. "To them bums? Why, I can get them knocked off for half that much."

Which was all the satisfaction to be got from him.

Headquarters, aware that as likely as not he would kill the two policemen rather than submit to their demands, sent a squad to rescue and arrest them. In the meantime the gangsters on the truck had appealed to Torrio, and soon headquarters heard their spokesman informing O'Banion:

"Hey, Dion, I just been talkin' to Johnny and he says to let the cops have the three hundred. He says he don't want no trouble."

He went gunning where and when he pleased, and for reasons as quixotic as the snubbing of a friend. Yankee

Schwartz, his shadow and man Friday, complained that Davy Miller had refused to speak to him, in public. Davy was one of the four brothers—the others were Hirschey, politician-gangster-gambler, once in booze partnership with Torrio and O'Banion; Frank, a policeman; and Max, a youngster. Davy, a prize-fight referee, was known as the best boy with his fists on the West Side.

O'Banion learned that he was to attend an opening night performance of a musical comedy at La Salle Theater, in the Loop. He let him see the show through, then, as he emerged into the brightly lighted lobby along with a thousand other first-nighters in formal dress, fired twice. Davy's brother, Max, who had accompanied him, leaped to his aid, and O'Banion donated him a bullet. His belt buckle probably saved his life, as the bullet struck it and caromed off to the floor. Davy was wounded in the abdomen and spent two critical weeks in the hospital. O'Banion sauntered away after the shooting, and was never prosecuted nor even arrested.

The same year, 1924, he engineered the $1,000,000 Sibley warehouse robbery, in which 1,750 cases of bonded whiskey were removed. A Federal grand jury indicted Lieutenant Michael Grady of the detective bureau and four of his sergeants on charges of convoying the stuff to the bootleggers' distribution stations. They were suspended pending their trial, at which they were acquitted. They were then reinstated and not long after Grady was promoted to a police captaincy. The Sibley profits were used to buy the Cragin distillery, the largest alcohol plant in the West. When E. C.

Yellowly, Federal prohibition administrator, was preparing to close it he was offered a bribe of $250,000 to let it run.

Chief Collins participated in another O'Banion adventure, at the Sieben brewery. His rôle was that of uninvited guest. He had received a tip that thirteen truckloads of beer were to be run. He was there when O'Banion and his men arrived to superintend the job. He then discovered that two of his policemen, assigned to guard the brewery for just such an eventuality, were conveniently absent. He tore their stars from their coats with his own hands. Assistant United States District Attorney William F. Waugh was offered $50,000 to prevent the case coming to trial.

"I told them," he said, " 'You're talking to the wrong man.' "

Yet it didn't matter. The laughing gods of fate that presided over the O'Banion career balked even the attempts of the Government to punish him.

This land-going buccaneer whose Spanish Main was all Chicago; this cock o' the walk who strutted high, wide, and handsome through the underworld of crime and the overworld of politics, was bad news, indeed, to the liegemen of Capone and Torrio. They resented his arrogance and envied his business success. Racial feeling was undoubtedly involved. Naturally, the Italians and Sicilians had drifted to Capone and Torrio and the Irish to O'Banion. Quarrels were frequent and on two occasions the Big Three had to resort to drastic measures to avert killings. The animosities thus engendered persisted through the bootleg war and invested it with its international aspect.

Torrio had not foreseen the possibilities of the Cicero beer concession under O'Banion direction. In April, when the gangs moved in, it was estimated to be worth $20,000 a month. By October O'Banion had developed it to a gross of $100,000 a month. He had proselyted in Chicago and induced fifty saloonkeeper friends to locate in the new oasis.

This rankled with the Capone-Torrio liegemen because he had evidenced no intention of declaring the combine in on it. Individual mutterings swelled into a hubbub of threats and long-suppressed rancor became open hostility. The bland Torrio hastened to approach O'Banion.

His proposal was that if O'Banion would split a fourth on the beer revenues he would cut him in on the combine's brothels in Stickney.

"Go peddle your papers, Johnny," said O'Banion.

Chief Collins' "arch criminal" would have nothing to do with trafficking in women.

The saying that everything O'Banion touched turned to money was never truer than in his Cicero beer business. It increased until it was yielding more than the combine's business in the much greater trade area of Chicago's South and West Sides. Torrio and Capone, brothers of the skin, suavely bided their time.

O'Banion had given Torrio a short answer and he figured that he had provocation. He was incensed at the Sicilian Gennas—the six brothers of the itching trigger-fingers. They were the combine's alky-cookers, their brother-in-law, Henry Spingola, having invented the process. They had at first been content to operate solely within that field, but with the taking of Cicero had gone in for bootlegging and had repeatedly encroached upon O'Banion's territory. His protests to Torrio had met with smiling promises, but no fulfillments.

Things were in that position when Torrio proposed the beer split. A conviction seized O'Banion that the combine was "trying to make a sucker of me." It smarted. A few shootings occurred with the Gennas and the limit of his scant forbearance was reached. He severed relations with the old confraternity of the Four Deuces in typically O'Banion fashion—a five-word sentence: "To hell with the Sicilians!" and issued orders to his willing crew to start muscling in and hijacking—blithely indifferent to the menace that dogged his footsteps, that was to overtake him in his florist's shop and present to Chicago an innovation in homicide —the handshake murder.

He was busy, anyway, with politics. The national, State, and county elections of 1924 being but two weeks away, the precincts of the Forty-second and Forty-third Wards were to be organized, as usual, to insure victory for his faction of the Republican party. One of O'Banion's proudest boasts, incidentally, was that he always delivered his borough "as per requirements."

A dinner during this hustings redirected Mayor Dever's attention to the gangster situation in such wise as to astound him. O'Banion was the headliner. It was held in a private dining-room of the Webster Hotel, 2150 Lincoln Park West, a swanky North Side neighborhood. The guest list—mostly O'Banion partisans —reads like a roster of the dramatis personæ of the scene in John Gay's *Beggar's Opera,* wherein cutthroats, thieves, and highwaymen rally round the wassail bowl to speed the jocund hours. Here it is:

Cornelius P. Con Shea, ex-inmate of Sing Sing for attempted murder of a woman; in charge of the teamsters' strike in Chicago in which twenty-one men were killed and four hundred sixteen injured; indicted for murder of Police Lieutenant Terence Lyons, but acquitted; secretary of the Theater and Building Janitors' Union.

Frank Gusenberg of the four aliases; burglar, robber, and stickup; brother of Peter Gusenberg, who served time in Joliet Penitentiary and Fort Leavenworth for complicity in the Polk Street station $400,000 mail robbery.

Two-Gun Louis Alterie, partner of O'Banion in booze, beer, and gambling deals, and president of the Theater and Building Janitors' Union.

Maxie Eisen, the Simon Legree of the pushcart peddlers; associated with O'Banion in the Cragin distillery.

Jerry O'Connor, Loop gambling-house proprietor and vice president of the Theater and Building Janitors' Union.

William Scott Stewart, a former assistant State's attorney, and counsel for Alterie.

Vincent the Schemer Drucci, erstwhile telephone-coin-box thief; crook and beer runner.

Earl Hymie Weiss, ex-burglar and safe-cracker, who motorized murder.

Into this assemblage was ushered Colonel Albert A. Sprague, Harvard graduate; wealthy; a distinguished civic personage; commissioner of public works in the Dever administration. He was the Democratic nominee for United States Senator against Charles S. Deneen.

With him were County Clerk Robert M. Sweitzer, unsuccessful candidate for mayor of Chicago on the Democratic ticket in 1911, 1915, and 1919, Chief of Detectives Michael Hughes, and Police Lieutenant Charles Egan.

Colonel Sprague delivered a talk and sat down with the gunmen, as did Mr. Sweitzer and the others. There was a copious flow of pre-war Scotch, wine, and beer. The dining-room was decorated with the national colors, festoons of tissue streamers in red, white, and blue.

Jerry O'Connor, the union's vice president, received a $2,500 diamond stick-pin, O'Banion a $1,500 platinum wrist-watch—and Alterie almost shot a waiter.

The garçons, as is customary, had chosen one of their number to pass the hat for tips. Alterie wasn't aware of what was coming off until the collector approached his table. He whipped out his two guns and vociferated:

"Hey, you, none of that racket stuff goes here!" Then to the diners, "Shall I kill him?"

"Naw, let him suffer," chortled O'Banion, and Alterie dismissed him with a playful whack on the head.

The only O'Banion notable Colonel Sprague didn't meet that night was Samuel J. Nails Morton, dude and front man of the North Side gang, who had won the French *Croix de Guerre* for leading a squad of the 131st Illinois Infantry over the top after he had been twice wounded. He returned home a first lieutenant. In 1921 he and Hirschey Miller killed a couple of policemen in a black-and-tan café. Twice they faced a jury and twice they shook hands with their twelve peers.

Nails was a well-known figure on the Lincoln Park

bridle paths, where the city's best people do their horse-back riding. He liked mettlesome steeds. A stirrup leather broke during a morning canter and he was thrown and kicked to death.

Alterie, cogitating this, called at the stables and rented Nails' mount, ostensibly for a ride.

"We taught that ——— horse of yours a lesson," he telephoned three hours later. "If you want the saddle go and get it."

He had shot the animal.

The mayor ordered Hughes to explain his presence at the O'Banion dinner. What he said to Colonel Sprague is not of record. Hughes' explanation was that he had been told that it was to be just a party for Jerry O'Connor, but that when he arrived and "recognized a number of notorious characters I had thrown into the detective bureau basement a half-dozen times I knew I had been framed, and withdrew almost at once."

Hughes was only an incident of a situation, which, as in 1923, was beyond the mayor's control. He was up against the system. Its contact with the criminal element, which prior to 1924 had been maintained with more or less stealth, took a social turn that year, assuming the form of testimonial dinners, at which politicians fraternized cheek by jowl with gangsters, openly, in the big downtown hotels. The lavish ostentatiousness and general prodigality of these repasts inspired a clergy-man to refer to them as "Belshazzar feasts." They became an institution of the Chicago scene and marked the way to the moral and financial collapse of the municipal and county governments in 1928–29.

As for Colonel Sprague's vote-seeking expedition into O'Banion's borough, it was barren of results. Mr. Deneen's plurality in the Forty-second and Forty-third Wards was 5,938. He polled 17,327 votes to Colonel Sprague's 11,389. State's Attorney Robert E. Crowe's plurality over Michael L. Igoe, Torrio's counsel in the O'Connor-Bucher-Meeghan slayings, was even greater—9,315. The two wards gave Mr. Crowe 18,-961 votes and Mr. Igoe 9,646.

That was November 4th. O'Banion was still boasting of it on November 10th, when Carmen Vacco, city sealer, and James Genna, of the six brothers, came in to buy flowers for the funeral of Mike Merlo, founder and president of the Unione Sicilione, who had died a natural death.

"I turned the trick," O'Banion chuckled. He was in high spirits, chock-full of banter, with the Irish grin working overtime.

Vacco, whom Merlo had put in office, gave O'Banion a $750 order. They were sparing no expense on Mike. A local sculptor had been commissioned to mold a life-sized wax effigy of him. It cost $5,000 and in the procession to the cemetery occupied a touring car, preceding the hearse.

Telling O'Banion to remain in the shop, as others of Merlo's friends would be in for flowers, Vacco and Genna left. Sure enough, within five minutes, the telephone rang and a masculine voice conveyed the information that the customers were on their way over.

O'Banion was in the rear of the shop, which was divided by a partition, clipping the stems of a bunch of chrysanthemums. With him was William Crutchfield, a negro porter. It was the noon hour.

A blue Jewett sedan, headed south, stopped, with engine idling, at the curb, directly opposite the entrance. It contained four men. One stayed at the wheel. Three alighted. Once in the shop they walked abreast. The man in the center was tall, well built, smooth-shaven, wearing a brown overcoat and a brown fedora hat. The other two were short and stocky.

O'Banion was saying to Crutchfield, "The floor is littered with leaves and petals, Bill. Better brush them up." He heard the customers enter and went to the front of the shop.

"Hello, boys! You from Mike Merlo's?" was his greeting. In his left hand he held his florist's shears. His right was extended.

"Yes," replied the center man, grasping the extended right.

This much Crutchfield witnessed, having swept up the litter and passing the swinging door, then partly open, at that moment. The rest he heard.

One, two, three, four, five, six times the guns spoke—two bullets in the right breast; a third through the larynx; a fourth to the left of it a bit; a fifth in the right cheek. The five were fired within as many seconds. There was a pause before the sixth. It was the finish shot, to make certain of the job. It was fired into the left cheek as O'Banion lay sprawled among his flowers. The revolver was held so close that the skin was powder-burned.

The center man had held O'Banion's right in a vise-like grip while the man on his left did the shooting.

The man on his right, presumably, had imprisoned O'Banion's left to prevent his drawing his emergency revolver. Obviously it had all been carefully rehearsed. The sedan had been driven around the corner and was headed west in Superior Street. Leaving the shop, the three ran to it, jumped in, and were whirled away. And soon the word was passing in speakeasies and club lounges:

"Deany's been bumped off."

Thus was the handshake murder introduced to Chicago. There were but two witnesses—Crutchfield, and an eleven-year-old schoolboy, Gregory Summers, stationed during the noon hour at North State Street and East Chicago Avenue, a hundred yards distant, as a junior traffic officer. He heard several shots, he said, and saw three men run out of the shop. "Two of them were dark and they looked like foreigners. The other man had a light complexion." Crutchfield, who had a close-up view, said that the center or tall man, "might have been a Jew or Greek, but the other two were Italians."

Today, more than five years after, the one contribution toward a solution of the crime is the deduction made by Captain William Schoemaker of the detective bureau—"Old Shoes,"—tough as mulehide, crotchety as a grizzly with a sore tooth, hated, feared, probably the greatest copper ever produced by the Chicago police department.

"Crutchfield's story," said he, "is that O'Banion went to meet the three men, holding the shears in his left hand, his right extended.

"O'Banion, above all things, knew he was marked for

THE SMILING FLORIST

One of the few pictures of Dion O'Banion, taken while
ruling the North Side gang. He carried three
guns but died without a chance to use any.

POLICE PROTECTION!

Nothing extraordinary about Capone's Chicago home at 7244 Prairie Avenue. The police car waited for his appearance after his release from a Pennsylvania Penitentiary. He didn't show up.

death. He knew it might come at any moment. Ordinarily, when talking to strangers, he stood with feet apart, the right hand on the hip, thumb to rear and fingers down in front. The left was usually in his coat pocket. In this position he was ready for instant action with the automatics in the specially tailored pockets.

"But we have him advancing to meet these fellows without hesitation—his right hand extended. He felt safe. He knew them—at least by sight—and did not suspect them."

Further than that the investigation could not progress. It encountered "the inevitable Italian wall of silence."

Torrio, Capone, and the Gennas were questioned.

"The day before he was killed I gave him an order for $10,000 worth of flowers," said Torrio. "Our boys wanted to send some floral pieces to Mike Merlo's house and we all chipped in and gave the business to Dion."

Cook County's coroner finally wrote it off, "Slayers not apprehended. John Scalise and Albert Anselmi and Frank Yale [of New York City, since killed] suspected, but never brought to trial."

The gangster funeral era dates from the O'Banion obsequies. He was laid out in a $10,000 casket, bought in the East and shipped to Chicago in a special express freight car. A sob sister described it as "equipped with solid silver and bronze double walls, inner sealed and air tight, with heavy plate glass above and a couch of white satin below, with tufted cushion extra for his left hand to rest on; at the corners, solid silver posts, carved in wonderful designs."

The remains were exhibited for three days at the undertaking establishment of John A. Sbarbaro, 708 North Wells Street. Mr. Sbarbaro was also an assistant State's attorney, he and William H. McSwiggin representing Mr. Crowe's office in most of the gangster-killing inquiries. A glimpse of the scene in Mr. Sbarbaro's mortuary chapel is afforded us by another sob sister:

"Silver angels stood at the head and feet with their heads bowed in the light of ten candles that burned in solid golden candlesticks they held in their hands. Beneath the casket, on the marble slab that supports its glory, is the inscription, 'Suffer little children to come unto me.' And over it all the perfume of flowers."

Mounted police cleared the streets the day of the funeral. Plain-clothes men mingled with the mourners and cautioned them against indiscriminate use of fire-arms. There were twenty-six truckloads of flowers—$50,000 worth. Feature pieces were a heart of American Beauty roses, standing eight feet high; a blanket of roses, orchids, and lilies, measuring seven by ten feet, sent to cover the grave at Mount Carmel; an arch from which swung two white peace doves; a huge wreath from the Teamsters' Union; and a basket of roses labeled, "From Al."

Torrio and Capone steeled themselves to attend the services. They knew what the O'Banions were thinking. They did not dare stay away. They sat opposite George Bugs Moran, Earl Hymie Weiss, and Vincent the Schemer Drucci at the mortuary chapel; rode with them to the cemetery; faced them across the grave at the cemetery. Then Torrio fled the city, with the

O'Banions in pursuit, trailing him to Hot Springs, Arkansas, to New Orleans, to the Bahamas and to Cuba, then back again to the United States; finally overtaking and shooting him down in the presence of his wife, in front of his Chicago home. So Torrio fades from the picture and Capone alone remains, in the rôle of General Al the Scarface.

O'Banion's death marked the beginning of the real Bootleg Battle of the Marne. Madison Street, extending westward from Lake Michigan and the Loop, and bisecting the geographical center of the city, was No Man's Land. Across it, the struggle deadlocked back and forth for four years and three months—from November of 1924 until February 14, 1929, when the killing of seven O'Banions in a North Clark Street garage (the Moran gang massacre) led to a truce.

In the fullest sense, it was a war for commercial supremacy. Capone's two chief objectives were the crushing of the O'Banions on the North Side—and their allies on other sectors—and control of the Unione Sicilione (the alky cooking-guild), Golden Fleece of prohibition Chicago. It comprises some 15,000 Sicilians, disciplined like an army; implacable of purpose; swift and silent of deed; the Mafia of Italy transplanted to the United States. Capone's ambition here caused endless bloodshed. Every man aspiring to its presidency died by the gun. The record is:

Angelo Genna, one of the six brothers, who sought to succeed Mike Merlo; killed May 26, 1925.

Samuel Samoots Amatuna, the next aspirant; killed October 13, 1925.

Antonio Lombardo, killed September 7, 1928.

Pasquale Lolordo, who succeeded Lombardo; killed January 8, 1929.

Joseph Guinta, killed May 8, 1929.

No matter. Ever in the background loomed the figure of General Al the Scarface, seeing to it that out of the slaughter there should arise a Capone man to head the Unione. One always did.

By the fall of 1927 the Torrio dream of a booze monopoly was an actuality. Capone altogether commanded the sources of a revenue estimated by government investigators at $105,000,000 a year, divided as follows:

Beer and liquor, including alky-cooking......	$60,000,000
Gambling establishments and dog-tracks......	25,000,000
Vice, dance halls, roadhouses, and other resorts	10,000,000
Rackets..................................	10,000,000

Of this, the take by police, city and county politicians, and dry agents was, of course, enormous. In addition there were legitimate expenses, such as the payrolls of the booze syndicate. No accurate estimate is possible as to the amount Capone was pocketing, but those in his confidence have put it at $30,000,000. Yet:

"If I had known," said Capone, the time they tried to bribe the chef in the Little Italy café to put prussic acid in his soup; "what I was stepping into in Chicago I never would have left the Five Points outfit."

There have been more attempts upon his life than upon that of any other gangster. He is the most-shot-at man in America. Except for the interlude in Eastern Penitentiary there has not been a second's peace of mind for him. Days he lived in an armored car; nights he slept with sentinels at his door. In 1927 there was posted an offer of $50,000 to any gunman who would accomplish his death. For all this writer knows the offer still stands.

After their chief's funeral, the O'Banions launched a furious offensive, whose climax was a daylight attack on Capone's suburban stronghold by eight carloads of machine-gun squads and sawed-off shotgun crews. Operating with soldierly precision, they poured a thousand slugs and bullets into a block of restaurants, shops, and hotels.

"This is war," editorialized a Chicago newspaper.

Nothing like it was ever known before in an American community in peace-time.

PART TWO

THERE were four Al Capones:

Al, the feudal baron of Cicero.

Al, the Michigan Avenue business man—booze and racketeer boss.

Al, the seigneur of a Florida estate.

Al, the home boy.

In Cicero, his abode was the Hawthorne Hotel, a three-story brick structure—really a garrison—with steel-shuttered windows and a heavily stocked arsenal at 4823 West Twenty-second Street, the central block of the suburb's main-stem thoroughfare. It was the Hawthorne that rubberneck bus ballyhooers called "the Capone Castle."

Entrance was through a passageway, twenty-five feet long, opening off the street, leading to the lobby, which was quadrangular in form. The chairs, settees, lounges —all the furniture, in fact, including the clerk's desk, the telephone switchboard and the cigar counter—were so arranged as to front on the passageway. The visitor, therefore, found himself in the center of a kind of stage, undergoing a visual onslaught. His coming had been tipped off by a lookout at the street door who had pressed a warning buzzer.

There were never fewer than a dozen ostensible idlers in the lobby—fellows with indigo-stippled chins and eyes as expressionless as those of a dead mackerel;

the Capone bodyguard. They gazed from behind newspapers and through a haze of cigarette smoke amid a silence that was ear-splitting. The bellhops, the room clerk, and the girl at the telephone switchboard were on the Capone payroll.

Here, as securely entrenched as in a fortress, Capone directed the bootleg war, as well as his various Cicero enterprises. Aside from vice, gambling, and booze, the chief of these was the Hawthorne Kennel Club dogtracks, a $500,000 project, with four hundred greyhounds to chase the electric rabbit.

Here, too, he indulged his hobby—passion, rather—of crap shooting. The Italians have a phrase for great art, *"il poco più,"* meaning "the little more." Capone addressing the dice in a hot crap game, coatless, vestless, collarless, the floor littered with greenbacks, was indisputably *il poco più.* He scaled the dramatic heights with his colloquies and pantomime.

Thespis could not approach the feeling with which, on hands and knees, he supplicated fickle, capricious Phœbe, or wheedled Little Joe from Decatur, or browbeat Big Dick. The pathos registered at Box Cars, Snake Eyes, or Two Rolls and No Coffee, was heartrending.

He thought in terms of the gran'—a thousand dollars —and never made a pass for under that amount except when his guests included persons "not in the bucks." The dice sessions often lasted all night and through to noon of the following day. The winnings did not interest Capone. It was the excitement. He was a gambling addict.

The bookies gloated when he hove in sight. He was

their meat. He would bet as high as $100,000 on a horse-race. He seldom played them across the board. He liked to "slap it on the nose." He was gullible as to sure things. If a tout happened to pick one that came in he would toss him a gran'. He estimated in 1929 that he had lost close to $10,000,000 to the bookies since coming to Chicago nine years before. His I. O. U. was par at any racetrack. In New Orleans after a losing day he wrote one for $500,000 and it was accepted without question.

But the stock market has yet to wean a dollar from him.

"It's a racket," says he.

Because of its distance from the city, the Hawthorne provided a discreet rendezvous for politicians, and so it was here that Capone entertained and conferred with Chicago and Cook County officialdom. The censorious were so unkind as to refer to it as his remote control. His election-eve dinners were famous—modern editions of the feasts of Lucullus—invitations to which were covetously regarded by the local Catos and Marcus Aureliuses.

Assistant State's Attorney William H. McSwiggin, who prosecuted John Scalise and Albert Anselmi at the first of their three trials for the murder of Police Officers Harold F. Olson and Charles B. Walsh, was not unfamiliar with his hospitality.

"Little Mac, a great friend of mine," said Capone. "Always trying to help somebody. I was talking to him in my hotel just before he was shot."

He meant the night McSwiggin was killed in company with two beer gangsters who had been trying to muscle in on Capone territory.

This is by way of preface to the occasion when Capone is generally conceded to have eclipsed his own record as genial host. It was the dinner celebrating the final acquittal of Scalise and Anselmi. A hundred thousand dollars had been spent in defense of his two ace killers. The case had dragged along, due to crafty legal tactics, for two years. The public furor had abated. The third jury had returned a jig-time verdict that Scalise and Anselmi had only defended themselves against unwarranted police aggression. Gangland had scored another victory.

The affair was exclusive. There were not more than a hundred present, but they were the Who's Who of later coroner's inquests—Antonio Lombardo, who assumed the presidency of the Unione Sicilione, always fatal; Pasquale Lolordo, who succeeded him, and followed him to the cemetery; Joseph Guinta, the dancing torpedo with the chilled-steel eyes; Anthony Ferraro, one of Lombardo's bodyguard; Hughey Stubby McGovern, William Gunner McPadden, and Theodore Tony the Greek Anton, who ran the restaurant above the Smoke Shop, Capone gambling joint operated by Frankie Pope, millionaire newsie.

Scalise and Anselmi, of course, were the lions of the evening. They sat at the speakers' table, drinking many toasts to the jury that freed them. The jubilation was hysterical. The only outsider there was a professional man, who attended as Capone's guest. His description, verbatim, was:

"If the dinner cost a jitney it cost $25,000. I have sat in at many political love feasts where wine flowed, but never, never as at this party. It was a deluge. At the climax of the festivities, the guests staged a sham battle with champagne, uncorking bottles by the case and letting the contents fly at one another. Wine spurted everywhere, and lay in puddles on the floor. The popping of corks was like machine-gun fire. Brut, Cliquot, Piper Heidsieck and Mumm's—$20 the quart F. O. B. Chicago. O God! O Montreal!"

However pleasant the social side of the Cicero picture may have been, the business side was something else again. The program outlined by Ed Konvalinka, the soda-jerker who became a Main Street Warwick with the election of the Capone ticket, had rough going occasionally. A recalcitrant alderman, for instance, opposed a measure favored by Capone. His colleagues argued vehemently, but he stubbornly refused to listen to reason. Word of his attitude reached Capone, who hurried to the City Hall, waited till he emerged from the meeting, and then gave him a sound drubbing. Another time Capone's merry-andrews stormed the hall while the council was deliberating and chased the members out in a body.

Robert and Arthur St. John, brothers, were two newspaper editors Capone could neither bribe nor intimidate. They fought him tooth and nail. Robert edited the *Cicero Tribune* and Arthur the *Berwyn Tribune,* weeklies. Berwyn adjoined Cicero on the west.

Threats proving unavailing, Robert was slugged and kicked by gangsters led by Capone in person. Arthur, crusading against the invasion of vice in Berwyn, was fired upon by a carload of men just before an election day and kidnaped. He was held incommunicado for forty-eight hours, until the polls closed.

In off hours, Capone was fond of visiting with Tony the Greek, the restaurateur, over Frankie Pope's place, whose T-bone steaks were chefs-d'œuvres. Although Capone was and is a gourmet of parts and relished these, it was Tony's company more than his cookery that attracted him. He had a real affection for the man. There comes to mind a Gilbert and Sullivan couplet, running, as accurately as memory can recall:

> When a felon's not engaged in his employment,
> His capacity for innocent enjoyment,
> Is just like any other man's.

In the rear of the restaurant was a table reserved for Capone's personal use. Curtains hid it from prying, possibly hostile eyes, and there he would spend whole evenings with his friend Tony. Needless to say, Tony was another who esteemed Capone "a right guy." He was of the species known as Capone fans, which numbers thousands in Chicago. He liked nothing better than to spin yarns of Capone's big-heartedness. One of these had to do with a bedraggled newsie on a rainy November evening. He ambled in with an armful of papers, and approached Capone's booth.

"How many you got left, kid?" asked Capone.

"About fifty, I guess," he answered.

"Throw them on the floor. Here," handing him a $20 bill, "run along home to your mother."

There was one story Tony never told. It happened on a bitterly cold night in January, when a blizzard howled off the lake and the streets were caked with ice. Few humans were abroad. The restaurant was deserted save for Capone and Tony in the booth. The bell attached to the door leading to the stairway tinkled.

"Customers coming up," said Tony. "I'll get their order and be back in a second."

Seconds became minutes, minutes hours, and he did not return.

The story Tony never told was set down by the coroner.

"Theodore Tony the Greek Anton, restaurant proprietor of Cicero, taken for a ride. Body found in quicklime. Slayers not apprehended."

Capone sat in the booth that night as the minutes lengthened, sobbing like a child. He knew what had happened. Enemy gangsters in their reprisals were striking at him through his friendships.

What price bootleg glory?

There were four Al Capones, and Al, the Chicago business man, was a man of two addresses and an alias. At the Metropole Hotel, 2300 South Michigan Avenue, he was Al the Big Shot of politics, booze, rackets, vice, and gambling. It was gangdom's G. H. Q. It is within walking distance of the Loop, in the city's finest boulevard, often called its Fifth Avenue, and which parallels that Grant Park where in 1933 is to be held the World's Fair. A frequenter of the Metropole during the Capone régime describes it thus:

It was garrisoned like Birger's blockhouse in the woods in Bloody Williamson county. The Capones occupied as many as fifty rooms on two heavily guarded floors. They operated their own private elevators and maintained their own service bars. Gambling went on openly and women visited the floors at all hours of the day and night. The aroma of highly flavored Italian foods brought in from the outside permeated the corridors. Nearly every hotel rule and regulation was violated daily.

On Sunday mornings especially the lobby of the Metropole was a beehive of activity. Prominent criminal lawyers and high officials of the police department, along with politicians and divekeepers waited their turn to consult with the Big Shot. Policemen in uniform streamed in and out. A blind pig operated in the lobby by a semi-public official did a land office business.

In an underground vault, especially constructed, were stored $150,000 worth of wines and liquors. The stock was constantly replenished. It was for the gang's private use. Capone himself occupied rooms 409 and 410, overlooking the boulevard. The hallway was patrolled by sentinels, posted at regular intervals as in an army. In an ante-room of the Capone suite was the bodyguard, equipped with the latest type of firearms.

A couple of blocks up the street from the G. H. Q., Al the Big Shot did a Hyde-and-Jekyll and became Al the doctor—Dr. Brown of 2146 South Michigan Avenue. A casual visitor, opening the door on which the unpretentious name was lettered, would have had no cause to suspect that he was in other than the reception room of a physician's suite. The furnishings were identical with those prescribed by the medical conventions, even to last year's magazines on the center table. The visitor might have observed that the thorough Dr. Brown had his own pharmacopœia—tiers of shelves against one wall behind a small counter, upon which in orderly array reposed rows of mysterious bottles, ranging in size from phials to quarts.

An annual business totaling millions was transacted here. The doctor subterfuge camouflaged the general offices of the Capone bootleg syndicate. The reception-room bottles contained stock samples of every known variety of liquor, and prospective customers were allowed to take them to their own chemists for analysis.

Here was a supertrust operating with the efficiency of a great corporation. It had a complete auditing system, maintained by a clerical staff of twenty-five persons. There were loose-leaf ledgers, card indexes, memorandum accounts, and day-books. No item was overlooked. Specifically, the records showed:

1. The names of more than two hundred well-known Chicagoans, and of many large hotels and drugstores, all patrons of the syndicate.

2. The names of police officers and prohibition agents on the syndicate's pay-off list.

3. All channels through which booze is brought from rum row, off New York City harbor, and from Miami and New Orleans.

4. Details of the management of four big breweries controlled by the syndicate and producing the bulk of Chicago's beer.

5. Loose-leaf ledgers showing the cost system used in disorderly houses.

6. Blue books of all the saloons in Chicago and outlying towns buying the syndicate's ale, booze, and beer.

The man in charge of the syndicate's offices and who had thus systematized its operations was Jack Guzik, admittedly the brains of the Capone organization. He is a brother of Harry, a convicted pander, pardoned by Governor Small before he had served any of his sentence. So highly does Capone esteem Guzik that once when his friend was ill in Michael Reese Hospital he stationed a twenty-four hour watch at his bedside to guard against assassination.

Guzik's standing in the community is such that when there was a wedding in his family in the summer of 1929, a morning newspaper made social mention of it, with a two-column picture, also noting that among those present were Aldermen John Coughlin of the First Ward and William V. Pacelli of Morris Eller's Twentieth Ward; Police Captain Hugh McCarthy and Ralph Bottles Capone, brother of the subject of this sketch—who was not present, being detained temporarily in Philadelphia.

Besides his sedentary duties at 2146 South Michigan Avenue, Guzik was in close contact with the various outside units of the syndicate, receiving reports in code of liquor shipments from across the Canadian border, and when they would arrive, as well as of those from Florida and New York City. He also kept in contact with the capable Mr. Danny Stanton, head of the Capone muscle department, whose activities were supported by such pillars as Hughey Stubby McGovern, William Gunner Padden, Frank Dutch Carpenter, Raymond Cassidy, and Thomas Johnson—all except Stanton now pushing up the daisies.

The syndicate was inconvenienced and dismayed when the police, responding to Mayor Dever's unremitting efforts to purge the city, raided its general offices and seized the records. Detective Sergeant Edward Birmingham, who participated in the raid, said he had been offered a bribe of $5,000 to forget the book-keeping system and the records.

It looked as if the administration were finally going to get somewhere. In the language of Mayor Dever, "We've got the goods this time." The evidence of graft and corruption among police officials and prohibition agents was damning. It was announced that the documents would be turned over to the Government for action.

They weren't. Municipal Judge Howard Hayes had impounded them the day after the raid, and at a special hearing, of which there was no formal notification, returned them to the syndicate without giving the Federal authorities opportunity to inspect them.

United States District Attorney Edwin A. Olson protested at what he described as a direct refusal to co-operate with the Government and made public a letter he had written to Judge Hayes asking him to withhold decision pending an investigation. The return of the records by Judge Hayes followed within sixteen hours a request from Federal officials at New Orleans for a transcript of them. The request, of course, was not granted.

In June of 1925 Capone decided to have his life insured, and so notified the Chicago office of a large company. A representative was sent to interview him.

"What is your occupation?" he asked Capone.

"Dealer in second-hand furniture," answered Capone.

"And he never cracked a smile," the representative reported.

The other questions being put and answered, Capone was told he would hear further from the company, which he did. Although actuaries do not classify his stated occupation among the hazardous risks, the application was rejected. He tried a half-dozen other companies with no better luck.

In the Chicago city directory of 1928-29 he was listed as a salesman.

"What is your business?" asked Assistant United States District Attorney Daniel Anderson during a Federal grand jury investigation of Chicago Heights booze cases.

"I must stand on my constitutional rights and refuse to answer anything particular about that," said Capone.

He had three portentous reasons for wanting his life insured—George Bugs Moran, Earl Hymie Weiss, and Vincent the Schemer Drucci. There had been four, but Two-Gun Louis Alterie had departed. It was gangdom and not the courts that rid the city of the blustering cowboy hoodlum.

Alterie had only affectionate memories of the courts. Their leniency toward gangsters was manifested in remarkable fashion in a case in which he was involved. He had made himself conspicuous after O'Banion's death. At the inquest he had dared the killers "to shoot it out at State and Madison." He had gone about town flourishing his side-arms in night-life places and reiterating the challenge.

Deputy Police Commissioner John Stege walked in on him one Sabbath morn in Ike Bloom's Midnight Frolics in Twenty-second Street and arrested him with a cocked gun on the hip. He was held at the detective bureau until Monday without being booked. His lawyer, William Scott Stewart, a former assistant State's attorney, then appeared before Judge William J. Lindsay of the criminal court to compel Stege to file charges. The judge ruled for Stewart and Alterie was charged with carrying a revolver and with disorderly conduct.

Quoting the conservative *Chicago Daily News* on the judicial procedure:

JUDGE GOOD TO ALTERIE

Scolds Police for Arresting Gunman: Frees Him on 2 Charges.

Reprimanding the police for "wasting their time" in arresting Louis Alterie, Judge William J. Lindsay in the criminal court this afternoon ordered that Alterie, pal of the late Dion O'Banion, and two others, be booked on two charges and released on $1,000 bonds. . . .

"Why do you waste your time on this kind of stuff?" demanded Judge Lindsay, as he acquiesced in the pleas of William Scott Stewart to have Alterie and the others booked. "Why, I have to carry a revolver myself because my neighborhood is so poorly policed. My home has been robbed and that is merely illustrative of the experience of hundreds of others."

Gangdom had other ideas. George Bugs Moran, the ex-convict, led Alterie aside in Friar's Inn, a couple of nights later, when Alterie was boasting of his standing, and said:

"You're gettin' us in bad. You gab too much. Beat it."

The implication was unmistakable. His own kind had sat in judgment on him. Moran was delivering its findings. Neither expert counsel nor friendly judges could help him now. He could go out on a train or in a coffin.

He chose the train, returning to the ranch in Colorado.

Capone wanted insurance, for the guns had roared again, with the vengeful O'Banions pushing the offensive. Hell-bent, the three musketeers, Drucci, Moran, and Weiss, had come riding across No Man's Land; over the Madison Street deadline; past the Capone G. H. Q. at the Metropole Hotel; on south to Fifty-fifth and State streets, where they had let Capone's sedan have it with sawed-off shotguns and machine guns.

"They let it have everything but the kitchen stove," commented an old bureau squad sergeant.

Slugs and bullets, at three-foot range, had raked it from stem to stern, riddling the hood and tonneau and demolishing the engine. The O'Banions had used a touring car with drawn curtains, driving slowly alongside the sedan and blasting away from the front and rear seats. Sylvester Barton, the chauffeur, was wounded in the back. He dropped to the floor and escaped further injury.

Capone missed death by minutes. He had been inspecting his booze and beer territory and had just stepped into a restaurant.

Within a week Torrio got his. The O'Banions, trailing him after Dion's wake and funeral from Chicago to Hot Springs, Arkansas, to New Orleans, to the Bahamas and Havana, Cuba, and back to Palm Beach, had at last overtaken him in front of his South Side home, at 7011 Clyde Avenue.

He and Mrs. Torrio had been shopping in the Loop and had returned with several parcels. She had stepped out of the car first and was halfway to the entrance of the building. Torrio was still inside the car collecting the parcels. On the opposite side of the street a gray automobile was parked. It contained three men. Two leaped from it, running. One, with a sawed-off shotgun, posted himself at the rear of Torrio's car, and the other, with a revolver, at the front.

They opened fire simultaneously. A charge of buckshot ripped through the body of the coach. Robert Barton, chauffeur, brother of Sylvester, was struck in the right knee. Torrio wasn't scratched. He dropped the parcels and started running for the apartment building. He was the apex of a triangle of which the gunmen were the base.

They concentrated their cross-fire on him. A .45 caliber bullet from the revolver buried itself in his left arm. He wheeled, still half running, to reach for his own gun, and a charge of buckshot caught him full in the front, shattering his jaw and piercing his lungs and abdomen. He folded up on the sidewalk.

It looked as if the mighty Torrio was about ready to strike out. As he lay unconscious, the O'Banion pistoleer dashed over to administer the *coup de grace*— a bullet in the brain. However, he had emptied his revolver and it was necessary to insert a new cartridge clip. As he was doing that, and the sawed-off shotgunner was reloading, their driver honked the horn sharply. Apparently it was a prearranged signal for flight. Both fled to the car, which disappeared around the corner.

"I know who they are," said Torrio, in Jackson Park Hospital. "It's my business."

Capone rushed to his bedside. The temperamental

Neapolitan was in tears and forgot himself so far as to blurt:

"The gang did it! The gang did it!"

He took command of the sick-room, employing extra private nurses and posting a bodyguard of four men—two in the room and two outside the building. Torrio insisted, too, that he be kept in an inside room. He was in the hospital sixteen days. When he left, February 9th, it was via a fire escape, to circumvent any designs of the O'Banions at another attempt on his life.

A tough egg, Torrio. Reared with the New York City Five Pointers, his playmates had been killers like Gyp the Blood and Lefty Louie, and with them he had participated in only his conscience knows how much crime. He was among those questioned in the murder of Herman Rosenthal, the gambler. Colosimo had brought him on to Chicago and the Mafia had ceased its persecution after three of its members had been assassinated. He was tough, all right, BUT——

"Johnny's the same as a lot of fighters in the ring," said a straight-thinking Chicagoan who knows him. "He can dish it out, but he can't take it."

Vainly the police questioned Torrio, Capone, and Barton, the chauffeur. They stuck by the code. No squawking for them. This was "their" business.

But seventeen-year-old Peter Veesaert, son of the janitor of a neighboring apartment building, was beholden to no such ethics. Three times in as many identification tests, he picked Moran as the revolver assailant. He had witnessed the whole attack. He recited in detail how Moran had been the first to leap from the gray automobile and open fire. He faced him at the detective bureau and said, "You're the man."

"Who? Me?" growled the ex-convict.

"Yes," the boy fearlessly insisted.

Moran was never indicted nor brought to trial.

Within seventy-two hours he was released on bonds of $5,000 by Judge William J. Lindsay, although police headquarters had asked that he be detained "pending the uncovering of more evidence." Assistant State's Attorney John A. Sbarbaro represented Mr. Crowe's office in the investigation.

Torrio refused to aid in the prosecution, and another finis was written by the Cook County authorities to a gangster shooting. Not by General Al the Scarface, though. In his ledger it was docketed, "Unfinished business." He was to wait a long time.

". . . can dish it out, but can't take it."

Torrio was using fire-escapes and Capone thought a portable fort would be comfortable to ride around in. He gave the order for his celebrated armored sedan. The body was of steel construction, the windows of bullet-proof glass, and the fenders non-dentable. The average family sedan weighs between 3,600 and 4,000 pounds. Capone's weighed seven tons. It cost him $20,-000. Shrapnel, buckshot, or machine-gun bullets would splatter off it as harmlessly as raindrops off a tin roof. It had a special combination lock so that his enemies couldn't jimmy a door to plant a bomb under him.

It became a familiar sight in Michigan Avenue, Lake Shore Drive, and Sheridan Road. Capone was fond of motoring and almost any evening might have been seen taking the benediction of the air; puffing his hefty black cigar as he lolled back against the overstuffed leather cushions in the rear seat; his eleven-and-a-half-carat diamond shining for all it was worth, which was $50,000.

Then there was the convoy. Preceding the portable fort was a scout flivver, which darted in and out of traffic, keeping a distance of a half-block, and performing somewhat the same duties as a destroyer to a battleship. Immediately following the fort was a touring car containing the Capone bodyguard. This convoy seemed superfluous considering the invulnerability of the new equipage, but Capone was taking no chances. His acute terror of death was demonstrated shortly before he got the armored sedan. He had been to the Criminal Courts Building. As he was leaving, a group of cameramen began shooting pictures. "Don't take my automobile license number, boys," he begged, but one fellow had already done so, and the picture appeared in an afternoon newspaper. Capone gave the car away and bought another, thus obtaining a new number. "That picture would have put me on the spot," he explained.

The appearance of the portable fort and convoy in downtown Chicago was always an occasion of public interest. "There goes Al," would fly from lip to lip, and pedestrians would crowd to sidewalk curbs, craning necks as eagerly as for a circus parade. It was a civic spectacle to linger in the recollections of strangers within the gates of America's second largest city during 1925, 1926, 1927, and 1928. If visitors were deprived of it in 1929 neither the Chicago police department nor the State's attorney's office of Cook County could be held accountable—much less the Federal prohibition authorities. The responsibility was Philadelphia's.

Said the *Chicago Tribune* at the time of his arrest there:

This is the first time Capone has been convicted of any offense and punished. So far as is known Philadelphia was out of his territory. He was found on the city streets with a gun in his pocket, but he was not wanted in connection with other lawlessness in Pennsylvania. It is not charged that he was in any of the city's own gangs of bootleggers, gunmen and corruptionists. . . .

He is in jail not because he was a successful and persistent violator of the Volstead act or because he was convicted of murder, but because he violated a Pennsylvania state law, the equivalent of which in Illinois he has always violated.

By common repute and common police knowledge he has been the head of a murderous gang living by defiance of federal law. The federal officers in Chicago knew him as such. The federal government has sent little bootleggers and distillers to jail. . . . But it has never given the chief gangster of the city enough disturbance to cause him really to notice it. . . . He has traveled from Chicago to Florida and from Florida while liquor was being wholesaled under his direction, a trade in which machine guns furnish the only sales resistance. . . .

Capone is in jail. It is not because of his years of violation of federal law, not because of the wealth he has made and distributed in such lawlessness, not because of his gang leadership and the murders committed, but because he had a pistol in his pocket when he came out of a Philadelphia moving picture theater.

The *Tribune*, whose policy is anti-Volstead, bears down upon the Federal authorities, to the exclusion of county and municipal authorities. In Chicago Capone's status was far above mere immunity to the law. There are many incidents illustrative of that fact.

A hoodlum had escaped from the Criminal Courts Building. A city-wide search was made for him. A squad of ambitious young coppers, acting on a confidential tip, raided the hangout of a South Side gang that was a subsidiary of the Capone organization. The hoodlum wasn't there, but several members of the gang were, and as the squad entered they threw their artillery on the floor. It consisted of automatics and a sawed-off shotgun, which the young coppers seized and took to their commanding officer.

"We got these off the ―― gang," they told him.

"Who gave you such orders? Take that stuff back," he said.

Soon the young coppers were advised that they were in bad and might be transferred to the bush. They should see Capone. He received them at G. H. Q.

"Well," he said, "I understand your captain wasn't to blame, and that you boys just made a mistake. I'm going to give you a break. After this, don't pull another boner."

Again, a henchman having been haled into court and held, contrary to his expressed wishes, Capone barked at one of the clerical staff at G. H. Q.:

"Get me Judge ――."

When he was put on the wire, Capone, without preliminary, said:

"I thought I told you to discharge that fellow."

"Oh," was the reply, "I was off the bench that day. I wrote a memo for Judge ――, and my bailiff forgot to deliver it."

"Forgot! Don't let him forget again."

A surprising incident occurred in May of 1927, when Commander Francesco de Pinedo, Mussolini's round-the-world flyer and good-will emissary, arrived off the city's front yard—Grant Park, at Monroe Street—in his Marchetti hydroplane, the *Santa Maria II*.

Pinedo's coming had been awaited for weeks. Chicago was his last scheduled stop in the United States. As he landed, sirens were blowing, whistles screeching, flags waving, and the populace huzzaing. The dignitaries comprising the welcoming committee were Dr. Ugo M. Galli, president of the local Fascisti; Leopold Zunini, Italian consul general, Judge Bernard P. Barasa to represent Mayor Thompson and the municipality, and, aboard the yacht of a millionaire radio manufacturer, Capone.

He was the first to greet Pinedo. The explanation for his presence given to the writer was that the police department had heard rumors of a plot to stage an anti-Fascisti demonstration and had appealed to Capone to make a personal appearance in the belief that it would serve as a more effective preventive of trouble than the detail of a hundred bluecoats.

There was no untoward happening except that Capone was reprimanded by a news cameraman for getting in his way when Pinedo stepped ashore.

"Hey, you, one side!" he bawled, and Capone meekly obeyed.

Ever since, in recalling the incident, the photographer groans:

"What a dumbbell I was—passing up a picture of Al welcoming a visitor to Chicago!"

AL CAPONE

Time had, indeed, wrought vast changes in our fellow townsman. Few now would recognize in the political Big Shot the roughneck bouncer of the Four Deuces, or in the tailored and chauffeured man about town the vulgar hoodlum who had flashed a deputy sheriff's star and waved a revolver at a common taxi-driver. It seemed unthinkable that Capone, the civic spectacle of the portable fort, could have been he who stooped to shoot a low bum like Joe Howard—"estate: 1 pair cuff buttons; cash, $17."

Getting a bit fastidious, too, as regards associates. Richard Bennett was having a party for Jim Tully, the novelist and playwright. Capone was invited.

"Who's going to be there?" he demanded.

The guest list was produced. He was noncommittal until his informant reached the names of the Byfields of the Hotel Sherman, on whose sixteenth floor are sequestered Chicago's mayor and Little City Hall.

"I hear both Frank and Jesse Byfield are good guys," he said. "I may go."

But he didn't. A theatrical press agent who loved his work not wisely, but too well, overdid his advance notices by announcing Capone's acceptance. That made it impossible. To have gone after the newspapers published it would have been to put himself on the spot.

It is a curious fact that Capone is the object of a sort of hero worship. People go out of their way to shake hands with him. The psychology of this is at least interesting. The writer is acquainted with a civil engineer of high repute who, on a business trip to Philadelphia, visited Eastern Penitentiary just to see him. He had not known him previously. He said he shook hands with him and told him, "Al, we're with you."

Wherever Capone went he was accorded preferential treatment. A typical instance was related by Westbrook Pegler, the sports writer, while in reminiscent mood:

"Last winter Mr. Al Capone, the doyen of the racketeers, was escorted to a seat within the working press reservation at the battle of the two home loving husbands [Stribling and Sharkey] in Miami Beach."

Mr. Pegler then draws certain conclusions, which, while not germane, are arresting:

"It is true that he was not there in an official capacity, but the public impression is such that persons are on official business at all times, wherever they may be.

"So when Dempsey, in his character as an official greeter for the Garden corporation, welcomed Mr. Capone and dusted off a chair for him, the scene was interpreted as a gesture of good fellowship and an exchange of amenities between two professions having much in common."

As usual the cameraman besought him to pose. One picture, which a newsreel sent around the country, was of "Gangland's King," as an inspired title-writer captioned Capone, standing with Jack Sharkey and Bill Cunningham, former all-American football player.

Capone's first stay in Florida was productive of a story frequently teacupped in Chicago's Gold Coast set because it concerns a family that is a member of it. Having decided to spend a winter on the Nile, the family advertised its Miami home for lease. A realty broker appeared with a prospect—season's rent in advance and no questions asked—and the deal was closed. Capone was, of course, the prospect. The best version of the story is that of Dick Little, who got it first hand from a friend of the lessors:

They went off to Egypt in fear and trepidation of what they would find left of their beautiful place when they returned. Furniture and china and *objets d'art* smashed, no doubt, with bullet holes through the taffeta curtains and the walls riddled. Why had they ever done such a silly thing! Their Egyptian winter was completely spoiled. . . .

At last they turned their faces homeward, and once through the customs made a beeline for Miami. But their beautiful place stood placidly in the Florida sunshine, just as they had left it; inside, the furniture, the curtains, the walls were unchanged.

Only in the silver chests there were eight or ten dozen new sets of sterling silver, and in the china closets stack after stack of new and beautiful china. They collapsed in chairs and stared at each other.

On the first of the month, however, there was some annoyance; the telephone bill arrived with a $500 long distance call to be paid. The lady of the house was furious. Her husband was more philosophical—had they not had their house returned to them in perfect condition after several months' occupancy by the Capones? . . . That afternoon a quiet little woman in the simplest of clothes drove up to the door in a high-powered motor car, and, announcing herself as Mrs. Alphonse Capone, requested to see the owner.

"I came," said the quiet little woman, "to pay our telephone bill. We did not know how much it would be when we left, but if you have it now I'll pay it."

The owner produced the bill and Mrs. Capone took a thousand-dollar bill from her pocketbook.

"Keep the change," she said, "I'm sure we must have broken something while we were here and I hope that will cover it."

Capone's next maneuver in Florida was to buy the Palm Island estate, three miles from downtown Miami. The transaction was conducted with much strategy, Capone's identity being concealed until the deal was closed.

The other millionaires on the island, if they had not known him by reputation, would have set him down as a quiet man of rather odd tastes. Wherever one roamed about the house or walled grounds there were bulky, hard-faced men—the Capone guards. He entertained extensively, his week-end parties often numbering seventy-five or a hundred guests. He was a gracious, affable host, anxious only to please those who might accept his hospitality.

As soon as the colony learned the identity of the newcomer there was a vehement protest. A delegation waited upon Solicitor R. R. Taylor of Dade County, Mayor J. Newton Lummus, Jr., and Chief of Police Guy C. Reeve of Miami. Mr. Taylor summoned Capone to his office and informed him that he was regarded as an undesirable.

"I am a property owner here," said Capone. "I have done nothing wrong. I don't intend to do anything wrong and I don't intend to leave. The only way you can get rid of me is to have the United States Supreme Court say there is a law to put me out."

He stayed, and as a result Miami became the winter Cicero of Chicago gangdom. Terry Druggan, hijacker and beer runner, bought an ocean-front place near Capone, and he and his pal and business partner, Frankie Lake, maintained open house during the tourist season. Hughey Stubby McGovern's mob moved in

and there was a general influx of gamblers and pick-
pockets to patronize the Hialeah racetrack and the
Miami dog-tracks. It pleased the Chicago police department.

Capone's Palm Island estate, his $20,000 car and
other minutiæ of affluence, engaged the attention of
the Intelligence unit of the internal revenue service.
An investigation was started that is still under way.
There is a suspicion that he is holding out in income
taxes. It is a Volsteadian paradox that the Government
in one rôle should stalk as criminals the class prohibition has enriched and in another should seek to
share in its gains. There is an element of comedy
in it.

"We believe Capone has had the advice of able lawyers in covering up his assets," an official close to the
office of the collector of internal revenue for the Chicago
district confided to the writer. He was discouraged.
"We know, for instance, that he owns a lot of Chicago
realty, but we can find little property in his name.

"His sources of income are known to us. We believe
he could cash in for $20,000,000. But where has he
hidden it? Our men get so far, then they find themselves in blind alleys. Just as an example we discovered
$100,000 in cash which his brother, Ralph, had secreted
in a safety-deposit box. Pin money. We get leads that
look good, but don't materialize.

"A theory which we have been investigating for
more than a year is that the bulk of his wealth is
handled by a bank which he controls through dummy
stockholders. Our information is that this bank is used
as a depositary by several bootleggers and racketeers.

If we can uncover it there will be some startling disclosures."

The official ended his talk with a grudging tribute. He said Capone had exceptional business ability and would have gone far in any legitimate line. Then he uncorked this:

"If he had only been honest, what a hero he would have made for a Horatio Alger tale!"

Heh, heh!

The reader has met Al, the feudal baron; Al, the business man; Al, the Palm Island seigneur. Let us present Al, the home boy.

Nine steps lead up from the sidewalk to the stoop of the two-story, two-flat, faced brick building at 7244 Prairie Avenue, on Chicago's South Side. There is nothing unusual about it or its surroundings. It is of the standardized type common to every American city and located in a typical city block.

Domiciled there, occupying both flats, were Capone and his wife, Mae; their eleven-year-old boy; Capone's mother, Mrs. Theresa Capone, widow of Gabriel; her daughter, Mafalda; her oldest son, John; and her youngest son, Matthew. Originally there were five sons, but Frank was killed in the Cicero election-day battling, and Ralph, better known as Bottles, lived elsewhere.

The Capone town house is in the Grand Crossing police district. South of it lies the Kensington district, commanded as this biography is written by Captain Michael Grady, who as a detective bureau lieutenant was indicted in the $1,000,000 Sibley warehouse liquor robbery. He and four of his squad sergeants were charged with convoying the stolen whiskey to the bootleggers' distribution stations. They were acquitted at their trial. O'Banion, indicted for the theft, was killed while the case was still pending.

He who is editorialized as "by common repute and common police knowledge head of a murderous gang" selected for his domestic fireside a locality securely remote from the scene of his professional activities. No gang shootings occur hereabouts. No aliens infest it. There are no alky-cookers, no gambling joints, no blind pigs. Life is tranquil, orderly, reposeful. It is a nine o'clock neighborhood—a refuge to which the tired business man may repair, certain of soothing easement from all cark and care.

Altogether there are thirty-four dwellings in the block. Of the householders, twenty-two own their own homes—sixty-six per cent and a fraction, a substantial ratio. An interesting coincidence is that three of these home-owners are members of the police department. At 7208, there are Henry Huttner, a policeman, and his wife; at 7212, Patrick J. Houlihan, a policeman, and his wife. They are on Capone's side of the street, ten doors north of him. On the opposite side, at 7211, there live Dominick Gavigan, sergeant of police, and Mrs. Gavigan. He is at this writing attached to the Gresham district, which adjoins Grand Crossing on the southwest.

So far as can be ascertained, the Capones are the only Italian family in the block. The others are of Scotch, Irish, or German ancestry. Their occupations conform to the typicalness of the block. They include a steam-fitter, a druggist, a grocer, the president of a clothing company, the efficiency expert of a publishing firm, a draftsman, a cement salesman, and two doors south of Capone, a retired Presbyterian minister.

The personal opinion in the block is that the Capones are good neighbors; that they bother nobody and mind their own business; that when the women folks do happen to borrow a cup of sugar, say, they return it promptly, heaping full.

If you had entrée when Capone was there, you would find him puttering about in carpet slippers and lounging robe—probably tuning in on the radio or more than likely playing games with his son, whom he idolizes. He would invite you to have a snack of spaghetti, and if you accepted, he would prepare it himself at the big kitchen range, an apron tied round his colloped neck. He prides himself on his spaghetti chefery. With the dish the guest could drink his fill of elegant Chianti.

The personal side of Capone teems with stories of his generosity. His sister, Mafalda, attended the Richards School at Twenty-fifth and Lime streets, whose student body is composed exclusively of girls between fourteen and sixteen years of age. Around Christmas time the Capone sedan would pull up at the entrance, jammed to the top with baskets of candy, fruits, turkeys, and gifts for every pupil and the teachers as well. Nobody was forgotten. Capone supervised the distribution, beaming like old St. Nick.

Urchins and hangers-on around the boxing shows always laid for him. He invariably bought an extra $100 worth of tickets, which he stuck in convenient pockets for expeditious disposal. Arrived at the arena, he would be hemmed in by a milling rabble, chorusing, "Hello, Al!" Shouldering his way through, Capone would accompany each ducat with a, "Hello, kid!" and, if the recipient impressed him as particularly seedy, a $20 bill.

A detective who is an authority on underworld conditions says he never double-crossed a friend, or for that matter anybody who played square with him. In the early days, leaders of a rival outfit with which he wished to affiliate notified him they would do so if he would kill two of his gunmen who had made themselves obnoxious. "I wouldn't do that to a yellow dog," said Capone. However, he was pitiless toward those who betrayed his trust, as Scalise and Anselmi learned.

Apropos, the phrase, "bulging hips," is often encountered as applied to gangsters. In Chicago no gangster carries a gun on the hip. The draw would be too slow. All use the shoulder harness, the gun, a .45, being holstered about four inches below the left armpit. A smaller one is generally carried in the right coat pocket. There is a tonsorialist in the basement barber-shop of a Loop hotel who has many gangster customers. His chair does not pivot. It is adjusted to face the door. Whenever it is occupied by one whose hand rests in the right coat pocket, those in the know are aware that that one is a gangster.

If you chanced to meet Capone and he had a growth of whiskers, you knew there had been another coroner's inquest. In the event of a death he never shaved from the day of its occurrence until after the funeral.

Although, following the slaying of their leader, the O'Banions launched a furious offensive—driving Capone into his portable fort and scaring Torrio so badly that when he went to the Lake County jail to serve nine months for operating a brewery he had the windows of his cell equipped with steel screens and hired three extra deputy sheriffs for sentry duty—the years of 1924 and 1925 passed without any counter-reprisals. The reader may reasonably inquire why.

The answer is that General Al the Scarface was exceedingly busy on another sector. The deadliest gang Chicago ever knew was threatening him on the west. The Gennas had risen; and turned on him.

These six brothers from Marsala, Sicily, had arrived as immigrants in 1910, and settled in Diamond Joe Esposito's old Nineteenth Ward, that vortex of the melting-pot across the river, in the Maxwell Street police district. It is a pot that always bubbles and frequently boils over, as it did in the aldermanic campaign of 1921, when thirty murders were committed.

Here Angelo, Mike, Antonio, Peter, Jim, and Sam quickly adjusted themselves—Peter as a saloonkeeper; James as a blind-pigger; Sam as a blackhander and ward heeler, abetted by Angelo, the clan's tough guy, and Mike. Antonio did the thinking for them.

Before Volstead, the Gennas were unheard of, but with prohibition came the magnificent opportunities for bootleg profits in the city that votes five to one wet and drinks that way. They specialized in alky-cooking, developing it on a huge scale. The Government unknowingly aided them, inasmuch as it granted them a permit for an alcohol manufacturing plant. By virtue of this permit they were enabled to accomplish wholesale distribution of bootleg alcohol along with the industrial product.

They soon discovered that the facilities of the licensed plant were inadequate to supply the constantly increasing illicit demand. They then hit upon the scheme that made their fortunes—importing poor Sicilian families and setting them up in tenements with an alcohol still for each family. The man of the house was paid $15 a day—a fabulous sum in his old-world eyes—and all he had to do was to smoke his pipe and keep the still stoked. The Gennas had a hundred of these in operation. Their profits were enormous.

The reader will appreciate the importance of alky-cooking when it is explained that laboratory analyses of liquor confiscated in Chicago—Bourbon, rye, Scotch, brandy, rum, and such—show that ninety per cent of it is synthetic; that is to say, alcohol with flavoring, coloring, and a fancy label added. The Gennas, with the political connivance of Diamond Joe Esposito, had entrenched themselves with the authorities.

They leased a three-story building at 1022 Taylor Street, four blocks from the Maxwell Street police station, and used it as a warehouse and headquarters.

"For six years," said the late Patrick H. O'Donnell, criminal lawyer, in an argument to a jury in a gang-murder case, "the Genna brothers maintained a barter house for moonshine alcohol; maintained it openly and notoriously, as public as the greatest department store in State Street."

Eventually, the Government got around to investigating the Gennas and obtained a twenty-five page confession from their former office manager, in which he named five police captains. The confession was an interesting contribution to prohibition as was and as is in Chicago. Here is part of it:

The warehouse was run night and day, with two twelve hour shifts. Heavy trucks, automobiles and lighter trucks were used in the distribution. The warehouse was run openly and in full view of everybody . . . unmolested by the state authorities other than an occasional raid.

But notification of twenty-four hours was always given to the Gennas. Sometimes the very letters sent out by the police to raid were exhibited to this affiant, and there would be a clean-up, then a raid, then a reopening. . . .

During all the period that I worked in said warehouse the entire Genna enterprise was done with the full knowledge, consent and approval of the police of Chicago in so far as the police were in touch with or in the neighborhood or had business under their jurisdiction.

The Gennas for said protection paid, monthly, large sums, which rose from a small amount in the beginning to about $6,500 in April of 1925. Moreover, said police received in addition thereto much alcohol at a discount price to permit the Gennas publicly to operate said stills and system of distribution.

These were the years, let the reader remember, when Mayor Dever was trying to enforce prohibition.

Each month said warehouse was visited by 400 uniformed police and by squads—sometimes four per month—out of the central bureau. It was visited, moreover, by representatives with stars but not in uniform, commonly known around the warehouse as representatives of the state's attorney's office of Cook county.

That police might not impose upon the Gennas by falsely representing themselves as assigned to the Maxwell street station, each month there came by letter or messenger a list of all stars worn by officers and men at the Maxwell street station. These were on short slips of paper and were taken by this affiant.

The entire list of stars was run off on the adding machine and the papers sent from the station were destroyed.

As each man came in for his pay his star was observed. If his star was upon the list sent in he was paid; his star number was inserted on a loose leaf ledger page, and the amount of the payment was put opposite his star number. I had nothing to do with paying the squads or higher ups [from central detail or headquarters and the state's attorney's office], but was held accountable for the money paid to them. . . .

On occasions when truckloads of alcohol would be going to different parts of the city and they would be intercepted by strange policemen, complaint was lodged by the Gennas. It was arranged then between the Gennas and the squads in the central detail as follows:

When a long haul was to be made through strange territory, the Gennas on the preceding night would call certain numbers and say, "Tomorrow at 7." On the next morning at 7 a uniformed squad of police would remain in the offing until a truckload of alcohol would start from the Genna warehouse. This squad would convoy them through the zones of danger. This affiant himself has called them, according to the number which indicated that the police were to convoy the alcohol for the Gennas.

This blunt recital of graft and corruption gives an idea of the extent of the Gennas' operations. By 1925 they were in the high noon of their prosperity. The money was rolling into their coffers at the rate of $100,-000 a month.

They had had their share, too, of coddling by the

AL CAPONE

authorities, and had sat down at their own Belshazzar feasts with the political great and the near-great.

A poplar tree stands in front of 725 Loomis Street, in the heart of Little Italy. Tenements, sweat-shops, and factories crowd about it. The earth in which its roots seek nourishment is trampled hard by children's feet, and no grass grows. The air reeks of smoke and impurities. The poplar's foliage, even in spring, is sparse and pallid, and its limbs misshapen. Winters, it sprawls against the smudge of sky like a talon.

From the beginning to the end of 1921 you might have seen a daily procession of beshawled women and shabbily dressed men hurrying up to it, fearfully scanning a paper tacked to its trunk, and hurrying on. Today they call it "Dead Man's Tree." On it, in advance, of course, and always correctly, were posted the names of those who were to die in the feud of the thirty killings in the Anthony D'Andrea-John Powers aldermanic campaign.

The prelude was two bombings—first, the home of Alderman Powers in September of 1920, next, the home of D'Andrea in February of 1921.

The names of some of the more important posted on the poplar tree, and the order in which they were slain, follow:

Paul A. Labriola, a lieutenant in the Powers political organization, and for fifteen years bailiff of the municipal court; March 8, 1921..

Anthony D'Andrea; May 10th.

Joseph Sinacola, D'Andrea henchman; July 7th.

Joseph Laspisa, D'Andrea bodyguard; July 27th.

Dominick Guttillo, Powers henchman; August 27th.

Joseph Marino, D'Andrea lieutenant; October 9th.

Nicola Adamo, Powers henchman; November 26th.

Two witnesses made positive identification of Angelo Genna as the killer of Labriola. He was indicted, tried, and acquitted. He was defended by Stephen Malatto, who had resigned as an assistant State's attorney shortly before the trial. Mrs. Nicola Adamo identified Jim Genna as one of the killers of her husband. He was tried and acquitted.

In October of 1924, about the time the O'Banions were entertaining Colonel Albert A. Sprague and Chief of Detectives Michael Hughes, the Italian Republican Club, in which the Gennas were directors, was giving a dinner in the Morrison Hotel for office-seekers and office-holders. All six Gennas were present, Jim being seated at the speakers' table. They had sold $5,000 worth of tickets. Also present were John Scalise and Albert Anselmi, and Sam Samoots Amatuna.

The guests included State's Attorney Robert E. Crowe; Thomas O. Wallace, clerk of the circuit court; John K. Lawlor, sanitary district trustee; and Bernard W. Snow, chief bailiff of the municipal court, and now the titular head of the Republican party in Cook County, chairman of the central committee. These represented the Crowe-Barrett faction, the latter being two brothers, Charles V. Barrett of the Cook County board of review, and George F. Barrett of the Fleming Coal Company, counsel for the sanitary district.

United States Senator Charles S. Deneen's faction was represented by James Kearns, clerk of the municipal court; Joseph F. Haas, county recorder; William C.

Scherwat, candidate for county clerk, and Diamond Joe Esposito.

The dinner caused the Better Government Association to forward a resolution to the United States Senate charging that "Chicago politicians are in league with gangsters and the city is overrun with a combination of lawless politics and protected vice."

This, then, was the background, political and otherwise, of the six Gennas in 1925. They were well-nigh as powerful in the old Nineteenth Ward and throughout the length and breadth of Little Italy as Diamond Joe Esposito himself. As for the social problem—and it is just as serious west of the river in melting-pot town, as north of the water tower in the Gold Coast district—it had been happily solved by the marriage of Angelo, the clan's tough boy, to Lucille Spingola. This automatically raised the Gennas to the level of fashionable respectability commensurate with their wealth. For pomp and circumstance, it established a precedent in Little Italy, where festas are common and tinseled splendor is the rule rather than the exception.

The comely Lucille was the younger sister of Henry Spingola, the big garage owner; lawyer and politician; a candidate in 1924 for State Representative, but defeated for the Republican nomination by William V. Pacelli of the Morris Eller faction.

The Spingolas, said those who knew, considered themselves a cut above the Gennas. Henry had been graduated from McKinley High School and also had his diploma from the John Marshall Law School. And he played pinochle at Mongelluzzo's cozy Italian restaurant at 914 South Halsted Street with such grand opera stars as Désiré Défrère, the famous baritone, and Giacomo Spadoni, the conductor. Whereas, but recently Angelo and his brothers were only the scum of the slums. But Angelo's gat ruled the Gennas' alky business, and those who were in it with them. And Henry was one. So Angelo married Lucille.

The wedding reception was held in Carmen's hall of the Ashland auditorium, on the West Side, and three thousand guests partook of the refreshments. "Come one, come all," said Angelo in the invitations that he advertised in the papers. The pictorial feature, one which diverted attention even from the bride, was the wedding cake, twelve feet high and weighing two thousand pounds. It was declared to be the largest and most elaborately decorated cake ever baked in Chicago. Let us view it through the eyes of a young lady reporter on that January day in 1925:

As the crowds of friends and relatives, including prominent persons from all over the city, gathered to do the bride and groom honor, they glanced first at the right side of the hall and then at the left. At one side stood the bride, who had just come from the wedding ceremony at the Holy Family church, where Father Ciofelletti had united her in wedlock to the young importer.

Down the hall stood the wedding cake, soaring majestically like a sculptured cathedral above the throng. Friends gasped first at the loveliness of the bride and then at the wonder of the cake.

The cake, which it took four days to bake, was comprised of 400 pounds of sugar, 400 pounds of flour, several buckets of flavors, seven cases of eggs, containing 360 eggs to the case, and other materials from the pantry, said the artist and sculptor, S. Ferrara.

The cake was baked in tiers from a recipe Ferrara brought from Europe, thirty years ago, and was decorated with hundreds of frosted motifs, roses, little windows with icing for window panes, and on top of it all was a miniature balcony, on which stood a doll-like bride and groom. Sketched in icing was the inscription, "Home Sweet Home."

Angelo and Lucille shook off the dust of the Sicilian colony and went to live on the North Side, at the Belmont Hotel, 3156 Sheridan Road, where Mary Garden has stopped during her grand opera engagements in Chicago. It is across the street from Mayor Thompson's home, and among Angelo's other neighbors were the J. Ogden Armours at 3400 Sheridan Road.

With such a social triumph as this wedding capping their varied achievements, it would have seemed that there was nothing more the six brothers could ask. That is where Capone enters. The Gennas' greatest ambition had not been gratified. They wanted to rule the Unione Sicilione, whose founder and president, Mike Merlo, had died in 1924.

The spell this office exerted upon the imaginations of men of the Gennas' race was irresistible and has a twofold explanation. One, of course, was the pecuniary attraction. The other, old as the ages, was its symbol to them of high place—a patent of distinction, setting its possessor apart from his fellows. Its appeal was to the childish vanity inherent in the human race. The result was no fewer than twenty-five killings in five years. Capone, the Neapolitan, cherished no sentiments regarding it. To him it was a business proposition.

Prior to Merlo's death, as the reader has seen, the Gennas were Capone's allies, but with his passing alignments shifted. Primarily, Capone, who had maintained close relations with Merlo, was determined to name his successor. He did not want the Unione to pass into the control of somebody who might use it against him. He did not trust the Gennas. His choice for the place was Antonio Lombardo, partner of Joseph Aiello—commission brokers and cheese merchants.

To this, the answer of the six brothers was thumbs down. They would tell the cockeyed world. Who was Lombardo? What was his business and political importance compared with theirs? They called a meeting of their henchmen and adopted resolutions of protest. The decision infuriated them. They considered it a personal affront. And there was the commercial aspect. With the Unione they would have a complete monopoly of the alky-cooking industry; without it, a powerful rival, backed by the Capone machine guns. The competition would be ruinous. Their financial life was at stake.

"Let's go," said the six brothers.

They went fast and far; they had seated Angelo, the tough boy, in the late Mike Merlo's chair before Capone suspected what was up. For the tactics of the Sicilian Gennas were not those of the North Side Irish. The O'Banions were straightforward foemen, fighting in the open, giving no quarter and asking none. The way of the Gennas was compact of guile, stealth, and cunning—the smiling lip and the treacherous heart. They were organized hypocrisy.

A factor favoring their scheme was the popularity they had acquired among their countrymen by their largesse. These were in the minority, but they were desperately loyal and determined. With the support of Angelo's dire reputation, they experienced no difficulty in imposing their will on the pro-Lombardo majority. Wherefore, the six brothers established their dictatorship of the Unione. In European chancelleries this exploit would have been described as statesmanship; in Chicago, gangland called it muscling in.

The reader now understands why in 1925 Capone did not retaliate on the O'Banions for blasting his car into the junk-heap and filling Torrio with lead. He was occupied with the Gennas to the exclusion of all other matters. The O'Banions would receive attention later, and how! As for the six brothers:

Angelo was the first to die. His honeymoon was in its fifth month the morning of May 25th, when he kissed his bride good-bye at the Belmont Hotel and climbed into his $6,000 roadster to go to the alky plant. It was the old story of sawed-off shotguns and a volley of slugs.

The inevitable touring car with stolen license plates slid into the offing twelve blocks south of his fashionable abode, and in Ogden Avenue, near Hudson, three glinting muzzles, poked over the starboard side, spoke their piece for the tough boy. The evidence at the inquest was nil and it was continued indefinitely.

Mike was next—within three weeks, June 13th—and all the thrills of blood-and-thunder fiction were packed into the circumstances of his death. It was that Day of the Sixty Shots. There are two mementoes of it at police headquarters, in the big glass case that holds the stars of officers killed in the line of duty. There is the star of Harold F. Olson and there is the star of Charles B. Walsh. There is a third memento in the criminal court records of Cook County—an acquittal for John Scalise and Albert Anselmi for the murder of the two police sergeants.

This starkest action-drama of the bootleg war opens with Capone's pair of ace gunners, Scalise and Anselmi, and Mike Genna driving south in Western Avenue, the city's longest thoroughfare, three miles west of State Street, which it parallels. At Forty-seventh Street they passed detective bureau squad No. 8, assigned to the Chicago Lawn station, and consisting of Olson, Walsh, Michael J. Conway, and William Sweeney. The squad was touring the district and its car was traveling north. Recognizing Genna, Conway, who was in charge of the squad, said:

"Hoodlums. We'll follow them."

Olson, at the wheel, turned quickly and headed south, clanging the gong as a halt signal for the gangsters' car, by now a block away. It only sped the faster. The chase continued for a mile and a half. Fifty-ninth Street was passed at seventy-three miles an hour with the gangsters still holding their lead.

A truck swerved into their path and their chauffeur, who was never identified, applied the brakes to avert a collision. The pavement was wet from rain. The car spun halfway around, hurdled the curb, and plopped down, facing northeast, beside a lamp-post.

Olson was just as prompt. He jerked the emergency and the squad car slid to a stop, facing west, a few feet away.

Thirty seconds had not elapsed since the truck had put an end to the chase, yet when the police pulled up,

AL CAPONE

Scalise, Anselmi, and Genna were out and on the opposite side of their car. Only their heads were visible. The chauffeur had disappeared.

"What's the idea?" asked Conway. "Why all the speed when we were giving you the gong?"

None of the officers had drawn their guns. Olson, the first to step from the squad car, had his left foot on the running board as the question was put. Conway was waiting for his answer and Olson's right foot was in midair, when Scalise opened fire with a repeating shotgun. Olson toppled, shot in the head. Scalise pumped his second charge at Walsh, who fell with a mortal wound in the breast. Anselmi cut loose with another weapon and Conway, the leader, dropped with a charge of buckshot in the chest.

The gangsters had accounted for three of the four officers. Only the young copper, Sweeney, was left. They probably figured that it was all over but the shouting as they waited to pick him off. Imagine their surprise when Sweeney suddenly leaped out of the bullet-riddled tonneau and came galloping at them with a gun in either hand.

They were three to one and they had two repeating shotguns and four sawed-off shotguns, besides their revolvers. They took it on high. Employees of a garage at 5940 South Western Avenue, who with hundreds of others had been eyewitnesses, saw them running like rats through a vacant lot and into an alley halfway up the block between Western and Artesian Avenues. They still carried their shotguns.

Sweeney, both guns going, was in full pursuit, and overhauling them. For as they gained the alley, he was close enough to see Scalise and Anselmi duck into the passageway alongside a house at 5941 Artesian Avenue. Genna was last, and before following them he whirled, aimed his shotgun at Sweeney and pulled the trigger. There was no explosion. It held only empty shells. Sweeney's reply was a bullet that plugged Genna in the leg.

Unable to run farther, Genna rounded the house and looked for refuge. A basement window caught his eye. Smashing the glass with his shotgun he dived in, with Sweeney not thirty feet away. At this critical moment reinforcements appeared for Sweeney. Policeman Albert Richert of the Brighton Park station, riding a Western Avenue street car, had seen him starting in pursuit of the gangsters. He jumped off the car and ran after him. At the same time, Mrs. Ellen Oakey of 2434 West Sixtieth Street, peering from a window, had called to her husband:

"George, look, there's a shooting!"

Policeman George Oakey, sixty years old, white-haired and a bit stooped, had long been retired from active duty. He sat nights at the outer desk in the State's attorney's office. He was up and at the door by the time his wife finished the sentence. A minute later she saw him in the street, making for the scene of the fighting. He had to cross the vacant lot through which Sweeney had chased the gangsters and there he found Scalise's repeating shotgun.

Thus it was that as Sweeney prepared to execute his next maneuver against Genna, Richert and Oakey joined him. It was a simple maneuver. It consisted of crashing the basement door, which was locked from the inside. The three brawny shoulders soon accomplished this. Genna was lying on the floor. In his right hand was a .38 caliber revolver, which barked just once, before Sweeney, Richert, and Oakey rushed him. He had only the leg wound, but the bullet had severed an artery and he was weak from loss of blood. The officers carried him out and summoned a police ambulance to take him to the Bridewell hospital.

His life was ebbing fast. He was limp when the ambulance arrived and the attendants laid him on the stretcher. Not too limp, however, to lift his uninjured leg and kick the man holding the right corner of the stretcher full in the face.

"Take that, you dirty son of a ——," he said, and fell back unconscious. Two hours later he was dead.

Hatless and breathless, their guns discarded, Scalise and Anselmi had fled north on Artesian Avenue to Fifty-ninth Street. They had tried to buy caps in a drygoods store, but the proprietor, suspicious, had shooed them away. They had then continued over to Western Avenue, and boarded a northbound street car. A flivver squad, dispatched from the West Englewood station, was told of this, and after a short chase the street car was overtaken and the two captured. No, they didn't know anything about a shooting. They were just a couple of boys looking for work.

For half an hour Olson, Walsh, and Conway lay where they had fallen, so swiftly had events taken place. Then, with a semblance of calm restored to the neighborhood, the citizens formed a volunteer relief unit. Olson and Walsh were conveyed in an automobile to the German Deaconess' Hospital, where they died

without regaining consciousness. Conway was taken to
St. Bernard's Hospital, where his life was despaired of
for days. He and Sweeney were promoted to the grade
of detective sergeants.

The diabolical irony of the situation into which
Mike Genna was plunged on that June morning may
now be set forth. Actually, Scalise and Anselmi were
taking him for a ride. It was to be his last day on
earth, no matter what. Mike, of course, was blissfully
ignorant of it as he earnestly battled the police side by
side with Capone's gunners.

General Al the Scarface was outsmarting the Gennas
at their own game of guile and cunning. For weren't
Scalise and Anselmi the Gennas' countrymen and their
good friends? Yea. Didn't they even keep their car in
the Spingola garage at 922 South Morgan Street? Yea.

What the Gennas forgot to reckon with, strangely
enough, was the characteristic of the smiling lip and the
treacherous heart. Scalise and Anselmi had the sinister
talents that qualified them as perfect torpedoes. In
underworld parlance, a torpedo is an Italian or Sicilian
sharp-shooter who can be relied on to execute a sentence of death without fail. He is as inevitable as the
mongoose. His method is devious and calls for an ac-
complice. He first wins his victim's trust. He will defer
a killing for weeks to accomplish that. Then one day he
will meet the victim and grip his hand firmly with the
greeting:

"Meester Blank, my fren'."

And while he grips, his fellow torpedo approaches,
generally, but not always, from behind, and fires the
death shots. O'Banion was a torpedo victim. The reader

will recall that the coroner named both Scalise and Anselmi as his killers.

The trap into which Mike Genna had walked with his eyes wide open was divulged by a prominent Italian to a friend at the detective bureau soon after the June 13th shooting.

"Mike," he said, "was on his way to execution, when the squad car officers were mistaken for enemy gangsters and fired upon. Momentarily, it upset the plans of Scalise and Anselmi, but in the end it was all right, as Mike was killed anyway."

Antonio, master mind of the Genna clan, was the third to die—a month later lacking five days, on July 8th. Antonio was quite a fellow—the Beau Brummell of the family—a good mixer and a shrewd business man of his kind.

He was a patron of the opera and a regular theatergoer, always in full dress regalia. He knew the head waiters in the hot spots of the night life. Most often he was to be found in the Valentine Inn, a bandbox café of the Loop, where Gladys Bagwell entertained.

Gladys was from the little town of Chester, down south in the Illinois corn belt. She was the daughter of the Rev. Mr. J. H. Bagwell, Baptist minister, and used to play the organ and lead the choir in singing every Sabbath morn at Sunday School and church services.

She tired of it and came to Chicago in 1920. Her ambition was to go on the stage. She made the rounds of the booking agencies, but there were no openings at that time, even for a winsome girl with a sweet contralto voice. She could wait. She would never let the folks in Chester say she had failed. She was youth and inexperience.

Up one flight and a turn to the left, where the incandescents wore green goggles in the crepuscular recesses of the booths; where the dance floor was no bigger than a billiard table; where setups were a dollar and you drew from the hip—there at the baby grand, playing jazz for the collegians and singing sentimental ditties for A. W. O. L. husbands—Gladys was still waiting when her man appeared.

Her man was Antonio. He was good to her. When the third Genna was bumped off, Gladys was discovered living in a $100-a-week suite at the Congress Hotel, with platinum bracelets, pearl necklaces, diamond rings, fur coats, and a wardrobe of pretty things for all occasions. In a downtown garage there was a sports roadster with her monogram on the door. She spoke of Antonio as "my fiancé." They were to have been married in November. He carried a key to the suite.

It was Gladys he asked them to notify as he lay dying in the hospital, and when she came, to lean over him with the question, "Who got you, Tony?" the lips that until then had remained sealed by gangdom's code, murmured:

"The Cavalier."

And that, it was learned months later, was Antonio Spano, imported from his native Sicily in 1921 by the Gennas solely because of his ability as a gunman and killer. His appellation of "The Cavalier" was a synonym of dread in Mafia circles, in which he was prominent. The Gennas trusted him as they did Scalise and

Anselmi. He was another torpedo. The police never apprehended Spano, due to their misconstruction of the term. They concluded a man named "Cavallero" was the killer, and based their whole search on that without regard to the Italian interpretation of the term in the sense of trusted friend or bodyguard—the counterpart of the French *chevalier d'honneur*.

It was the Cavalier, then, who telephoned Tony the morning of July 8, 1925, requesting that Tony meet him at Grand Avenue and Curtis Street, on the near northwest side of the city.

"Two of the Gennas had been killed in as many months," a police informant explained. "They were frightened and suspicious. Tony never would have gone there for George Bugs Moran or Schemer Drucci of the O'Banion gang; or for any of the Capones, and that included Scalise and Anselmi. But he would go for the Cavalier. And he did."

He drove over in his car. There, at the rendezvous, was the faithful Spano, waiting with outstretched arm. He grasped Tony's right hand in a vise-like grip, the while exclaiming:

"Meester Genna, my fren'."

Out of a doorway, two figures with .38 automatics materialized. They eased over within three feet of Tony and let him have it in the back.

That was the police reconstruction of Tony's end and that was why, they said, Tony, as he lay dying, murmured to Gladys:

"The Cavalier."

Overnight the power of the once mighty Gennas waned. Three of the six brothers were dead, and the word was passed that Peter, Jim, and Sam were marked. They didn't wait to see. They fled to the old home town of Marsala, Sicily. Jim was in such a hurry that he left his wife behind to sell the $50,000 worth of furnishings of their apartment at 925 Lakeside Place, on the North Side.

The truest indication of the Gennas' decline in civic and political importance was at Tony's obsequies. Whereas Angelo had rated a $10,000 bronze casket, $25,000 in floral offerings, and a magnificent turnout— all the honors, in other words, of a first class gangster burial—Tony was put away with few flowers, with no crowds, and in an ordinary wooden coffin. His funeral was a flop.

Chicago was rid of the six brothers, but not of their followers. Some of these were secretly ambitious, none more so than the music-loving Sam Samoots Amatuna of the lavender color schemes in shirts, ties, socks, and cars. He had been the Gennas' pay-off man when their alky-cooking industry was flourishing, and the best police department money could buy was the Maxwell Street station. In his evening hours he was manager of Citro's restaurant, a political rendezvous.

Samoots saw in the fall of the House of Genna his opportunity to get in the bucks. He would seize control of the Unione Sicilione. Barnum was right. He found willing listeners in Eddie Zion, the roadhouse keeper, and Abraham Bummy Goldstein, better known as Pete the Peddler, who ran a wildcat distillery.

Samoots hastily recruited the shattered remnants of the Genna gang, descended on the headquarters of the Unione, and, with a show of artillery, declared himself president. He moved into the office occupied by the late Angelo Genna. The date was July 22d. To quote from the coroner's records:

November 13, 1925: Sam Samoots Amatuna, successor to Angelo Genna as president of the Unione Sicilione, killed as he sat in a barber chair getting a shave and manicure.

November 17, 1925: Eddie Zion, roadhouse keeper, friend of Samoots Amatuna, killed as he returned from Amatuna's funeral.

November 30, 1925: Abraham Bummy Goldstein, killed in a drugstore in the valley by two assailants who stole a shotgun from a detective bureau squad car parked near by.

So ends the tale of the quest of the Gennas and their henchmen for the Golden Fleece of prohibition Chicago.

Capone's personal choice, Antonio Lombardo, was the next incumbent of the office, and it is significant that with his accession the killings ceased for three years, and there was a semblance of peace. It recalls the saying that Capone's name in certain quarters was a better insurance of law and order than was a police department.

With Lombardo finally seated and the Gennas quieted forever, Capone was free to direct his attention to the O'Banions. He owed them a few calls, which he intended to repay as soon as possible. They beat him to it. His escape from death was even closer than the day they sent his car to the junk-heap.

PART THREE

WITH the thumb and trigger-finger of his right hand, Al Capone gripped the handle of a coffee-cup, his forearm describing the arc of a circle as he lifted it to his lips. Shoulders stooped, head inclined, he lifted it with the calm deliberation of one whose mind is temporarily detached from the world of large affairs and intent upon the agreeable humdrum of revictualing the inner man.

Beside him was Slippery Frank Rio, alias Cline, the savage wop, member of his personal bodyguard, who later served the year's prison term with him in Philadelphia. The hands of the eight-day clock above the cash register in the Hawthorne Restaurant, Cicero, indicated 1:15 P. M. The two men faced front, a precaution dictated by long gangland experience, and they were seated at the last of fifteen tables lined against the west wall. A lunch counter runs the length of the east wall. The interior of the restaurant is twenty-five feet wide by fifty feet deep.

Al never tasted his coffee. He set the cup down with a thud on the white-tiled table-top and cocked an ear. His right hand glided across his chest, under his coat, to the left armpit.

Typewriters!

Rio was quicker. His revolver drawn, he was half risen from his chair, his eyes on the double doors lead-

113

ing to the street. He held the attitude while all about him pandemonium reigned. Waiters ran for the kitchen. Diners—it was the busy period and the place was crowded—ducked under tables and lay flat on the floor.

Typewriters and ukelele music. Nearer, now—louder. Right in front of the restaurant. Past it. Dying away. Gone. Silence.

Al rose and started for the double doors. Before he had taken a step, Rio was on top of him. He made a flying tackle, landing on Al's shoulders and hurling him to the floor. He climbed astride him, pinioned his arms, and, gazing down into his astonished countenance, said:

"It's a stall, boss, to get you out. The real stuff hasn't started. You stay here."

Fast thinking, that. Al stayed, on the floor, with the rest of the diners. Rio's premonition was correct and balked the boldest attempt ever made upon his life. It was the day of the O'Banions' raid on the feudal baron's stronghold, and for the uninitiate it may be explained that in gangster vernacular a Thompson sub-machine gun is never anything but a typewriter and the drum holding the fifty or one hundred bullets a ukelele.

The three musketeers—Moran, Weiss, and Drucci—chose a golden autumn afternoon for their incredible exploit, when Cicero was *en fête* for its big occasion of the year—the fall meet at the historic turf course of Hawthorne. The track is forty-five minutes west of the Loop and a mile and a half south of Al's headquarters.

Thoroughbreds were there from all over the country, including entries from Mr. Silk Hat Terry Druggan's Sanola Farm stables. He will be recalled as a partner of Mr. Frankie Lake of the Cook County beerage, their fortunes having attained dimensions where they could indulge their hobby of horse-racing. In fact, their fortunes had interested the Government so much that Mrs. Mabel G. Reinecke, then collector of internal revenue, had filed suit to recover from them $517,842 in income taxes.

They were Al's bosom pals and business associates, as was also, by the way, the mysterious Louis Barko, who had no string of horses, but kept books on them when not otherwise employed.

Of the legitimate racing men who chanced to be around when the ukelele music started there was Clyde Freeman of May, Louisiana. He and his wife and their five-year-old boy, Clyde, Jr., were sitting in their car. They had eaten and were preparing to go to the track, where the first field was to be sent away at 2:30 P.M. They played the rôle of innocent bystanders.

Let the reader visualize the block. In the process, doubtless, there will come to mind the good, old-fashioned movie of Western life—the main street of bars, dance halls, and general store—the cowboys riding full tilt down it, firing their six shooters into the air. Yet that is mild—vapidly so—compared with the reality of events in Cicero the afternoon of September 20, 1926.

The locale is the forty-eight-hundred block of West Twenty-second Street, just across the western city limits of Chicago; a boulevard eighty feet wide with a double-tracked street-car line in the middle. The attack centered on the Hawthorne Hotel, midway of the block, at 4823–27, on the south side of the street. The building is in the shape of a square U, the two wings extending back to a third unit in the rear connecting them. A spacious courtway thus separates the second and third floors. The first floor is roofed and this provides for the twenty-five-foot passageway leading from the street entrance to the lobby.

Let the reader remember that the attacking party came from the west, moving east on Twenty-second Street to Chicago—none knows how far. The block consists of one, two, and three story buildings. On the far west corner, on the hotel's side of the street, is a hardware store; then a radio shop; then a paint and varnish store; then a small drygoods store. Next it is the Anton Hotel, run by a Capone henchman, and adjoining it, the Hawthorne. The street frontage of both hotels is given over to shops—a barber, a delicatessen, a laundry—and finally the Hawthorne Restaurant, three doors east of the Hawthorne Hotel entrance. Next it is a fifty-foot vacant lot used for parking cars.

The north side of Twenty-second Street was neutral territory and does not enter into the action story. It may, however, be briefly sketched to give the reader the complete picture. Its general architectural features were the same as those of the south side. Near the far west corner was a garage; then a red brick flat building; next it, a florist's; a lady barber; the Pinkert State Bank; a lingerie shop; a confectionery; a restaurant; a cigar store; and a corner pharmacy. Doctors, lawyers, dentists, and real estate brokers occupied the second-floor offices above these.

AL CAPONE

An average business block of an average suburb, a stranger would have said. All the commonplaces of America's Main Street, even to the women with market baskets and babies, and the red and green automatic stop-and-go traffic light at the intersection of Forty-eighth Avenue.

Here it was that the O'Banions' offensive in the Bootleg Battle of the Marne reached the peak of its fury. Twice before they had invaded Capone's Chicago territory—once to riddle his sedan at Fifty-fifth and State streets, once to shoot down Torrio. Now they were to play the ukeleles right on the doorstep of his Cicero abode.

They came in eight touring cars. The methodical fashion in which the attack was delivered convinced the police that it had been carefully rehearsed. Every maneuver was timed. The lead car was a block in advance of the other seven. It was the decoy, to draw the Capones to the doors and windows, and its typewriter was the one first heard by Al and Rio. It was shooting blank cartridges. It was equipped like a detective bureau squad car with a gong on the left running board. The gong was going as it sped through the block at fifty miles an hour.

Thirty seconds behind it came the other seven cars. The interval between each was not more than ten feet, and as they entered the block they slowed down to fifteen miles an hour. They passed the hardware store on the corner, the radio shop, the paint and varnish store, and the drygoods store without opening up. But when the first car came abreast of the Anton Hotel, a machine gunner began spraying its façade up and

117

down and across in the manner of a fireman at the nozzle of a hose.

When this automobile arrived in front of the Hawthorne Restaurant, it stopped, the others moving up to close their intervals. Then from five cars streams of bullets poured into every door and window from the Anton to the restaurant where Al and Rio lay on the floor under the rear table.

The sixth car halted directly at the entrance and passageway leading to the lobby of the Hawthorne Hotel. A man in a khaki shirt and brown overalls stepped out, strode over to the door, knelt on the sidewalk, and coolly aimed a Thompson sub-machine gun. The seventh car apparently contained the rear guard of the attackers, for its occupants, who were armed with sawed-off shotguns, did not participate in the shooting. When the khaki-shirted artillerist went into action they maintained a close watch over him.

He used a ukelele with one hundred shells, and his typewriter was set for rapid fire. That means six hundred shots a minute including reloading, as an expert can slide in a new drum in four seconds. So the O'Banions' serenade of Capone's personal headquarters in Cicero lasted a little less than ten seconds.

It was intended for the lobby and the artillerist's aim was perfect. As he pressed the trigger he moved the gun slowly back and forth the width of the passageway. The results are still visible—neat horizontal lines of .45 caliber bullet holes against the wall, some the height of a man's waist, some breast-high.

The reader will understand just how deadly was that serenade when it is explained that Thompson sub-machine gun fire will cut down a tree trunk twenty-four inches in circumference at a distance of thirty feet, and will penetrate one-quarter-inch steel armor-plate.

There was no encore to the serenade. As the last bullet left the drum, the artillerist leisurely rose and returned to the car, and the driver honked the horn three times. This seemed to be the preconcerted signal for departure, for the cavalcade immediately got under way, moving east on Twenty-second Street toward Chicago. It was soon lost to view.

Police estimates were that a thousand shots were fired. Every pane of glass in the guest rooms of the Anton and Hawthorne hotels exposed to the street was shattered, as well as the doors and windows of the barber shop, delicatessen, and laundry in the latter building. Woodwork was splintered and plastering chipped off walls and ceilings. The Hawthorne Restaurant, where bullets sang over the heads of Al and Rio and threescore other diners, suffered similarly.

"This is war," declared the *Chicago Herald and Examiner* in its leading editorial the morning after.

Strangely enough, nobody was killed. The instinct of self-preservation sent people scurrying to safety as soon as the decoy car appeared and kept them there till all danger was past. Clyde Freeman, the Louisiana racing man, and Mrs. Freeman and their five-year-old boy, were the only neutrals that did not make a getaway. The attack was in full swing before they realized what was happening. They were compelled to sit in their automobile, which was parked near the entrance of the Hawthorne Hotel, from start to finish of it.

One bullet bored Mr. Freeman's hat, another grazed

his son's knee, and a third clipped the boy's coat. A fourth struck Mrs. Freeman in the arm, and flying glass from the windshield was imbedded in her right eye. Their automobile was riddled.

Al was among the first to emerge from the restaurant when the O'Banions left, and he immediately began inquiring about casualties. He did not know the Freemans, but when he learned of Mrs. Freeman's injury, he introduced himself and insisted on assuming financial responsibility for it. It is a matter of record that he paid out $10,000 to specialists to save the sight of her eye. He also reimbursed the shopkeepers for damage sustained.

Another victim was the mysterious Mr. Louis Barko, who described himself as "just a lone-wolf gambler." He stopped a bullet in the shoulder. He was a permanent guest of Capone's Cicero hostelry and he interested the chief of detectives of that day, William Schoemaker.

"This fellow," said Shoes, as soon as he set eyes on Barko, "is one of the four men that tried to kill Earl Hymie Weiss and Schemer Drucci a month ago in Chicago. We pinched him running away after the shooting, and he gave the name of Paul Valerie, 3533 Walnut Street, a fake address.

Shoes had established a major link in the series of retaliations between the Capones and the O'Banions, for it was the attempt on the lives of Weiss and Drucci that led to the machine-gun raid on Al's Cicero stronghold.

This attempt was outstanding for two reasons: (1) It demonstrated gangland's complete disregard for the law in settling its differences; (2) it was as spectacular an exhibition of gunnery as was ever witnessed in downtown Chicago streets, with the possible exception of the killing of Antonio Lombardo in the Loop, a few steps from the world's busiest corner.

Drucci was living at the Congress Hotel, of Republican national convention fame, which fronts Grant Park for the whole of the five-hundred block in South Michigan Avenue. He and Weiss had breakfasted together and then had started out for a stroll. Because of the early morning hour—10 o'clock—they probably thought no enemy gangsters would be astir.

Both, of course, had their automatics harnessed under their left armpits, and Drucci was carrying $13,200 in bills in an inner coat pocket. They headed south. It was a fine, sunshiny August day. The boulevard was filled with cars of business and professional men bound for the Loop. Nobody noticed the two O'Banions—apparently—and they arrived without adventure at Michigan and Ninth Street, an intersection corresponding somewhat in prominence to Forty-second Street and Fifth Avenue, New York City.

The Standard Oil Building, which houses the offices of the sanitary district trustees of Chicago, is located on the southwestern corner. Drucci would never admit that this was his destination. He would only say that he was going to close a real estate deal and that the money was for that purpose.

The peculiar fact was that he and Weiss were "put on the spot" exactly in front of the building's entrance. It excited so much comment at the time that Morris Eller, then a member of the district, who was in his office when the shooting occurred, issued a statement denying that Drucci was en route to see him.

Also among those present was John A. Sbarbaro, assistant State's attorney and the undertaker who buried Dion O'Banion. He said:

"I had gone to the district offices to confer with President Lawrence F. King. I was talking to Trustee Eller when the shooting began. I went down to see what it was about."

A car with four men drove up to the curb as Weiss and Drucci crossed Ninth Street. One remained at the wheel. The other three, each armed with a brace of revolvers, opened fire. Weiss ducked, which is a tribute to his sagacity, rather than a reflection on his valor. That was never impeached. He knew when and where to use a gun.

The impetuous Drucci whipped out his .38 and waded in. He was one against three, but no matter. Two of them leaped from the car to get better aim and Drucci danced about like a fancy boxer to keep both, as well as the gunman in the car, in front of him. The sidewalk, which had been thronged, was cleared at the first shot, pedestrians seeking cover in doorways, alleys, and office buildings. Automobile traffic on that side of the street halted abruptly.

The popping of the revolvers could be heard for blocks. Altogether thirty bullets were fired. Many went wild and a few cracked into windows and drilled holes in the tonneaus of cars parked near by. None of the participants were wounded, but an interested spectator, James Cardan of 6807 South Aberdeen Street, was hit in the leg.

The shooting ended as suddenly as it started, due to the fact that the police unexpectedly hove in sight. The gunmen's car sped away without waiting for the two who were battling with Drucci on the sidewalk. He ran to an automobile occupied by C. C. Bassett of 9545 Calumet Avenue, pointed his empty revolver at him and commanded:

"Take me away, and make it snappy!"

Before Bassett could comply, a squad of detectives had surrounded the car and placed Drucci under arrest.

"It wasn't no gang fight," he hastened to say. "A stick-up, that's all. They wanted my roll."

The fleeing Barko, alias Valerie, was seized and Chief Schoemaker had Drucci look him over.

"Never saw him before," said Drucci.

He was only according Barko the gangland amenities, which Barko promptly repaid within a month, following the machine-gun raid on Cicero.

Chief Schoemaker knew Barko as the one Capone man who had actually seen the raiders. He was on the sidewalk when they arrived, making for the hotel. The bullet that lodged in his shoulder caught him as he dodged into the entrance. The chief took him to headquarters and brought in Weiss, Drucci, George Bugs Moran, and Peter Gusenburg for his exclusive inspection.

"Never saw them before," said Barko.

And that was that—as far as the police could get with those particular shootings.

It was Peter Gusenburg, by the way, who was to die with his brother, Frank, and five other O'Banions in the St. Valentine's Day massacre in a North Clark Street garage, two years and seven months later. This was to shock even the hard-boiled ex-convict Moran into forgetting the code of silence and exclaiming:

"Only the Capone gang kills like that!"

Barko "never saw them before," but three weeks to a day after the O'Banions' shelling of Cicero, the guns roared curtains for Earl Hymie Weiss, in a daylight ambuscade of devilish ingenuity; the most scientific killing, in fact, of Chicago's gang warfare, surpassed in boldness of conception only by the St. Valentine's Day massacre.

Weiss, the Pole, was the antithesis of Capone, the Neapolitan; unemotional, of a cold ferocity that made him a dread figure to both friend and foe. He was a combination of brain and brute and said to be the only man Capone ever really feared. He maintained headquarters as Big Shot of the Northsiders on the second floor of the two-story building at 738 North State Street housing the florist shop of William F. Schofield, partner of the late Dion O'Banion. Here, opposite the Holy Name Cathedral, Dion was torpedoed, and here his successor died.

The torpedo stratagem never would have fooled the abysmal-minded Weiss, himself the founder of a new school of lethal technique with his "taking-him-for-a-ride" formula, which not only motorized murder, but also made the solution of the crime practically impossible. A stolen car, or, if the slayers used their own, stolen license plates; the victim in the front seat; assassins in the rear; a bullet in the head at a convenient spot; body tossed out in an unfrequented street, or alongside a quiet country road—that was Weiss' invention, now used by gangland throughout the U. S. A.

Original means would have to be employed to get such a fellow, something unlike anything that had characterized the one hundred and thirty killings since the bootleg war started in September of 1923.

A few days after the raid on Cicero, a young man giving the name of Oscar Lundin applied for a room at 740 North State Street, next door to Schofield's shop. He wanted the second floor front, but it was not available. He took a hall room until it should be. The tenant moved out Tuesday, October 5th, and Lundin moved in. In the meantime, a woman had rented a third floor back room at No. 1 West Superior Street, which intersects State on the south of the florist shop.

Lundin's room commanded a slanting sweep of the front of the shop, enough to rake it with machine-gun fire; that of the woman, the rear door and the alley approach. Neither of these participated in the ambush. Their mission was simply to rent the rooms; to "front" to the landladies. They then vanished. Their identities were never disclosed.

Testimony of witnesses at the coroner's inquest was that the killers resembled Sicilians. The police recalled that Capone had gone east following the Weiss-Drucci-Moran attack on his car and the shooting of Torrio and had returned with fifteen of these human robots of the trigger. Ostensibly they were to augment his bodyguard, which in the spring of 1926 was increased to eighteen men.

Presumably, six killers were assigned for the Weiss job, as in each of the rooms three chairs were found grouped at the windows, with a semicircle of cigarette butts—hundreds of them—on the floor about each chair. The vigil began October 5th and lasted until the afternoon of Monday, October 11th, the killers waiting for the propitious moment, or probably for a time when the street was clear of pedestrians.

Thus, for seven days Weiss was a living dead man, walking in and out of his headquarters under the muzzles of Thompson sub-machine guns not fifty feet away—guns equipped with drums holding a hundred .45 caliber steel-jacketed bullets—and those of revolvers and sawed-off shotguns. This is known because the weapons were left behind.

The ambush at No. 1 West Superior Street was not utilized, the men at 740 North State turning the trick. Weiss and four companions, stepping from his car, were approaching the shop to enter and ascend to the second floor. The four were W. W. O'Brien, a criminal attorney; Benjamin Jacobs, politician of the Bloody Twentieth Ward, and O'Brien's investigator; Patrick Murray, beer peddler, allied with Weiss; and Sam Peller, Weiss' chauffeur.

Weiss sprawled on the sidewalk with ten bullets in his body, dying without regaining consciousness. Murray stopped seven of the .45 caliber steel jackets and fell dead in his tracks. Attorney O'Brien, Peller and Jacobs were seriously wounded, but lived. Lived but told no tales. They hadn't seen a thing; couldn't identify the killers; didn't know what it was all about. And another coroner's inquest petered out like a Cubs' rally in a world series.

General Al the Scarface, in shirtsleeves and house

slippers, received callers at the Hawthorne Hotel, Cicero, the day his hated foeman was laid on an undertaker's slab without having had opportunity either to draw his automatic or finger the rosary he always carried. The undertaker was John A. Sbarbaro.

"I'm sorry Weiss was killed," he said, "but I didn't have anything to do with it. I telephoned the detective bureau I would come in if they wanted me to, but they told me they didn't want me. I knew I would be blamed for it, but why should I kill Weiss?"

"He knows why," said Chief of Detectives William Schoemaker, and minced no words in accusing Capone of the double murder. Chief of Police Morgan A. Collins was just as explicit. His theory was that "Capone played safety first by importing the killers, expert machine gunners, and then hurrying them out of town."

Mark the ambiguous situation: The two heads of the city's law-enforcing agency express positive opinions as to Capone's guilt, yet he is not molested. He even solicits an invitation from the detective bureau to come in for questioning and is snubbed. The reader may well be curious. Let Chief Collins explain:

"It's a waste of time to arrest him. He's been in before on other murder charges. He has his alibi. He was in Cicero when the shooting occurred."

The Chicago police department had surrendered to Capone—unconditionally. Its morale was sapped. It could fight the underworld of crime, but not the overworld of crooked politics; and the alliance between the two had become plain to the dumbest copper on a beat. The sapping process had been going on for months and its cumulative effect was unknowingly voiced by Chief Collins in the Weiss case with his, "It's a waste of time to arrest him."

The débâcle of the police department may be said to date from a triple machine-gunning the night of April 27, 1926, when there died William H. McSwiggin, assistant State's attorney of Cook County; Thomas Duffy, barber, beer peddler, and precinct captain in McSwiggin's faction of the Republican party, and James J. Doherty, gangster, whom McSwiggin had previously prosecuted for murder, Doherty being acquitted.

They were riding about together, for reasons never satisfactorily explained, visiting the saloons and speakeasies of Capone's West Side territory. Duffy and Doherty were henchmen of the brothers Myles and Klondike O'Donnell, the guerrillas of the bootleg war, aligned sometimes with the O'Banions, again with the Capones, depending on the financial advantages presented—but generally going it alone.

They had had a sort of entente with Capone when he entered Cicero, but had called it off. Now they were his bitter enemies and business rivals. For months they had been muscling in on the West Side beer trade while he was busy with Weiss, Drucci, and Moran on the north. One of the customers they had taken away from him was Harry Madigan at 5615 West Roosevelt Road, Cicero.

"When I wanted to start a saloon in Cicero more than a year ago, Capone wouldn't let me," Madigan told Chief of Detectives Schoemaker. "I finally obtained strong political pressure and was able to open. Then

Capone came to me and said I would have to buy his beer, so I did.

"A few months ago Doherty and Myles O'Donnell came to me and told me they could sell me better beer than Capone beer, which was then needled. They did and it only cost $50 a barrel, where Capone charged me $60.

"I changed, and upon my recommendation so did several other Cicero saloonkeepers."

The O'Donnells manifested as little regard for Al's sinister reputation as had their fellow Irisher, Dion O'Banion. Their audacious invasion of Cicero was a challenge to his gang leadership and an assault upon his personal dignity. It was as if they had tweaked his nose.

Around eight o'clock the night of April 27th, McSwiggin and his party, in a new Lincoln sedan belonging to Doherty, parked in front of Madigan's saloon. With them were Myles O'Donnell, whom they had picked up along the way, and Edward Hanley, a former policeman, Doherty's chauffeur.

Their intention, the police surmised, was to drop in on Harry for a few social drinks and a friendly word or two, as a token of mutual good-will and business esteem. It is a custom much in use amongst enterprising beer merchants with good cash customers.

McSwiggin, Duffy, and Doherty, alighting first, had not cleared the narrow strip of parkway between the curb and sidewalk when they were caught by a stream of machine-gun bullets fired from a car that had sneaked up alongside, halted momentarily, then sped on. They fell, mortally wounded. Hanley, still at the wheel, and O'Donnell, just stepping out, escaped injury.

Duffy managed to crawl to the shelter of a tree, behind which he died. In a pocket of his vest was found a paper calling for the transfer of a police sergeant. Hanley and O'Donnell lifted Doherty and McSwiggin into the sedan, probably in the belief that they still lived, and drove west to Berwyn, where the bodies were tossed out. They then headed north for Oak Park, where the sedan was abandoned.

This crime, with its ugly political implications, roused Chicago temporarily from its sodden lethargy. The public clamor was such that a special prosecutor, former Judge Charles A. McDonald, was assigned to conduct an investigation. Five special grand juries were impaneled in the course of it, Mr. McDonald and his two assistants drew $34,125 from the county for their services; the mountain labored and this is what it brought forth:

"On the whole, a review of years past gives no special occasion for alarm at the present moment. Crime in volume and type wheels and rotates in cycles. . . . The situation is well enough in hand to encourage the hope that there will be no outbreak on any such scale as in the recent past. . . ."

This in the year 1926, when sixty-four gang slayings were committed in Chicago, with prosecutions in only three cases and all resulting in acquittals. The triple killing in which McSwiggin died never reached the prosecution stage. "Too much dynamite in it," as one sage observer commented.

Capone was the first man sought by the police,

owing to the effective work of Chief Schoemaker's men, which disclosed that A. V. Korecek, a West Side hardware dealer, had sold three Thompson sub-machine guns to a member of Capone's gang.

Supplementing this evidence was the story of a Cicero citizen who said that he was in a restaurant in that town the night of April 27th and that he saw Al, his brother Ralph, and three others of the gang in agitated conversation. At the conclusion of it, Al went to a panel in the wall and got a machine-gun. His companions armed themselves with revolvers. They then made a hasty departure. It was 7 o'clock, an hour before the triple killing.

So certain did it seem that the authorities finally had the goods on Capone that on May 5th a formal announcement was issued, which the newspapers considered so important that they put it on page one. Here it is:

It has been established to the satisfaction of the state's attorney's office and the detective bureau that Capone in person led the slayers of McSwiggin. It has become known that five automobiles carrying nearly thirty gangsters, all armed with weapons ranging from pistols to machine guns, were used in the triple killing.

It also has been found that Capone handled the machine gun, being compelled to this act in order to set an example of fearlessness to his less eager companions. The five automobiles, it has been learned, were used in hours of patient trailing of the doomed O'Donnell gang and later to make sure of escape.

Al had disappeared. Much police activity ensued. Squads raided hangouts throughout the county. Roadhouses immune hitherto were rudely entered at all hours of the day and night, and the press was duly informed of each and every movement. In Chicago, murder cases are tried in the newspapers long before they reach the courtroom. The police department and the State's attorney's office thus perform the double service of obliging both the public and criminals at large. It had been proclaimed in fat blackface type that "a secret warrant was issued for Al Capone charging him with murder." The extent to which Al benefited is of course speculative, but the fact is that no trace of him was obtained.

Days became weeks. Weeks drifted into months. April passed into May, May into June, June into July; August was only five days away when he sent word that he was emerging from his retreat. He had been waiting for the public clamor to subside—as had also others as prominent in politics as he was in gangdom.

On Thursday, July 29th, Capone with his counsel, Attorney Thomas D. Nash, appeared before Chief Justice Thomas J. Lynch of the criminal court. Assistant State's Attorney George E. Gorman stepped to the bar and said:

"This complaint [the warrant charging murder; Capone was never indicted] was made by Chief of Detectives Schoemaker on cursory information and belief. Subsequent investigation could not legally substantiate the information."

Whereupon Chief Justice Lynch dismissed the case and Capone was free to resume business at the old stand. In the court room was McSwiggin's father, Sergeant Anthony McSwiggin of the detective bureau, a stalwart old copper with a record of long and honorable service.

"They pinned a medal on him and turned him loose," he said.

The slaying left him a broken man, mentally and physically.

"They killed me, too, when they killed my boy," he used to repeat.

Mr. Gorman's little speech to the judge cost the taxpayers of Cook County $200,000. That is to say, the outlay in salaries to members of the police department and the State's attorney's staff for the three months' work on the case, and the current expenses of other parts of the legal machinery, approximated that sum.

"They made me the goat," said Al. "McSwiggin was my friend. Doherty and Duffy were my friends. Why, I used to lend Doherty money. Just a few days before the shooting, my brother Ralph, Doherty, and Myles and Klondike O'Donnell were at a party together."

No information was forthcoming from the O'Donnells, although Myles had been an eyewitness and an intended victim. The law of the code prevailed with them.

The triple killing produced the first of the Capone legends—stories not authenticated, but zealously circulated around night clubs and in speakeasy bars by those supposedly "in the know." It was that Sergeant Anthony McSwiggin journeyed to Cicero, cornered Al in the Hawthorne Hotel, and called him murderer;

that Al drew his automatic, presented it to the distraught father, and said, "If you think I did it, shoot me."

So profoundly did the crime impress itself upon the public consciousness that the phrase, "Who killed McSwiggin?" has taken its place in the Chicago idiom as a term of banter, and is as much a commonplace with grown-ups as is, "Who killed Cock Robin?" with the children.

The damning circumstances of the young prosecutor's death and the studied impotency of the State's attorney's office to get at the facts that shouted of corruption in high places had the inevitable reaction in the police department that has been mentioned— the demoralization that was expressed by Chief Collins in the Weiss case with his, "It's a waste of time to arrest him."

This was the period when the wags began labeling Al "the mayor of Crook County," and asserting Chicago had been sold down the river—of bootleg booze. The politicians were vaguely troubled. Al was looming too large for solid ivory comfort. He might become a campaign issue. Yet they were helpless, although they did not realize it. The situation was already beyond their control—it was the Frankenstein monster they had fabricated.

Weiss' death removed the biggest threat at Capone's ascendancy, and he entered the zenith of his career. No more would the three musketeers ride hell-bent across the No Man's Land of Madison Street, nor would the Northsiders again prove formidable. Their stamina was literally shot to pieces. They lacked a leader. Neither Moran nor Drucci was of the stuff to enable them to regain their prestige.

Apropos, it may be explained that only four men were ever recognized as Big Shots in Chicago gangland—Capone, Torrio, O'Banion, and Weiss. They embodied the qualifications that the appellation implied—executive ability, political acumen consonant with the times, commanding personality, and an instinctive hardihood that compelled respect and obedience among their followers. In the beginning, in 1923, there were many lesser chieftains, but as the elimination process of the bootleg war continued, these gravitated to one camp or the other until in the fall of 1926 a gangster was known either as an O'Banion or a Capone man.

The significance of Weiss' death, therefore, is obvious. Capone's power on the north was undisputed, and his reputation enhanced accordingly. He was also supreme on the west. The killing of McSwiggin, Doherty, and Duffy had put a quietus on the O'Donnells. The south was his, from the Loop to Chicago Heights. There remained only the great Southwest Side—and the perfidy of Polack Joe Saltis. That startled him as much as the revelations attending its discovery shocked the city.

Saltis, the behemoth Pole, of the stolid mien, overstuffed jowls, and lumbering gait, was and is one of the bizarreries of prohibition. Before the World War he was plodding along as a neighborhood saloonkeeper —first in Joliet, then over back of the yards, in the section where is concentrated the bulk of the Slavic population, whose men, women and children earn their livelihoods by the sweat of the brow in the packing plants and factories.

Now the candy kid out there, in the Thirteenth Ward, was a vest-pocket gladiator named John Dingbat O'Berta, ambitious politically, having run for alderman as well as State senator, and for a time a Republican committeeman. He married the dashing widow of Big Tim Murphy, racketeer and organizer of the Street Sweepers' Union, after Tim had been machine-gunned.

Volstead, far from slaking the thirst of Dingbat's constituency or Saltis' clientele, seemed to intensify it. The demand for beer was overwhelming. There were more than 200,000 parched throats southwest of the yards. If there was one thing Saltis comprehended, it was the public thirst. He knew that the public invariably would quench it. He saw opportunity beckoning. He knew his breweries. He approached his friend, Dingbat, who was sympathetically inclined. Thus was formed the commercial partnership of the behemoth and the bantam.

So well along on easy street were they within a year that Saltis bought himself a country estate in the Eagle River country of Wisconsin, where the wealthy sportsmen relax, and Dingbat took up golf. By 1925, when Capone was rising to power, they were firmly established, their milk route, as gangland calls it, numbering some two hundred saloons. Al did not bother them, other than to receive from Saltis a pledge of allegiance and a gentlemanly cut of the profits.

Besides, he was busy in 1925 with the Gennas and in 1926 with the O'Banions. If Saltis ever came to mind it was not as a source of worry, because Saltis

was his ally. So he thought until the October afternoon
that Weiss died, and search of his clothing and the
safe in the florist shop disclosed two remarkable documents.

Saltis and his chauffeur and bodyguard, Frank Lefty
Koncil, had been indicted and were on trial for the
murder of John Mitters Foley, one of a minor gang that
had attempted to invade their southwestern territory. In
Weiss' pocket was found a list containing the name of
every man called for jury service in the trial—those accepted, those rejected, and those not examined. In the
safe was a paper with the names of all the State's witnesses. It was also learned that Weiss had raised a
$100,000 defense fund.

The disclosures were doubly sensational in that they
bared the conspiracy against Capone and the collusion
between attachés of the Criminal Courts Building and
gangland to thwart justice.

"Weiss and Saltis had joined forces to put Capone
out of business," said Deputy Commissioner of Police
John Stege.

"Very disquieting rumors referring to the bribery
of this jury have been prevalent," Prosecutor Lloyd D.
Heth informed Judge Harry B. Miller, presiding at
the trial, the day following the disclosures. "If we had
definite proof we would set it up in the form of an
affidavit and ask that a mistrial be called. I suggest the
court call in the entire jury, tell them of the rumors,
and ask whether any of them has been approached to
return a particular kind of verdict."

Judge Miller did so, and each of the jurors denied
that he had been approached. The trial proceeded, but

was abruptly halted the second day when one of the jurors became violently insane. A new jury was sworn in and again the trial was resumed. On November 9th a verdict of not guilty was voted.

"I expected a different verdict on the evidence presented," said Judge Miller. "I think the evidence warranted a verdict of guilty."

John Dingbat O'Berta had been indicted with Saltis and Koncil for Foley's murder, but had been granted a separate trial. With their acquittal, however, his case was stricken from the calendar with leave to reinstate, and there it rests.

A hundred thousand dollars might buy Saltis an acquittal from the law for murder, as it had Scalise and Anselmi, but not one from Capone for a double-cross. He knew he was a dead man as soon as he should leave the protection of the county jail, unless he squared himself. But how to do it? The slow-witted Saltis was in a quandary. He appealed to Dingbat. Promptly the bantam answered:

"Maxie Eisen."

There was reassurance in the mere mention of the name. The sly and wily Maxie, fish-market racketeer, to whom every pushcart peddler in Maxwell Street paid tribute, was the keenest thinker in the Chicago underworld, not excepting Jack Guzik. He had been identified with the O'Banions, but when the shooting became promiscuous after the killing of Dion, had decided that a trip around the world would be healthful. He returned the day Weiss was machine-gunned. The coincidence alarmed him.

Dingbat would see his pal, Maxie. He found him

eagerly disposed, his mental processes accelerated in proportion to his alarm. This conference, which had historic consequences, is illustrative of the difference in minds. Dingbat saw only the plight of an individual. Maxie perceived a complete situation. Dingbat looked no farther than the personal safety of Polack Joe. Maxie was alert to the safety of all concerned—all for one, and one for all, against the common enemy, the law.

"The idea," said he to Dingbat, "is to call the war off. You're a bunch of saps, killing each other this way, and giving the cops a laugh. There's plenty of jack for everybody, as long as prohibition lasts. I'll talk to the boys."

His proposal was received with hearty enthusiasm by Moran and Drucci; likewise by the guerrillas, Myles and Klondike O'Donnell. They were willing to accept any terms within reason. Maxie was ready to talk turkey with the Big Shot.

An ordinary fellow would have gone direct to Capone. Not Maxie. He went to Antonio Lombardo, whom Al had seated as head of the Unione Sicilione. The cheese merchant and partner of Joseph Aiello in the commission brokerage firm was the pivot man of the Capone organization. Al leaned upon him for counsel in all matters, reposing a childlike trust in his business judgment. Maxie knew (1) that Lombardo would be in sympathy with his mission, and (2) that a word from him to Al would sink in and produce results.

"Things are worse than when I left," remarked Maxie, speaking as the returned tourist. "These shootings aren't doing anybody any good."

Lombardo agreed.

"I talked with Moran and Drucci, and the O'Donnells," added Maxie, casually. "They're sick of it. So are Saltis and O'Berta."

Lombardo's eyes lighted, but he was noncommittal. Maxie guilelessly changed the subject, and after a proper interval withdrew. He had not long to wait. Lombardo telephoned him the next day. Al wanted to see him. Another Eisen idea had gone over.

With his olive branch in one hand and the white flag of truce in the other, the self-appointed pacificator again repaired to the cheese merchant's office to elaborate his proposal and views. Al was impressed from the start.

"You're right," he assented, "we're a bunch of saps, killing each other."

The discussion, which amounted to a pourparler, was frank, earnest, and harmonious. At its conclusion Al asked Maxie's advice as to the next step, which was precisely what Maxie wanted him to do.

"You fellows should get together and have an understanding," he said.

It was jake with Al, if Maxie could arrange it. Maxie could.

There followed two more pourparlers, to adjust preliminary details, and on Wednesday, October 20, 1926, the gangsters' peace conference was held at the Hotel Sherman, in the shadow of the City Hall, across the street from the office of the chief of police. For the first time in years Al enjoyed the unpretentious status and prerogative of a common, ordinary citizen: He went abroad unattended and unarmed. His entourage of fifteen Sicilian gunmen, imported from New York,

140

had a night off. One of those preliminary details was a stipulation that there should be neither bodyguards nor gats.

Maxie, as chairman, sounded the keynote of the occasion in his opening address, when he said:

"Let's give each other a break."

The sentiment, which evoked loud cheers, kindled the enthusiasm of the delegates, and sent them into their humanitarian deliberations imbued with a spirit in keeping with the aims and purposes thereof.

Some years ago a clergyman wrote a book, *If Christ Came to Chicago*. One wonders what the good man's reaction would have been could he have walked in on this conference. Here sat Al Capone, "by common repute and common police knowledge . . . head of a murderous gang"; beside him, Antonio Lombardo, to die by the gun in a rush-hour killing in the Loop; Jack Guzik, brother of Harry, the pander, and manager of the Capone bootleg syndicate; Ralph Sheldon, gangster and beer and alky peddler.

Opposite them, handclasp distance across the table, sat George Bugs Moran, burglar, robber, and ex-convict; Vincent the Schemer Drucci, crook, jewel thief, election terrorist, cop-hater, and shootin' fool. Thirty-one years old and with just six months more to live. He was to curse a flatfoot once too often and get four bullets from the automatic of youthful Danny Healy of the detective bureau. Moran and Drucci were the sole surviving leaders of the North Side crowd the Capones had been so industriously engaged in exterminating since 1924.

Next, reading from right to left, were William Skidmore, pot-bellied ex-saloonkeeper, ward heeler, and court fixer; Christian P. Barney Bertsche, highwayman, safe-blower, whilom inmate of a half-dozen penitentiaries; and Jack Zuta, divekeeper and their muscle man. They were specialists in vice and gambling. They had operated under the ægis of O'Banion, and in the heyday of the swashbuckling Irisher's régime had figured many a time and oft in dirty work at the crossroads for the Capones. Now a new deal was on. They were willing to forget bygones, shake with Al, and tell him he was a great guy.

At the head of the table was Maxie, in his dual rôle of chairman and proxy delegate for the absent brothers. These were Saltis and Koncil, still in jail and glad of it, and the O'Donnells, whose fortitude had not regained par since the triple slaying of Duffy, Doherty, and McSwiggin.

Here they sat—Al and the gentry of the new era: thieves, highwaymen, panders, murderers, ex-convicts, thugs, and hoodlums—human beasts of prey, once skulking in holes as dark as the sewers of Paris, now come out in the open, thrust up by Volstead and corrupt politics to the eminence of big business men. Here they sat, partitioning Chicago and Cook County into trade areas, covenanting against society and the law, and going about it with the assurance of a group of directors of United States Steel or Standard Oil transacting routine matters.

The latter analogy is rather apt. The history of the development of the bootleg industry in five-to-one-wet Chicago is essentially that of any industry dealing in a basic commodity. Its trend was toward combination and centralization of power. Its methods of restraining competition were more primitive than those, say, of Standard Oil. In place of the rebate, the pipeline, and unfair price-cutting, it used the bullet. Like Standard Oil it became a supertrust, and there the analogy ends; for whereas the courts in 1911 dissolved Standard Oil, this group was apparently beyond the jurisdiction of any tribunal in the land.

Perhaps one of the outstanding facts of the so-called peace conference was that this bootleg monopoly had finally been established after almost four years of bloodshed and a toll of one hundred and thirty-five lives, and that its boss was Al Capone. Evidence of that was irrefutable. The delegates yessed him pro and con. Their compliance with his wishes was sycophantic. He dictated the peace-pact terms and they accepted them without a murmur. Really, be it said to Al's credit, there was nothing in them to murmur about. They were liberal and equable, as far as they went. They stipulated:

1. General amnesty.

2. No more murders or beatings.

3. All past killings and shootings attributed to gunmen affiliated with Chicago mobs to be looked on as closed incidents.

4. All ribbing (malicious gossip) carried between the factions by meddlesome policemen, or presented through the medium of the press, old telegrams and letters and other documents, dated prior to the peace treaty, to be disregarded.

5. Leaders of factions to be held responsible for any infractions of the pact, and unfriendly activities of the

rank and file to be reported to the delegates for disciplining by the respective leaders.

In the partitioning of the city and county, however, Al revealed himself as the practical-minded executive. From there on the meeting was a delimitation conference.

To the north, Moran and Drucci were circumscribed to the Forty-second and Forty-third Wards. All the territorial acquisitions and beer-selling privileges south of the Madison Street deadline for which O'Banion and Weiss had fought and died reverted to Capone. And their vice and gambling concessionaires, Skidmore and Bertsche, were informed that they would have to see Al concerning future operations.

Saltis was ordered to stay in his own backyard, southwest of Packingtown, restricting himself to his milk route of two hundred saloonkeepers among the Slavic population.

For Myles and Klondike O'Donnell, the guerrillas, there was only ominous silence. The assumption was that they were still on probation.

Capone was supreme on the west, from the Loop to Cicero, and on the south from the world's busiest corner to the Indiana boundary line at the lake and 106th Street, and on down to Chicago Heights. He was the John D. Rockefeller of some 20,000 anti-Volstead filling-stations. He was sitting on top of the bootleg world.

Amply as the foregoing glorifies the American gangster, it must needs have one more fact to complete the story. It is by way of a demonstration of Capone's might. So critical was the situation in 1926 that the editor of the *Chicago Tribune*, a wet newspaper, had appealed in March to the Coolidge administration, saying:

"President Coolidge placed the full weight of his administration, and the vast power of the federal government behind the move to rid Chicago of the gangs of alien gunmen who are terrorizing that community."

But the slaughter had continued, at the rate of six a month.

United States District Attorney Edwin A. Olson had charged before the United States Senate prohibition inquiry committee that "Chicago is crime-ridden and the police wink at violations of the prohibition law." The Better Government Association had carried a petition to Washington. Chief Morgan A. Collins had reorganized the police department to "run gangsters forever out of the city."

The slaughter had continued. Al spoke and it stopped. For more than two months not a gun barked. Up to October 21st there had been sixty-two murders. From then until December 30th, with the exception of a nondescript not identified with any faction slain December 19th, there wasn't a single gangster killing. Chicago had the unique experience of going seventy days without a bootleg inquest for the coroner.

Maxie Eisen was pretty well satisfied with the peace-conference results. The amnesty clause delighted him. He had delivered for his friend Dingbat, and, incidentally, had made the world a safer and a happier place, for Maxie. Saltis and Koncil could emerge from the county jail in safety, which they did. It looked like a soft winter.

Alas for the credulous Maxie! The gangster bumped off December 30th was Hillory Clements, one of Ralph Sheldon's outfit, which made it bad; and Ralph was a graduate member of Regan's Colts, which made it worse—for Saltis et al.

East of Polack Joe's domain, and directly back o' the yards, lay the bailiwick of the lusty-blooded Irish larrikins who loved a fight better than nobody's business. They were an institution, these Regan's Colts, dating from the nineties, when they were the Morgan Athletic Club, and each year traveled to Sante Fé Park on the Sante Fé railroad for their annual picnic. On one such hilarious occasion they tossed all the plush-covered seats out of the train windows and almost wrecked the coaches. The railroad filed a damage suit against the Morgan Athletic Club, which promptly disbanded and became Regan's Colts.

They were staunch allies of Capone and had supplied his organization with pillars like Mr. Danny Stanton, head of the muscle department, and the Messrs. Hughey Stubby McGovern, William Gunner Padden, Frank Dutch Carpenter, Raymond Cassidy, and Thomas Johnson.

The trouble was, the Regans would never take Saltis seriously. Which was "okey" before prohibition when he was just a plodding saloonkeeper at 51st and Artesian. Then Joey Brooks, toughest hombre back o' the yards, used to get beered up, as the boys tell it, and go over and "pull Polack Joe's shirt-tail out."

Joey was the cause of the first bad blood between Saltis and the Regans, for one winter's night in 1925 he was killed as he sat in his car talking with County Highway Policeman Edward A. Harmening, who was also killed. The double murder was never solved by the police, but the Regans charged it to the Saltis crowd. And in April of 1926 Ralph Sheldon had received a fiendish warning. John Tucillo—brother-in-law, by the way, of Diamond Joe Esposito—and Frank De Laurentis, two of Sheldon's booze runners, were taken for a ride in their own automobile, after which the machine, with the bodies in it, was driven back and parked in front of Sheldon's home. The theory was that Tucillo and De Laurentis had invaded Saltis territory.

Wherefore, with this atrocious occurrence in mind, the reader may readily surmise that the killing of Hillory Clements was bad news, indeed, for the gangsters' peace pact as well as for Saltis et al. Two months and twelve days after his death, the coroner of Cook County entered the following items in his record:

"March 11, 1927: Frank Lefty Koncil, henchman of Joe Saltis, gang leader, killed in auto ambush. Slayers not caught.

"March 11, 1927: Charles Big Hayes Hubacek, member of Saltis gang, killed with Koncil. Slayers not caught."

The reprisals put Polack Joe in his place. Never again did he stray from his milk route to annoy Capone's South Side allies. With him disposed of Al was free to prepare to meet an old friend, Mike

Hughes, whom the reader may remember for an ex-change of pleasantries. It was Mike, serving as chief of the county highway police, who said:

"I have chased Capone out of Cicero and for that matter out of further business dealings in Cook County."

It was Al who replied:

"Chase me out of Cook County? Well, he hasn't done it and he won't do it. I'm getting sick of fellows like Hughes using me to attract glory to themselves."

The point is that on April 5, 1927, William Hale Thompson had been elected mayor. In his campaign speeches he had referred to Hughes as "Go-Get-'Em-Mike," had said he would appoint him chief of police and that he would "drive the crooks out of Chicago in ninety days." Hughes succeeded Morgan A. Collins April 14th.

The years of 1927, 1928, and 1929 were to prove memorable for the subject of this sketch, as well as for Chicago, Philadelphia, and the world at large.

Mayor Thompson, self-styled Big Bill the Builder, was for America First, and Capone was for America's Thirst. They weren't so far apart, at that.

PART FOUR

IN a general way, the world knows two Chicagos—
the chamber of commerce Chicago, and the political
Chicago—both being the quintessence of hokum. The
difference is that the one is genteel hokum and the
other vicious hokum.

The Chicago that is—living symbol of America—
of no yesterdays, only tomorrows—exuberant ado-
lescence—"laughing," says Carl Sandburg, "laughing
the stormy, husky, brawling laughter of youth; half
naked; sweating; proud to be hog butcher; toolmaker;
stacker of wheat; player with railroads, and freight
handler to the nation. . . ."—so big; so mighty; so
toweringly prophetic; so unconquerably strong; so
starkly beautiful—the city known to those who love
and understand it—the Chicago that is strides on regardless of the one and despite the other.

The chamber of commerce Chicago is compounded
of the fine-spun phrase; the platitudes and super-
latives of the after-dinner speaker. It tends to gloze the
realities. It is in the manner of the railroad executive
who sat in at President Hoover's prosperity conferences, following the collapse of the stock market in the
fall of 1929, joined in the yea-man chorus on 1930
expansion programs to avert unemployment, and returned to lay off 1,500 shopmen. The chamber of commerce Chicago has men for citizens' advisory boards,

reception committees, loud-speaker occasions, world's fair commissions, but none for practical duty in the trenches. It is a dress-suit leadership, admirable as far as it goes. The dire need is for a shirtsleeve leadership by men of the stature of Charles G. Dawes.

Political Chicago, which is continually puzzling outside observers, is a stage for much buffoonery and mountebanking, with mediocrity entrenched in office, and venality and waste the rule rather than the exception. The condition is chargeable, of course, to the voters themselves, whose attitude of unconcern is proverbial, the resultant being a species of slacker citizenship reflected not only at the polls, but also in jury service in the criminal courts.

In some respects Chicago is a national symptom; a sermon, if you like, on what's wrong with urban America.

The vaunted "I will" spirit is nonexistent except in private initiative and enterprise. Political Chicago is full of sound and fury at election times, beating the tomtom of issues; otherwise boring in for more party spoils; an ugly picture, but not without its uses—in it every city may recognize something of itself. The paradise of the gangster, the extortionist, the polls terrorist, the bomber, and the racketeer. The last two work together, the bomber supplementing the racketeer. The official record lists one hundred and fifteen bombs exploded in 1929, the average property damage per bomb being $1,713, a total of $197,109, with no convictions.

Scotland Yard, London, in 1928, the latest year for which official figures are available, investigated eighteen murders, obtaining convictions of eleven of the murderers. The other seven committed suicide. In 1928 there were 200 murders in New York City, with seven convictions. In Chicago there were 367 murders, 129 of which were either unsolved or the principals not apprehended. Of those arrested, 37 were acquitted, 39 received jail sentences, 16 were sent to insane asylums, 16 committed suicide, and 11 (gangster cases) were killed. There were no executions. In other words, on the 1928 record, a murderer had a 300-to-0 chance that he would not be sentenced to death in Chicago.

Entering 1930, the municipality, in a political sense, was a moral bankrupt; a financial bum; flat broke; literally a panhandler on the doorsteps of its bankers; its plight incomparably worse than that of New York City in the days of the Tweed Ring. On the record of its electorate it was the sap town of America.

Floating debts totaled $280,000,000, with 40,123 public employees—police, firemen, schoolteachers, janitors, clerks—unpaid, their back salaries aggregating $11,275,500. The board of education was in arrears $480,000 in coal bills. That was disclosed when one firm—the Reiner Coal Company—served notice that it would deliver no more fuel without a settlement in District No. 5, comprising 71 schools on the South Side with a combined enrollment of 98,382 pupils. Also the board was without funds to pay for free textbooks distributed in the classrooms, having owed $872,422 for them since March of 1929.

In the county, 3,862 employees were unpaid, and 1,642 widowed mothers, dependent upon county mothers' pensions, were destitute. Chicago banks had refused to buy any more of the tax anticipation warrants, of which they had already bought $185,000,000 worth.

A citizens' rescue committee of business and professional men was formed to extricate the municipality from what was described as "the most serious situation which has ever confronted an American city." Although there had been a reassessment, and a consequent delay in collecting 1928 taxes, statisticians stated that the books showed that the city and the school board had been overspending for years, and that even with the 1928 and 1929 taxes collected there would still be a deficit of $27,641,000.

This story is not concerned with scrutinizing the political career of William Hale Thompson, or that of any other man. It is interested in him and others as phenomena rather than as personalities. It seeks to point no moral, only to present, with as much fidelity as lies within the writer's power, a canvas of events; to let the reader see the Chicago scene of 1927 and the first four months of 1928—a period so weird that the world sat back and gaped, incredulous.

The story is concerned with Mayor Thompson's last administration because it was coincident with the apotheosis, as it were, of the gangster, when the shadow of Al Capone was cast across the City Hall and County Building as the Frankenstein monster of politics, and the voters rose in revolt.

Even so, they did not suspect Capone's actual status. That was not revealed until months later, when the

Illinois Association for Criminal Justice, a non-political body, headed by Rush C. Butler, president of the Illinois Bar Association, issued the first chapter of its report of a one-year investigation of organized crime, and stated that Capone "contributed substantially" to the Thompson mayoralty campaign fund. Estimates of the amount varied, the highest being $250,000, which seems excessive. A hundred thousand dollars would be nearer the mark. At least, the late William E. Dever refused a campaign contribution of that amount from vice and crime interests.

Capone received, the report stated, the gambling privileges of the South and West Sides and the booze concession for the Loop—around one hundred and twenty-five speakeasies in thirty-five square blocks, which Capone controlled while in Eastern Penitentiary through Jack Guzik. His beer trucks rumbled through the downtown streets as openly as milk-wagons, re-calling a remark by Patrick Roche, formerly of the Intelligence unit of the internal revenue service, but then chief investigator of the State's attorney's office:

"A one-legged prohibition agent on a bicycle could stop the beer in the Loop in a day," then, pausing for an impressive second, "if he were honest."

The Thompson platform, adopted in December of 1926, had a "Crime" plank, which read:

"The people of Chicago demand an end of the present unprecedented and appalling reign of crime. . . . The chief cause of this condition is not at the bottom, not with the mass of the police department, but it is at the top, with the powers, seen and unseen, which rule the force. . . . When I was mayor I was held responsible for crime conditions, and properly so, and I accepted that responsibility without trying to shift it to the courts or to other governmental agencies. . . . With practically the same men as are now in the police department, I drove the crooks out of Chicago, and will do so again if I am elected mayor."

His campaign manager was Homer K. Galpin, formerly chairman of the Cook County Republican central committee, who fled the city in 1928 when ordered to appear before the grand jury to testify as to sources of campaign contributions, and remained in hiding a year. He was mentioned by Baseball Commissioner Kenesaw M. Landis—then a Federal judge—in his testimony before the Daugherty investigating committee of the United States Senate in the case of Phillip L. Grossman, a West Madison Street saloonkeeper, whose place was a notorious hangout for criminals. Grossman was pardoned by President Coolidge before he had served a sentence imposed by Judge Landis. The judge named Mr. Galpin, Fred Upham, and George F. Barrett as "active in efforts to procure the pardon." In another inquiry, before the Brookhart investigating committee, Brice F. Armstrong, prohibition agent, testified that "eight breweries are running now in Chicago under protection," and that, "Homer K. Galpin is the man who tells them where, when and how to go."

The Saturnalia, some have called this last administration. Its overture was a shooting and it opens with song; sounds of revelry by night in the Louis XIV room of the Hotel Sherman. Let us listen in:

AL CAPONE

America first and last and always;
Our hearts are loyal, our faith is strong;
America first and last and always;
Our shrine and homeland, tho' right or wrong.

Stout hearts and willing lungs were abetting the voices, which numbered possibly one thousand and five hundred, with that raspy Sweet-Adeline quality of hoarseness peculiar to election-day vocalism:

United we stand for God and country;
At no one's command we'll ever be;
America first and last and always;
Sweet land of freedom and liberty.

The campaign anthem. Its singing ceased as a man with a megaphone mounted one of the tables where the returns were being checked and bellowed:

"The lead is now 52,000."

Victory. Yells from the men, shrieks from the women; clinking of glasses; backslapping; foot-stamping; bedlam.

A door swung wide. William Hale Thompson entered the room, grinning, waving his sombrero; his smallish, close-set, roving eyes two glittering gimlet points; his huge, paunchy frame fairly rocking with the relish of it. Above the hubbub boomed his stentorian bass:

"Tell 'em, cowboys; tell 'em! I told you I'd ride 'em high and wide!"

It was his first public utterance as mayor-elect of Chicago for the third time; date, Tuesday, April 5, 1927.

He was jubilant for several reasons. His "Bust King

155

George on the Snoot," or America First doctrine as enunciated in the campaign theme song, had triumphed; likewise the proposition of "No entangling alliances." "I stand," his platform had stated, "for the principles laid down by George Washington." British spies and propagandists were to be silenced. He had found evidence of their pernicious activities everywhere.

"I've got a lot of stuff I've been bottling up on the University of Chicago," he revealed at one meeting. "The university is in a conspiracy to distort American history in behalf of the king of England."

William McAndrew, superintendent of schools, he discovered to be a "stool-pigeon for King George." His platform declared regarding Mr. McAndrew, who had been associate superintendent of schools of New York City from 1914 until 1924, when he was brought to Chicago, that "he has encouraged the circulation of unpatriotic propaganda in our schools to poison the minds of our children against the founders of our country."

Yes, he was riding 'em high and wide. Even Oscar Carlstrom, attorney general of Illinois, indulged in eulogy in introducing him to an audience of ex-service men:

"I am glad to see you here in behalf of a friend of mine . . . Big Bill the Builder, who loves the little children . . . Big Bill the American, who stands for America First."

A year later, when these two political bedfellows had fallen out, the attorney general was to assert:

"He's been chasing a phantom King George up the

alleys, and turning the city over to crooks and gamblers until today conditions are anathema in the eyes of Chicago."

In the 1927 mayoralty election Mr. Thompson's opponents were William E. Dever, Democrat and incumbent, and Dr. John Dill Robertson, Independent, health commissioner in the previous Thompson administrations, whose campaign manager was Fred Lundin. The two were originally Mr. Thompson's warm cronies and Mr. Lundin had been his political mentor and godfather.

A few glimpses of the hustings may not be amiss to provide readers living at a distance with a better Chicago background. The defection of Dr. Robertson and Mr. Lundin grieved Mr. Thompson so sorely that he was led to express himself in public. He obtained two plump rats, appropriated the stage of a Loop theater, and, to quote from a newspaper account:

Big Bill Thompson put on his rat show yesterday at the Cort Theater. With two big rats from the stockyards, one named Fred, after Fred Lundin, and the other Doc, after Dr. John Dill Robertson, the former mayor kept his audience interested as he addressed his remarks to the two rodents.

"This one," he said, indicating the rat named after Dr. Robertson, "this one is Doc. I can tell him because he hadn't had a bath in twenty years until we washed him yesterday. But we did wash him and he doesn't smell like a billy goat any longer.

"Don't hang your head, now, Fred," he said, addressing the other rat. "Fred, let me ask you something: Wasn't I the best friend you ever had? Isn't it true that I came home from Honolulu to save you from the penitentiary?"

Big Bill then related how he lived up to the cowboy code of

standing by his friends and came home as a character witness in the school-board graft trial.

Thompson said he had six rats to start with, but that Fred and Doc ate up the other four, which were smaller.

Mr. Lundin's comment on this was that Mr. Thompson was using "the guttersnipe talk of a hoodlum." Dr. Robertson raised the cry of "Who killed McSwiggin?" and charged that in 1921 "Thompson appointed Charles C. Fitzmorris, a Democrat, chief of police, during whose reign began the formation of the multimillionaire crime ring."

"The Doc is slinging mud," replied Mr. Thompson. "I'm not descending to personalities, but you should watch Doc Robertson eating in a restaurant—eggs in his whiskers, soup on his vest; you'd think the Doc got his education driving a garbage wagon."

Dr. Robertson's statement concerning Mr. Fitzmorris, himself a newspaperman in 1910 and now a millionaire, recalled the testimony of Mayor Dever in 1926 before the United States Senate prohibition inquiry committee. It was that when he assumed office in 1923 "sixty per cent of the police were engaged in the liquor business; not in connivance, but actually," and that "Chief Collins' predecessor [Mr. Fitzmorris] had acknowledged that to be true."

The forensic activities of Mr. Thompson against King George irked Mayor Dever, who hinted that they were nothing more than a smoke screen—hokum.

"I have tried," he said, "to confine this campaign to the issues and the interests of Chicago, but in that I have found no combatant. I thought the square thing to do was to get into the ring with Bill with the gloves, but he would not come into the ring. He has been throwing tacks from the outside. I have never respected him. I do not respect him now. I shall not respect him whether he wins or loses."

Said Judge Harry B. Miller of the superior court of Cook County:

"If Thompson wins Chicago will have a Fatty Arbuckle for Mayor."

The vote was, Thompson, 515,716; Dever, 432,678; Robertson, 51,347.

Mayor Dever had tried conscientiously to enforce prohibition; Dr. Robertson had campaigned on a platform of "Smash the crime ring"; Mr. Thompson had proclaimed, "I'm wetter than the middle of the Atlantic ocean."

The Saturnalia, then, has for an overture a shooting —the killing on April 4th, the day preceding the election, of Vincent the Schemer Drucci. Members of his gang had raided the offices of Alderman Dorsey R. Crowe of the Forty-second Ward, a Dever supporter. Chief Collins had received information of a plot to kidnap the alderman and his co-workers. He had issued orders for a roundup of thugs and hoodlums.

A detective bureau squad commanded by Lieutenant, William Liebeck sighted Drucci at Diversity Parkway and Clark Street, on the North Side. With him were his friend, Henry Finkelstein, proprietor of a nightlife café, and one Albert Single of Peoria. Drucci was relieved of a .45 automatic and the three were taken to the bureau. There, although twenty minutes had not elapsed, Lieutenant Liebeck was notified that Drucci's

attorney, Maurice Green, was waiting at the Criminal
Courts Building with a petition for a writ of habeas
corpus.

He and Policemen Danny Healy, Matthew Cunningham, and Dennis Kehoe, driver, thereupon reloaded
their prisoners into the squad car for the trip to that
building. Healy, a clean, high-spirited young fellow
who despised gangsters, had killed one of the Armitage
Avenue car-barn bandits and had mastered Polack Joe
Saltis in a personal encounter. He was assigned to
guard Drucci, who knew him by reputation. Healy's
story of what happened was:

"When Drucci got into the car, he said, 'You ——,
I'll get you. I'll wait on your doorstep for you.' I told
him to shut his mouth. Drucci said, 'Go on, you kid
copper; I'll fix you for this.' I told him to keep quiet.
Drucci said, 'You take your gun off me or I'll kick hell
out of you.' He got up on one leg and struck me on
the right side of the head with his left hand, saying,
'I'll take you and your tool [revolver].' He said, coming
toward me, 'I'll fix you,' grabbing hold of me by the right
hand. I grabbed my gun with my left hand and fired
four shots at him."

Like Mike Genna, Drucci died cursing a copper.

His attorney, waiting impatiently in the Criminal
Courts Building to "spring" his client, learned that he
was in the county morgue. He immediately sought to
have Healy arrested on a charge of murder, but was
unsuccessful.

"I don't know anything about any one being murdered," said Old Shoes (Chief of Detectives William
Schoemaker). "I know Drucci was killed trying to take

a gun away from an officer. We're having a medal made for Healy."

The solicitude of politicians for gangsters and their kind was shown in the case of Drucci's friend, Finkelstein. As soon as word of his arrest got around there interceded in his behalf State Representative Harry Weisbrod, Alderman Jacob M. Arvey, and Moe Rosenberg, brother of Sanitary District Trustee Michael Rosenberg. Their pleas before Judge William J. Lindsay obtained his release on bond.

Drucci lay in gangster state for a day and a night in a $10,000 aluminum and silver casket in the chapel of Assistant State's Attorney John A. Sbarbaro's undertaking establishment. The American flag was draped over the remains and there were $30,000 worth of flowers—a heart of blood red roses, inscribed, "To my darling husband"; a huge circlet of pink roses sent to "My boy"; a chair of purest white and deepest purple flowers, with the inscription, "Our pal"; there were broken wheels of flowers, shafts of flowers, Bibles of flowers, and just plain flowers.

Present at the wake were George Bugs Moran, sole survivor of the three O'Banion musketeers; Julius Potatoes Kaufman, Frank and Peter Gusenberg, Benjamin Jacobs, politician wounded in the machine gunning of Weiss, and James Fur Sammons.

In the procession to Mount Carmel Cemetery, the American flag enfolded the hearse. The floral gifts filled twelve automobiles and preceded the funeral car. The body was placed in a vault pending the purchase of a mausoleum.

Mrs. Cecilia Drucci, the widow, very blonde (Chicago gangsters prefer blondes), contributed a perfect epitaph. The obsequies were over and she was preparing to leave the cemetery.

"A policeman murdered him," she said, "but we sure gave him a grand funeral."

When Morgan A. Collins retired on April 14th, Michael Hughes succeeded him as chief of the city's $15,000,000 police department, and custodian of its fine collection of clues. His induction into office was noteworthy for its civic éclat. There was a testimonial dinner, attended by two thousand five hundred persons, at which he was presented with a diamond-studded gold star. His announced policy was that crime suppression would be of first importance and prohibition enforcement of second. In this, of course, he was only supplying a carbon copy of a major plank in the mayor's platform.

"We'll put the police back traveling beats instead of sniffing around for a little home brew or frisking pantries for a hip flask," was Mr. Thompson's oft-repeated campaign utterance. He denounced the police under Collins as "snoopers against personal liberty."

The inference was plain. America First Chicago was to be free of entangling alliances with the Eighteenth Amendment—and the mayor's critics could scan that plank with a fluoroscope for hokum. He was sincere, personally as well as politically, in saying that he was "wetter than the middle of the Atlantic ocean." The Little City Hall on the sixteenth floor of the Hotel Sherman was the foremost oasis of the Loop. No one liked a Bourbon highball better than he; none was freer with his hospitality. Considering the hypocrisy in high places, the mayor's open drinking, openly arrived at, always impressed the writer as refreshing.

Certainly, in that he was an office-holder, it was hardly ethical—but it was consistent in the city where one out of every three persons is a prohibition law-breaker in one form or another.

The "no snooping" corrected the rankest absurdity in the office of chief of police. It sanctioned, so to speak, the booze cupboard. For ten years, with the possible exception of Collins, with whose personal habits the writer was not familiar, every chief has had his private stock and dispensed it to newspapermen and others. Watching an official with a gold star on his chest comfortably downing snits of whiskey while his men are out dry-raiding the city, is a rare experience.

As a policy for the practical operation of a police department, the winking at the Eighteenth Amendment was something else again. Chief Hughes was letting the administration chart an ambiguous course for him. Events were to prove that prohibition enforcement and the crime problem were integrated. In endeavoring to differentiate, he was to find himself in an impasse.

Of that, naturally, he was unaware, when, on April 28th, fourteen days after assuming office, he issued the statement that "frightened by the police drive, the gunmen, bandits and other world characters are on the run already." Viewed in perspective, with the knowledge of the Capone campaign contribution, the efforts of Chief Hughes and the department to cope with the gangster situation in 1927–28 assume a tragi-comic aspect.

Undoubtedly, he was spurred by the mayor's pre-election assurances. He felt that he had a definite commitment. He was Go-Get-'Em-Mike, who was to drive the crooks out of Chicago in ninety days. Before he could organize further than on paper for that undertaking his attention was diverted by a series of murders so singular as to challenge the best minds of the force.

On the evening of May 25th a home-bound pedestrian stumbled on the body of a man at Desplaines and DeKoven streets. The neighborhood, half industrial, half residential, southwest of the Loop, across the river, is a huddle of factory and tenement buildings by day, and by night a Limehouse backdrop; a place of skulking figures, dimly seen in the shadows of tortuous areaways and narrow alleys. Doors open unexpectedly into halls and covered staircases leading to impenetrable mystery. Lights glimmer from bleary panes, behind which humans are pigeonholed. One of those murky purlieus, this Limehouse backdrop, where anything might happen—where the wary citizen never ventures without having secreted his money in his shoe.

The victim of the murder wore tailored clothes of expensive texture and a three-carat diamond solitaire ring, and his hip pocket yielded a roll of hundred-dollar bills totaling $1,200. So robbery was not the motive. That in itself, in that neighborhood, lifted the crime into the category of the unusual. The man was a stranger, which was curious, but the thing that focused interest was a nickel—a nickel clutched in the right hand. It had been put there after death and the fingers bent over to hold it.

Speculation was still busy with this case, when, on August 11th, every angle of it was duplicated—only this time it was a double murder. Then, on September 24th, occurred another—the fourth of the series. As with the first victim, the three men were strangers, all well dressed, all carrying large sums, which were intact, and in the right hand of each was clutched a nickel.

Seeking light, the chief bethought him of an extraordinary youth, born James DeMora, now answering to the nom de guerre of Jack McGurn. He was not hard to find. He was skipping rope in the Metropole Hotel, 2300 South Michigan Avenue, G. H. Q. of General Al the Scarface.

The mild pastime of skipping the rope may seem irrelevant to the rôle of a suspect in a four-man murder case. Yet if the reader had accompanied the police to the Metropole he would have discovered two rooms equipped with punching bags, horizontal bars, trapezes, rowing machines, and other gymnasium paraphernalia.

Capone's gunmen were required to keep conditioned. They followed a schedule of training as methodical as that of college football athletes. Experience had taught him that their professional value, based on that quality commonly described as nerve, was in direct ratio to their physical fitness. It might be only the imperceptible tremor of a trigger-finger, or the slightest wavering of an eye, or a split second of hesitancy at the crucial moment in any of a score of unforeseen emergencies; yet the cost of the lapse would have to be reckoned in lives and money.

Thus much the canny Scarface had learned, and had profited accordingly. His system was an important factor in producing the bootleg gangster typified in McGurn, the antithesis of that popular fancy. The picture of a furtive, sallow-faced creature, with cap and pulled-down visor and cigarette drooping from listless lip, gives way to that of an upstanding, square-shouldered fellow, in his teens or twenties, keen-eyed, ruddy-cheeked; a smart dresser, with a flair for diamonds and blondes; always occupying choice seats at prize fights, wrestling matches, football and baseball games, the racetrack, and the theater; knowing the night-club head waiters and receiving their deferential ministrations.

McGurn in many respects is as dramatic a figure as Capone. He commands special attention by reason of his melting-pot background. He is Chicago born and reared. His life history is an open book—that is to say, the adolescent period—an unusual circumstance, and affording opportunity for interesting research. He is a sociological document, revealing how at least one gangster got that way.

James De Mora, eldest of six children, was the son of Angelo De Mora, the grocer. His boyhood was spent in the backyard of Halsted Street called Little Italy, Chicago's most congested district; its ramshackle, firetrap structures, devoid of all pretense at hygiene, and wedged wall to wall and end to end, cover almost every available square foot of every lot and block. Its atmosphere in summer is fetid and stifling, mothers with their babies sleeping on the sidewalks and front stoops. It offers no sweep of playground, no breathing space, no sunlit freedom to the growing child, except in its streets and alleys. Life is raw and squalid in Little Italy.

The boy James, report cards show, was an eager pupil at the neighborhood school, quick to learn and of retentive mind. He was a leader in playground sports

and was particularly fond of boxing. Indeed, he became
the school champion, easily outpointing opponents
twenty and thirty pounds heavier. As he grew older and
his ability increased, his admirers urged him to join an
amateur athletic club. He did, and mastered more of
the rudiments of fisticuffs, while adding to his string of
victories. He had the true fighting heart. A fight pro-
moter heard of him and gave him a tryout, and he
turned professional, a welterweight, adopting the ring
name of Jack McGurn.

His father, Angelo the grocer before prohibition, had
become Angelo the sugar dealer after its advent; caught
up and carried along on the wave of get-rich-quick
frenzy that swept all Little Italy with the rise of the
alky-cooking industry. Angelo sold sugar to the Gennas,
which implies no more reproach than to say that Samuel
Insull, who built Chicago's $30,000,000 opera house,
sold gas to Abraham Bummy Goldstein (Pete the Peddler) for his wildcat distillery at 1154 Hastings Street.
A police raid there disclosed that Bummy in one month
had used $1,700 worth of gas.

Angelo sold sugar, and business competition was a
sanguinary enterprise. He was found shot to death the
morning of January 8, 1923, in front of his store at
936 Vernon Park Place, a half-block from his home.
Jack was then nineteen. With the widowed mother and
the five other children, he attended the inquest. He was
silent and preoccupied.

Had he any suspicions as to who killed his father?
"No."

Was he not fearful, having become head of the house,
for his own life?

"I'm big enough," he said with ominous quiet, "to take care of this case myself."

The prize ring never saw him again. His friends missed him at the usual neighborhood haunts. If they wondered what had happened to him, it was not for long. Out of the underworld jungle began emanating police reports of the boy turned gangster—McGurn picked up in the Loop, carrying a revolver; McGurn arrested in a room in a West Side hotel, with his fifteen-year-old brother, Antonio, and an arsenal consisting of a Thompson sub-machine gun with loaded magazine attached, a .45 caliber automatic pistol, a rifle, and a quantity of dumdum bullets; McGurn wounded by a spray of machine-gun bullets while in a telephone booth in a hotel near the North Side; McGurn's automobile riddled with shotgun slugs.

Summarizing the findings in the investigation of the Moran gang massacre, for which McGurn and the late John Scalise were indicted, Dr. Herman N. Bundesen, Cook County coroner, wrote:

"It is known he is suspected of having had a hand in the killing of some fifteen other gangsters [which would give McGurn around twenty-two notches]. He is generally regarded as an expert machine gunner. It is believed he got his start as a killer after his father was shot to death."

McGurn's professional value was top because of his invincible nerve. There was no likelihood that he would ever collapse under the strain and "go cuckoo," the big dread of every gangster boss. For it is axiomatic that "if a gunner goes cuckoo, he turns yellow," which means that he will weaken in a pinch and squawk.

Therewith is disclosed a little-known phase of underworld life. The gangster boss is always vigilant for the telltale symptoms of a collapse among his killers. They manifest themselves in the trite details of daily habit—lighting too many cigarettes and tossing them aside after a few superficial puffs; drinking coffee in jerky sips; failing to pull the tie up snugly to the collar in dressing.

Detecting any of these symptoms, the boss redoubles his vigilance. The patient may snap out of it. If after a week's observation he has doubts as to his condition, he stages a conclusive test, in this wise: A party is organized to make the rounds of the whoopee spots. The patient is taken along. Apparently by accident, he meets half a dozen pretty girls in different places. Each one is nice to him. Each one, in fact, tries to vamp him. They are plants. If he does not react, that settles it; the boss knows the worst has come to pass— "When a guy don't fall for a broad, he's through"—his killer has turned yellow. The remedy follows. He is bumped off. His colleagues get him drunk and take him for a ride. It happens often in Chicago.

McGurn was Capone's chief gunner's mate, and the police wanted to question him in the four-man murder case, because it looked as if somebody was out to get the Scarface. Identification had disclosed each victim as a professional killer. Number 1 was Antonio Torchio of New York; Numbers 2 and 3, taken for a ride together August 11th, were Anthony K. Russo and Vincent Spicuzza of St. Louis; Number 4 was Samuel Valente of Cleveland.

The five-cent pieces in their hands were expressive

of their slayers' contempt for them; tantamount to a derisive sneer and a slap in the face. It is an extreme gesture of contumely, which the gangster does not employ except when he is beside himself with rage. Trouble was brewing.

Chicago in 1927 and 1928 was tagged in underworld jargon as "hot" for any outsiders who had no business there, so well had Capone consolidated his gains and systematized his overlordship of vice, gambling, and booze. Only real money could have induced the four killers to take a chance. Who had offered it? The police learned nothing from McGurn, although the coroner recorded him and Scalise as suspects in the Torchio job.

Trouble was brewing. The ukelele music started suddenly for members of the old Genna outfit. Six were slain within a month and a half—Lawrence La Presta, on June 1st; Diego Attlomionte, June 29th; Numio Jamericco, June 30th; Lorenzo Alagno, also June 30th; Giovanni Blaudins, July 11th; Dominic Cinderella, July 17th.

For the first five, the coroner entered the notation, "Slayers not apprehended," but in the case of Cinderella, a saloonkeeper, whose body was trussed in a sack and tossed in a ditch, he again had occasion to mention McGurn, and with him one Orchell DeGrazio. They were arrested, but freed for lack of evidence.

Events moved swiftly. The morning of November 22d newsies greeted Chicagoans with cries of "Cops ordered to kill killers!" "Gunmen defy police; invade law's stronghold!" The story they were crying began:

"Chicago gunfighters almost achieved the ultimate in assassination yesterday, when they silently encircled the detective bureau and waited patiently for the opportunity to kill Joseph Aiello, hitherto only a modest claimant to gang honors, who became by this stealthy swarming of the clans, a new and astonishing figure in the stratum of bullets, booze, gambling and vice."

And farther along:

"Summed up, from police information, the situation is one involving perhaps $75,000,000 a year, the profits of gambling and vice and booze in Chicago. It is for control of these profits that there has been launched a new war between one group headed by William Skidmore and Barney Bertsche and another group ruled by Al Brown [Capone] and Antonio Lombardo."

The Aiellos were making their bid for gang leadership. Primarily they wanted to seize the Unione Sicilione. They had reorganized the old Genna outfit, and had effected a coalition with George Bugs Moran of the O'Banion remnant on the North Side and with William Skidmore, Barney Bertsche, and Jack Zuta on the West Side. These had accordingly repudiated the peace pact of October, 1926, and the Capones regarded it as treachery.

It was the last threat of any consequence at Capone's power. It was elaborately conceived and aimed at the extinction of both Capone and Lombardo, whom he had seated as president of the Unione Sicilione in November of 1925.

If Capone had kept a diary, 1927 would be ringed in red as the banner year for plots against his life, the instigators of all of them being the Aiellos. First they tried to bribe the chef of the Little Italy café with $10,000 to put prussic acid in his soup, but the chef weakened and confessed. Then they offered $50,000 to any gunman who would "show us a Capone notch." It was this that brought the professional killers to town —and to the county morgue. Finally they devised two machine-gun ambuscades—one for Lombardo, in a flat opposite his home at 4442 Washington Boulevard, and one for Capone, in the Loop—room 302 in the Atlantic Hotel, at 316 South Clark Street, commanding the entrance across the way to his favorite loafing-place, the cigar store of Michael Hinky Dink Kenna, at 311 South Clark Street. These ambuscades provided the climax of the plottings, and knowledge of them caused the demonstration by Capone gunmen at the detective bureau when they learned of Aiello's presence there. They had been after him for months, but hadn't caught up with him.

Of the Aiellos there were the four brothers—Joseph, Dominick, Antonio, and Andrew—and a score of cousins, Joseph being the head of this Sicilian family clan. He had originally been Lombardo's business partner and they had prospered as cheese merchants and commission brokers. Both were active in the affairs of the Unione Sicilione during the régime of Mike Merlo, its founder and, by the way, the only one of its six presidents from 1924 to 1929, to die a natural death.

Stern and just in his administration of the office, Merlo's rule was absolute. He was a shrewd politician —he had put Carmen Vacco in as city sealer of Chicago—and he was zealous of the interests of his people, most of whom were first-generation immigrants. To their simple minds he represented mysterious authority and influence. They venerated him, ignorant, of course, that he was exploiting them for their votes.

As long as Merlo lived there was no discord in the Unione Sicilione, but immediately after his death began that struggle for leadership with which the reader is familiar. All the arts of political intrigue were utilized by men ambitious for the post, and by their families and friends.

Lombardo, with Capone's help, emerged victorious. For a time the Aiellos supported him, and he and Joseph maintained their business relationship. But Joseph was jealous. He had had an insight into racial politics and the game fascinated him. His ambition, stimulated by the persuasions of his followers, overmastered his judgment. He quarreled with Lombardo. They dissolved their partnership, and the Aiellos launched their conspiracy.

Not content to confine it to Chicago, they sent members of the family to Cleveland and St. Louis to organize rivals to the local branches of the Unione Sicilione. A dozen killings resulted in St. Louis, culminating in the slaying of two Aiello kinsmen as they were eating in a restaurant in Springfield, Illinois, en route to Chicago.

Chief Hughes' men, always surprisingly well informed in gangster skullduggery adverse to Capone, suddenly raided the flat opposite Lombardo's home, at 4442 Washington Boulevard, and uncovered the machine-gun ambuscade. Next, they went to 7002 North Western Avenue, ten miles away, found a cache of dynamite and percussion caps, and a clue that sent them to the Rex Hotel, at 3142 North Ashland Avenue.

There they captured Angelo La Mantio, twenty-three years old, a Milwaukee gunman, and with him four of the Aiello clan. A trifle soft for the job he had undertaken La Mantio admitted to the police that he had been hired to do away with Capone and Lombardo, and divulged the ambuscade in the Atlantic Hotel.

With that the action shifts to the detective bureau. La Mantio and Joseph Aiello had not been there an hour when a policeman standing at a window saw a half-dozen taxis stop on the opposite side of the street, discharging between twenty and twenty-five passengers— all men. He assumed that there had been a raid somewhere and that officers were bringing in prisoners. But not for long.

The men hurriedly put their heads together, gesticulating excitedly and darting glances at the bureau. Then they separated, some sauntering up and down the sidewalk; some loitering at the curb and in doorways; some stationing themselves at the street corners; while others crossed over to disappear in an alley alongside the building, into which opened its rear exit. The policeman called to a fellow officer. As he did so three men headed directly for the bureau's front entrance, one of them transferring a revolver from an armpit holster to the side pocket of his overcoat.

"Louis Campagnia," exclaimed the fellow officer. "It's the Capone crowd."

Which was the way headquarters was first apprised of the gangland episode now chronicled in police lore as the Siege of the Detective Bureau. The place was completely surounded.

The two officers ran to the street and brought back Campagnia, Frank Perry, and Samuel Marcus, mem-

174

bers of the Capone bodyguard imported from the East. A pair of .45 automatics apiece was found on Campagnia and Perry, but only one gun on Marcus. The discrepancy was explained five minutes later when he whipped a sawed-off Colt from inside his shirt while being questioned in the chief of detective's office. He was overpowered before he could use it. His intention, apparently, was to shoot his way to liberty.

The three were put in a cell adjoining that of Joseph Aiello, and a policeman who understood the Italian language was disguised and placed within hearing. Aiello at once recognized his enemies.

"Can't we settle this?" he pleaded. "Give me just fifteen days—just fifteen days—and I will sell my stores and house and leave everything in your hands. Think of my wife and baby and let me go."

The Capones laughed.

"You dirty rat! You started this. We'll end it. You're as good as dead."

Upon his release from custody, Aiello, wild-eyed with terror, begged for police protection. He was escorted to a taxi and told to beat it. He fled Chicago; went in a hole, as the underworld saying is, for eighteen months, or until May of 1929, when Capone was jailed in Philadelphia. His brother Dominick elected to stay to conduct their business affairs, and was shot to death. So was finis written to another quest for the Golden Fleece of prohibition Chicago, and to another conspiracy to depose Capone.

By the terms of the 1926 peace pact, Skidmore, Bertsche, and Zuta had been relegated to the district north of the Madison Street deadline—largely the

Forty-second and Forty-third Wards—but after tying up with the Aiellos they had stepped across, and Zuta, the divekeeper, had essayed the rôle of muscle man— touring the territory with a crew of gunmen, spotting gambling places and resorts, and exacting tribute from the operators. The Capones bombed their headquarters at 823 West Adams Street, wrecking the building. It was a warning, and sufficed. The three scurried for cover to their North Side district and remained there.

Matters vital to Capone's peace of mind had likewise been satisfactorily adjusted in Cicero. A Federal grand jury in October of 1926 had voted indictments in seventy-eight liquor cases. The defendants included Ed Konvalinka, whom the reader will remember as the soda-jerker who became a Main Street Warwick; Mayor Joseph Klenha; Police Chief Theodore L. Svoboda; and Capone—Klenha had been Konvalinka's candidate on the ticket sponsored by Capone's gunmen in the election of April 1, 1924. The charges were conspiracy and there were two key witnesses—John Costenora, a Cicero saloonkeeper, and Santo Celebron, a bartender. Because of the congested calendars of the Federal courts, a year elapsed before the cases were called for trial. When they were, it was learned that Castenora and Celebron had been killed. The Government had to dismiss the cases for lack of evidence.

Also there had been the Cicero graft investigation, Special State's Attorney Charles A. MacDonald having obtained evidence in the form of canceled checks showing payments of large sums of money by Capone and associates to city officials. But though the names were written on them, none of the witnesses summoned before the grand jury could identify them—not even Alfred Pinkert, vice president of the Pinkert State Bank of Cicero—and the investigation had fizzled.

The Pinkert State Bank was across the street from Capone's Hawthorne Hotel headquarters. In one of its safety-deposit boxes Government agents, delving for income-tax information in 1929, discovered Ralph Bottles Capone's $100,000 cache; they learned further that in 1927 and 1928 he had made deposits of $974,000 in five different banks under as many different names. A by-product was the disclosure that his brother Al had exercised his rich man's option for a hobby and had chosen racing, establishing the Arsonia stables, with seven thoroughbreds.

In December of 1927, a looker-on at the Chicago scene would have concluded that Al Capone was pretty comfortably ensconced, pretty well content with himself and the world. The Aiellos had been routed. A quietus had been put on Skidmore, Bertsche, and Zuta. Professional killers from other cities had been taught a lesson. A couple of murders had made Cicero safe from the United States Government. Capone was master of all he surveyed.

Gone, too, were many of that company of magnificent scoundrels that in 1920 had gloried and drunk deep at the long mahogany bar of the Four Deuces—his own brother, Frank; three of the six deadly Gennas; Walter O'Donnell of the South Side O'Donnells; Sam Samoots Amatuna; Vincent the Schemer Drucci; Samuel J. Nails Morton; Earl Hymie Weiss; and Dion O'Banion —yea, even old Joe Howard—"estate: 1 pair cuff buttons; cash, $17." Gone with "yesterday's sev'n thousand years." He could paraphrase Omar: "The moving trigger-finger writes. . . ."

Municipal cabinet member without portfolio, commissioner of lawlessness—and mayor of Crook County, the columnist wags had dubbed him. In the public mind, both here and abroad, his name had became synonymous with crime and corruption—and with prohibition as is.

The looker-on, then, would have been as astounded and puzzled as was the citizenry when Capone abruptly announced on December 5th that he was shaking off the dust of Chicago, leaving for Florida, and, "I don't know when I'll get back, if ever."

He aired his favorite grievance:

"The coppers won't have to lay all the gang murders on me now."

He revealed his mental anguish because the world did not understand him:

"My wife and my mother hear so much about what a terrible criminal I am, it's getting too much for them, and I'm sick of it myself.

"The other day a man came in and said that he had to have $3,000. If I'd give it to him, he said, he would make me beneficiary in a $15,000 insurance policy he'd take out, and then kill himself.

"Today I got a letter from a woman in England. Even over there I'm known as a gorilla. She offered to pay my passage to London if I'd kill some neighbors she'd been having a quarrel with."

Capone did not go to Florida. He went instead to Los Angeles, accompanied by his wife, son, and a two-man bodyguard. They left Chicago December 10th.

They were back December 18th. Los Angeles had received them with a reception committee headed by Chief of Police James E. Davis.

"You're not wanted here," he quietly informed Capone. "We're giving you twelve hours to leave."

Capone was indignant, but submissive. There was talk of riding him out of town on a rail. He boarded an eastbound Santa Fé train December 14th.

"We were just tourists," he said. "I thought Los Angeles liked tourists. We no sooner got there than the newspapers started writing stuff about me, and then I got the bum's rush. And somebody stole my wine. A swell dump."

In the interim Chief Hughes had spoken:

"Capone can't come back to Chicago."

With the idea of sidestepping Hughes and slipping quietly into the city, Capone and his party debarked from the train at Joliet, where is located the Illinois State Penitentiary. John Corcoran, its chief of police, met them, relieved Capone and his bodyguard of their several pieces of ordnance, and charged them with gun-toting. Fines totaling $2,601 were assessed.

"I'm a property owner and a taxpayer," was Capone's rejoinder to Hughes. "I guess I can return to my own home."

Well, yes. But the chief could post a twenty-four hour detail in front of his house at 7244 Prairie Avenue. He could have bluecoats stalking him all over town. He could harry him day and night. Which he did, inspiring a Rialto poet to commit a parody on "Mary's Little Lamb":

179

AL CAPONE

Capone had a flatfoot pair whose dogs did fret them so;
For everywhere Capone went those cops 2 had 2 go.

The chief won. Capone resumed his wanderings, heading for Florida and St. Petersburg this time. The news preceded him. The police met him at the station and trailed him so assiduously that he stayed only overnight. He tried Miami. Women's clubs, churches, and business men's organizations protested; he was ordered on his way. Nassau learned that he was dickering for a home in the Bahamas. The colonial governor proscribed him. New Orleans heard he was coming and issued a warning. The world seemed to have a set opinion regarding Capone, even though it did not understand him.

The looker-on at the Chicago scene might likewise have inferred by now that the authorities of Capone's home town had discovered him to be an undesirable. Right. *Et tu!* A belated discovery.

Chief Hughes, a veteran of the police department, had wide and intimate knowledge of gangsters. He knew Capone's background. He had worked on the Big Jim Colosimo case in 1920. He had investigated Capone on his first serious murder rap—that of old Joe Howard in 1924. He had expressed his attitude toward him in his declaration as chief, pro tempore, of the county highway police in the winter of 1926–27, that he had run him "out of Cicero and for that matter out of further business dealings in Cook County." Yet as Mayor Thompson's Go-Get-'Em-Mike, who was to drive the crooks out of Chicago in ninety days, he had tolerated Capone and his swarm of killers for eight

180

months; he had been so clement, in fact, that Capone could boast in Los Angeles, as he could later in Philadelphia:

"I have no police record in Chicago. I have never done time."

Seeking explanation of this toleration and clemency one recalls the report of the Illinois Association for Criminal Justice. To quote the exact language:

"In circles close to Capone, it was well known that he had contributed substantially to the Thompson campaign. . . ."

That refers to the mayoralty campaign of 1927. The reader will note its unqualified nature. So far as the writer knows Mayor Thompson offered no denial at the time of its publication in June of 1928. His campaign manager, Homer K. Galpin, as has been related, fled the city when sought for questioning as to sources of contributions.

Why, then, after eight months, in December of 1927, the bum's rush for Capone? Why the sudden determination to purge Chicago of his presence? A primary election was approaching. Could that be the answer?

The America First machine was facing a fight to retain its city, county, and State patronage—a fight that was to center in the offices of United States Senator, governor, and State's attorney. In addition there were to be elected ward committeemen and delegates to the Republican national convention at Kansas City.

Capone had grown too big for political comfort—too big to explain away. He was bigger than the administration, bigger than any issue. His shadow across the City Hall and County Building was lengthening, broadening. He was a fact—a terrible fact—and a symbol. He was subsidized criminality. He was the breakdown of law and order. He was organized violence expanding from booze and vice into the polling-booth, the jury room, the witness chair, into the trades and professions and industries. He was the extortionist—the racketeer, so-called—preying upon the city's economic life. He was rule by the gun.

As such he had become page-one news in the press of two continents. His armored car and bodyguard had been commented on by newspapers of London, Berlin, Paris, Edinburgh, and Rome. Chicago was being depicted as the crime capital of the world, with a murder rate exceeding that of New York City, and bombings in proportionate volume.

Here was Capone, and there was the plank in the mayor's platform:

"The people of Chicago demand an end of the present unprecedented and appalling reign of crime."

And here was Chief Hughes—in a predicament. He had followed the course charted for him by the administration of no entangling alliances with the Eighteenth Amendment; he was trapped between the Scylla of crime suppression and the Charybdis of prohibition enforcement; he was alone and friendless—as events were to prove—on the deep and treacherous sea of politics.

Presumably, the dénouement at the detective bureau, when Capone's gunners surrounded it to try to kill Joseph Aiello, decided the administration to get rid of him. Such a demonstration—a criminal tour de force—had never before been witnessed in Chicago. The contemptuous flouting of the law, the brazen indifference to the authorities, startled the public—sent a shudder through the city—and focused attention anew on the gangster menace.

If the administration hoped by the move to remedy an embarrassing situation, it was disappointed. The effect was just the opposite. Capone's odyssey caught the popular fancy. He was likened to "The Man Without a Country," and his wanderings were faithfully and fulsomely recorded by a gleeful press, lavish in its ridicule of Chicago. Finally, with the aid of subterfuge and the connivance of a scheming broker, Capone bought the villa on Palm Island, Miami Beach, and as a property owner successfully defied the whole commonwealth of Florida to oust him.

A month after his unceremonious exit from Chicago, a singular occurrence served to revive discussion of him. On the evening of January 25th a pair of bombs was tossed—one at the home of Charles C. Fitzmorris, city controller, and in the previous Thompson administration chief of police, the other at the home of Dr. William H. Reid, commissioner of public service, formerly smoke inspector. He was to be tried, with six police captains, in 1929, in the slot-machine-racket case —involving the alleged operation of 8,000 machines about the city with a daily take of as high as $50 each. The case was to fail when the witness relied upon by the prosecution to obtain a conviction refused to testify.

Controller Fitzmorris and Dr. Reid were the most influential of the mayor's advisers and the ranking members of his cabinet. Therefore it was apparent that the purpose of the bombs was political.

"This is a direct challenge from the lawless," said the mayor. "We accept the challenge." And he added, somewhat cryptically: "When our fight is over, the challengers will be sorry."

He was photographed by an evening newspaper, standing at a patrol box, taking personal charge of the investigation.

The challengers' reply was another bomb, February 11th, this one tossed into the apartment building occupied by Lawrence Cuneo, brother-in-law and secretary of State's Attorney Robert E. Crowe.

A week's interval, and a fourth bomb reached its destination—the undertaking establishment of John A. Sbarbaro, where so many notables of the bootleg war had reposed in gangster state. Mr. Sbarbaro, formerly one of Mr. Crowe's assistant State's attorneys, was now a municipal judge, having been elected as an America Firster.

Washington's Birthday of 1928 saw police guards stationed at the homes of Mayor Thompson; State's Attorney Crowe; City Sealer Daniel A. Serritella; Bernard P. Barasa, the administration's contact man with the Sicilians and Italians; Morris Eller, formerly sanitary district trustee and a candidate again on the America First ticket, his son, Emmanuel Eller, judge of the superior court, and Chief Hughes.

"I am completely baffled," said Chief Hughes. "I have been unable to obtain any clues as to the identities of the bombers or their motives."

Capone was sunning himself in his Palm Island, Florida, villa by the sea, telling friends:

"I like it down here. It's warm—but not too warm."

AL CAPONE

Up to now Mayor Thompson had been largely occupied with national affairs. The Mississippi River had overflowed, with disastrous consequences, April 30, 1927, a few weeks after his election, and he had immediately assumed leadership of the flood-control relief program in Congress. This had necessitated frequent trips to Washington and through the Southern States. He had, too, originated the "Draft Coolidge," idea, and there was the America First movement. The three combined made heavy demands upon his time.

He traveled more than 15,000 miles from April to February, spending nearly three months out of town. His official itinerary:

Date	1927	Destination	Purpose
April	18	New Orleans	Flood control
May	27	Phelps, Wisconsin	Hunting
June	9	Washington, District of Columbia	Flood control
July	12	St. Louis	Flood control
July	26	Mackinac Island	Vacation
August	17	Toledo, Ohio	America First
August	25	Springfield, Illinois	State Fair
September	6	Eleven cities; seven states	Flood control
October	2	Manitowish, Wisconsin	Fishing
October	7	Huron, South Dakota	Hunting
October	30	Toledo, Ohio	America First
November	7	Washington, District of Columbia	Water meters
December	3	Boston and Washington, District of Columbia	America First

	1928		
January	19	Springfield, Illinois	To see Gov. Small
February	1	New Orleans	Flood control
February	8	Springfield, Illinois	To see Gov. Small
February	22	Washington, District of Columbia	Flood control

These junkets were invariably festal events, the mayor being accompanied by delegations of followers numbering from one hundred to one thousand. Special trains were used, with red, white, and blue streamers on the sides of the coaches. Music was furnished by the police octet and harmonica band. For fifteen or twenty minutes before departure the junketers, assembled in the train-shed with megaphones, would join in singing "America First," led by the mayor.

In a statement issued August 20, 1927, dealing with State politics, he declared emphatically that he was not and would not be a candidate for President of the United States.

"I deeply regret," it read, "that the rumor will not down that I am a candidate for any higher office than that of mayor of the city of Chicago. . . . For me to be a candidate myself would be to inject a personal political ambition to the detriment of the success of the principles, and I hope that my friends who consider this statement definite will refrain from further remarks that would indicate otherwise."

In 1918 he had been an unsuccessful candidate for the Republican nomination for United States Senator from Illinois.

The America First Foundation had been established and was launching a nation-wide campaign for membership. The mayor was president. The secretary, John J. Murphy, outlined its aims—"to teach respect for the flag, train youth and aliens for citizenship, and instill in the public mind the ideals of George Washington, Abraham Lincoln, and Big Bill Thompson."

Locally, the mayor had announced a new slogan,

"Make Chicago Hum!" which was to be the motto of his administration. He elaborated on it:

"Open the waterway, to make Chicago hum. Settle the traction question, to make Chicago hum. Get rid of the bread lines, to make Chicago hum. Speed the great public improvements, to make Chicago hum. Chase out the crooks and gunmen, to make Chicago hum."

A victory banquet had been held at Fred Mann's Rainbo Gardens at which he had been presented with a Lincoln sport coupé. He changed it for a touring car, and had the left side of the rear seat raised with an extra cushion. A spotlight was installed in the back panel of the front seat. Evenings, with the top down, when starting for a ride, he would say to the chauffeur, "All right," and the chauffeur would press a switch and a flood of light would illumine his torso and features.

"The people like to see their mayor," he explained.

J. Lewis Coath, self-styled "Iron-Handed Jack," had been elected president of the board of education, and William McAndrew, superintendent of schools, had been suspended and was on trial for insubordination as a preliminary to his being ousted permanently.

Corporation Counsel Samuel A. Ettelson, in collaboration with Milton Weil, music publisher, who had composed "America First," was writing a song that was to rank with it as a campaign document. The title was "Big Bill the Builder." There were four verses and as many choruses. The first verse read:

Scanning hist'ry's pages, we find names we love so well,
Heroes of the ages— Of their deeds we love to tell,

AL CAPONE

But right beside them soon there'll be a name
Of some one we all acclaim.

And then the first-verse chorus:

Who is the one, Chicago's greatest son?
It's Big Bill the Builder;
Who fought night and day to build the waterway?
It's Big Bill the Builder.
To stem the flood, he stood in mud and fought for all he's worth;
He'll fight so we can always be the grandest land on earth;
He's big, real and true—a man clear thru and thru—
Big Bill the Builder— We're building with you.

U. J. Herrmann, yachtsman, sportsman, owner of
the Cort Theater, and the outstanding figure of the
Loop and Rialto, had been appointed book censor of
the Chicago Public Library. Information had reached
the mayor that there was being conducted there "what
appears to be a school or course for pro-British, un-
American propaganda."

A self-made Chicagoan, who started life as a bill-
poster, Sport, as everyone calls him, is a forthright
man of blunt speech and plain taste, impatient of affec-
tation. Many stories are told about him, the best
known having to do with a visit to New York City.
Arrived at the Commodore Hotel, he was standing at
the clerk's desk, pen in hand, ready to register. He
noticed the last entry:

"Grosvenor Thistlewaite, and valet, Boston."

He wrote:

"Sport Herrmann, and valise, Chicago."

As soon as he was notified of his appointment as book

188

censor Sport announced that all seditious volumes found on the shelves of the library would be burned in a lake-front bonfire. Two separate petitions for injunctions to restrain him were at once filed. The mayor issued a denial that he had ordered the torch. Sport receded from his position and the incident was closed.

So much for the political aspect of the Chicago scene. The gangster aspect was being enlivened by Polack Joe Saltis, South Side gunman and beer peddler, who was poking fun at the police with habeas corpus writs. The daily press was featuring the holding of Sunday court to free him and two of his henchmen after they had been picked up in a raid. One account reads as follows:

First intimation that friends of Saltis had set the machinery of the courts in motion to save Joe the possible discomfiture of a Sunday night in a cell developed when Judge William J. Lindsay telephoned Chief of Detectives William E. O'Connor at noon.

"A writ has been sworn out," Judge Lindsay informed the detective chief. "You must either book Joe and the others or release them." . . .

Judge Stanley H. Klarkowski of the criminal court unexpectedly put in an appearance at the police station, accompanied by a bailiff and a court clerk. He set up court in the station squadroom and then dispatched a specially sworn bailiff with writs to bring in Saltis, Sullivan and Conlon. . . .

Half an hour later Saltis and his friends were at liberty. . . .

A similar method of impromptu writ procedure . . . was used by Judge Emmanuel Eller a week ago. Judge Eller opened court at his home at 1 A. M. on Sunday, December 4, and ordered the release of Willie Druggan, brother of the notorious Terry Druggan, who was held for inquiry into a mysterious shooting of a third Druggan brother.

Another case occurred last Wednesday night when Judge William J. Lindsay appeared at midnight at the detective bureau and ordered Chief O'Connor to produce Robert Long, a thief suspect.

Saltis was enlivening the scene in still another way. He was demonstrating how to evade a jail sentence. Two weeks after his acquittal of the murder of John Mitters Foley, Saltis had been arrested. November 29, 1926, armed with a .45 automatic. On December 10th, Municipal Judge George A. Curran sentenced him to serve sixty days in the Bridewell and to pay a fine of $50 for carrying concealed weapons. Saltis' attorney was W. W. O'Brien, who represented him in the Foley trial and was wounded in the machine-gunning of Earl Hymie Weiss.

O'Brien, when Judge Curran imposed sentence, made a motion for a new trial, which was overruled. He then took an appeal to the appellate court, and Saltis was allowed his freedom on his original bond.

The appellate court sustained Judge Curran. O'Brien took an appeal to the State supreme court. On April 26, 1927, that court handed down a decision reaffirming the municipal-court conviction.

With Saltis still at liberty, the case was next appealed to the United States Supreme Court, the chief contention being that since Saltis' life had been threatened, he was entitled to carry a gun for self-protection. On May 15, 1928, that court denied the appeal, dismissing as "frivolous" the contention that Saltis had a right to go armed.

In the meantime, O'Brien had filed an application

for a pardon with the State board of pardons and paroles. It was not granted. A year and five months had elapsed since Judge Curran imposed sentence, and that would have been the maximum period Saltis could legally have avoided serving the jail term.

However, when the United States Supreme Court handed down its finding he fled the city for the north woods of Wisconsin and did not return until December 16, 1928, going to the Bridewell December 21st, after two years and eleven days of hide-and-seek with the law.

A new spirit was abroad in Chicago; animating discussions in homes, clubs, and public places; energizing reflection; rallying opinion. The mass consciousness had been stirred. People were thinking. Voices other than those of politicians were making themselves heard.

The Rev. M. P. Boynton, once an ardent supporter of Mayor Thompson, and for thirty years pastor of the Woodlawn Baptist Church, was preaching a sermon on local conditions, quoting a statement that "the fraudulent vote cast in the last [1927] mayoralty election was more than 100,000," and that "this was sufficient to throw the election which ever way the men responsible for those frauds wanted it to go."

He emphasized the fact that "no one seems to know anything about the recent bomb outrages, while a group robbing a mail train is almost at once run down by the police, indicted and put behind the bars under bonds of $100,000.

"Why can the police in our city so quickly apprehend one gang and be so ignorant of and helpless in the hands of another gang?"

A town meeting of lawyers, judges, and business men was being called by Silas H. Strawn, president of the American Bar Association. A few hours before it convened there was a triple slaying in Chicago Heights, three men who were attempting to hijack a Capone booze truck being taken for a ride.

Mr. Strawn, who had just returned from China, thought crime was no greater in Chicago than elsewhere, but "there is more than there should be." Chief Hughes had statistics to show that he had reduced it, and said Chicago was maligned. He made a plea for three thousand more policemen. T. E. Donnelley, chairman of the citizens' committee, could not believe that crime had been reduced materially. He foresaw a long hard fight against it, "or else the criminals will be running the country."

G. L. Hostetter, executive secretary of the Employers' Association, addressing a luncheon meeting of the Chicago Association of Commerce, listed sixty-one rackets levying tribute on as many lines of legitimate enterprise. He cited specific cases of rule by the gun—that of a man who tried to start a small window-washing concern without the ante to the racket boss, and was murdered; that of another who attempted to haul machinery, and was murdered; that of an independent junk-dealer who stood in the way of a monopoly of the waste-paper business, and was murdered.

"In one instance," he said, "we find collusion between union organizers and one of our beer gangs in an effort to unionize the employees of a manufacturer."

Frank J. Loesch, president of the Chicago Crime Commission, was voicing a distinctive characteristic of slacker citizenship, although he did not so describe it. He merely said:

"There are too many good citizens asking for and receiving from judges improper excuses from jury service. About forty per cent of those summoned for jury service in the criminal court are excused."

Congregations of five hundred churches were holding prayer services for Chicago's "deliverance from political corruption at the April primaries." Typical of the invocations was that of the Rev. John Thompson of the Chicago Methodist Temple, the Loop's skyscraper church, whose gold-leafed spire and cross rise serenely above the turmoil of hived humanity, at Clark and Washington streets, cater-cornered from the City Hall and County Building:

"O Thou that didst care for Nineveh, and didst spare it, and Thou that didst weep over Jerusalem, dost Thou still brood over these great modern cities? We pray Thee to rule over Chicago—this young and strong, good and bad, city—and out of man's worst, bring Thine own best."

Within two weeks the sawed-off shotguns roared a finis to the devious career of Diamond Joe Esposito, fifty-eight poisoned slugs, fired at almost point-blank range, burying themselves in his pudgy body. United States Senator Charles S. Deneen hurried home from Washington, and the fight was on.

Esposito's death was of tremendous significance. He was a leader in the Deneen faction of the Republican party, opposing the America Firsters. In the old Nineteenth Ward—now the Twenty-fifth—the Italian district, he was by way of being a political, social, and business institution. "Dimey," they called him. His name was a household word. No christening, no wedding, no funeral, no saint's day, was complete without Dimey's presence. In the Christmas holidays· he gave his annual party and played Santa Claus for the poor children. He was the ward's godfather.

The result was apparent at election times. Like his friend, Big Jim Colosimo, and like Mike Merlo, Esposito, in the vernacular of the Chicago ward heeler, was a sheepherder: he delivered votes.

His career has a bearing on this story. Fifty-six years old, he was born in the town of Accera, seven miles from Naples, April 28, 1872. In 1895, when twenty-three years old, he emigrated to America. He worked as a day laborer in Boston and Brooklyn, saving his money. He came to Chicago in 1905, settling in the old Nineteenth Ward and opening a bakery. In 1910 he bought a saloon and restaurant at 1048 West Taylor Street. It was there in 1917 that one Cuono Coletta shot up a spaghetti party, Joe's brother, Sam, losing a finger. Coletta's head was blown off by a guest who happened to have his artillery handy.

In his· exploiting activities, Esposito went a step beyond Colosimo. Whereas Big Jim had banded his fellow countrymen into the Street Cleaners' Social and Athletic Club, but had eschewed the labor game as too dangerous, Diamond Joe organized his constituents into the International Hod Carriers' Building and Construction Laborers' Union, becoming their business agent and treasurer. He also founded, and was president of, the Circolo Accera, composed of men and women from his Italian birthplace and its environs.

AL CAPONE

He was indicted for murder in October of 1908. The charge was that he had shot Mack Geaquenta, a barber, during an argument over a woman. The bullet struck Geaquenta in the mouth and he died without regaining consciousness. The shooting occurred in August. The case was not called for trial until June of 1909. The State's witnesses, whose testimony had brought about the indictment, weakened in their identification of him in court, and the case was stricken off, with leave to reinstate.

In 1913 he married a pretty sixteen-year-old Italian girl, Carmela Marchese. He was then forty-one. The wedding, according to his own estimates, cost $65,000, of which $40,000 went for wine. The celebration lasted three days, the entire Nineteenth Ward participating.

Esposito's début into politics was spectacular. In 1920, he entered the lists as a Deneen candidate for Republican ward committeeman against Chris Mamer, a veteran campaigner and the Thompson entry. That year—it was during Mr. Thompson's second administration—with one exception the Thompsonites made a clean sweep of the thirty-five wards then comprising Chicago. The exception was the Nineteenth, where Esposito beat Mamer hands down. He was the only Deneenite to win. It attracted city-wide attention to him.

The victory, with its attendant celebrity, caused him to open the Bella Napoli café at 850 South Halsted Street, celebrated for its cuisine and as a rendezvous for politicians. The manager was Tony Mops Volpi, a deputy sheriff, whose appointment Esposito had obtained, and who was later sent to prison for complicity in a counterfeiting plot. Dry agents raided the place in June of 1923, seizing a quantity of wines and liquors, and it was padlocked for a year. Esposito pleaded guilty to violating the prohibition laws and was fined $1,000.

In the meantime, with Senator Deneen's support, he had again sought office, as a candidate for Cook County commissioner. He won the nomination, but was defeated in the election.

Too shrewd to become openly involved in the bootleg war, he operated always with the factor of safety in mind. He was associated with the Gennas before their break with Capone; he sold sugar to the big alky-cooking syndicate in Melrose Park, a suburb northwest of Cicero; in Chicago Heights, Capone territory, he owned the Milano café, where dry agents found a 1,000-gallon still, 3,800 gallons of alcohol, fifteen barrels of wine, and two barrels of whiskey.

His brother-in-law, John Tucillo, a booze runner for Ralph Sheldon of the Capone South Side outfit, was taken for a ride and his body left in a car in front of Sheldon's home, in one of the most atrocious reprisals of the bootleg war. Another brother-in-law, Phillip Leonatti, was shot to death in his cigar store. These facts will suffice to acquaint the reader with Esposito's political and business background.

The social side of him was unique. He had a passion for festal entertaining. For twenty years his annual St. Joseph's Day parties were the outstanding events of the Nineteenth Ward. It was as a dinner host, however, that he excelled, and the biggest affair at which he ever presided was the victory banquet in February of 1925 to celebrate Mr. Deneen's election to the United

States Senate. It was given in the Gold Room of the Congress Hotel. More than one thousand five hundred guests, including all the precinct captains and their families, assembled, and Mr. Deneen was presented with a bronze bust of himself.

Local notables present were Municipal Court Judges John J. Lupe, Edgar A. Jonas, William E. Helander, Joseph W. Schulman, William L. Morgan, George A. Curran, John A. Bugee, Francis B. Allegretti, William R. Fetzer, and George B. Holmes; Circuit Court Judges Victor P. Arnold and Hugo M. Friend; Superior Court Judge Harry B. Miller; County Recorder Joseph F. Haas; State Supreme Court Clerk Charles Vail; Municipal Court Clerk James H. Kearns. Father Francis Breen invoked the divine blessing.

The friendship and alliance of Senator Deneen—a parliamentarian dry who voted for the Jones five-and-ten law—with Esposito provides another of the anomalies of prohibition as is.

Deneen was present in November of 1925 at the christening party for Esposito's son, Charles Anthony, who was named for him. It was held at the Bella Napoli café, from which the Federal padlock had been removed a twelvemonth previously.

Esposito was perhaps the most pampered of his kind in Chicago. In 1923, after he had been fined for violating the prohibition laws, he went to Italy—his first and only journey to the land of his birth. Arrived there, he received a testimonial that he cherished until his death. It was a scroll bearing his photograph, with American and Italian flags intertwined. Inside was a message of good-will, with assurances of welcome upon

197

his return. On the back were the signatures, among others, of Governor Len Small, Mayor Thompson, Senator Deneen, and County Clerk Robert M. Sweitzer.

One by one, Esposito had seen both friends and enemies die by the gun—Big Jim Colosimo, with whom he had worked as a day laborer in Brooklyn, at whose funeral in 1920 he had served as pallbearer, and who had introduced Torrio to Chicago; Paul A. Labriola and Anthony D'Andrea, victims of the aldermanic campaign of the thirty assassinations in 1921; Sam Samoots Amatuna; three of the six Gennas—Tony, Mike, and Angelo. He had seen them die, and on the morning of March 21, 1928, he had had his own warning, over the telephone—a seven-word message:

"Get out of town or get killed."

His associates implored him to leave.

"I can't go," he told them. "Just today, my boy Joseph was taken down with scarlet fever; and I promised Senator Deneen I would run for ward committeeman."

A determined contest was being waged by the America Firsters for that post, their candidate being Joseph P. Savage, a former assistant State's attorney.

"But," remonstrated Esposito's friends, "you ought to go down to that farm of yours [near Cedar Lake, Indiana] and raise chickens for a while."

He shook his head. He had a two-man bodyguard, the brothers Ralph and Joe Varchetti. He wasn't afraid. In the evening he visited his headquarters, the Esposito National Republican Club, at 2215 West Taylor Street, a few blocks from his home, at 800

South Oakley Boulevard. He left the club with the Varchettis.

To quote verbatim from Ralph Varchetti's testimony at the inquest:

We went back to the drugstore, and after staying about fifteen minutes, Dimey said, "Let's go home," and we started off, putting him between us.

We met a woman on the way—she was an election clerk, and Dimey told her to do what she could in the primary to win him votes—and we stopped for a few minutes while he talked to her. Then we went along Oakley, and when we got about to 810 South Oakley, we heard a shot. I thought it was a blowout.

Then there were more shots, and Joe says, "O my God!" and I knew he was hit. I dropped to the sidewalk and lay flat, with my face in the dirt. I could see Dimey twisting and sinking to the sidewalk. The shots came in bursts of fire from an automobile which had driven alongside of us, from behind.

When the firing stopped a second, I looked up and they fired again. I dropped flat, and this time waited until they were gone.

I got near Dimey and tried to wake him. He was gone.

Only meager descriptions were forthcoming from the Varchettis—three men in an automobile; they didn't recognize them; they couldn't identify them; they didn't notice the make of car. The only clues were two sawed-off double-barreled shotguns and a revolver, which the assassins tossed out as they sped away.

The girl bride of 1913—now a woman of thirty-one—had seen it. She had been hearing whisperings. She was keeping vigil at a front window, with the three children—Joseph, thirteen; Jeanette, nine; and Charles, three. She ran to the sidewalk.

"Oh, is it you, Giuseppe?" she wailed, and saw that it was he.

There he lay, on his back, the diamonds that had gained him his nickname glittering in the moonlight—the $5,000 solitaire ring on his right hand; the belt buckle, with the initials J. E. patterned in diamonds; the tie-pin and the shirt studs.

"He was so good to the Italian people and this is what he got for it," she moaned; then, in an access of grief, "I'll kill! I'll kill them for this!"

She didn't. Her lips were sealed at the inquest. She maintained the tradition of the "Italian wall of silence." The police had their theories—booze, politics, the Mafia—but no solutions. The coroner finally wrote it off, "Slayers not apprehended."

Diamond Joe was laid to rest in Mount Carmel Cemetery beside Mike Merlo, Dion O'Banion, Vincent the Schemer Drucci, and others. Among those attending the funeral were Senator Deneen, Assistant United States District Attorney William Parello, Chief Justice Harry Olson of the municipal court, Judge William J. Lindsay of the criminal court, and Bernard P. Barasa.

His death keyed a campaign that was to be memorable for invective and violence. Senator Deneen, still noncommittal in public but vehement in private, seeking to hold aloof from the local mêlée, returned to Washington, but not for long. A twin bombing—with "pineapples"—within five days brought him back on March 26th.

One bomb, charged with dynamite, wrecked the front

of his three-story frame residence at 457 West 61st Street. The only persons there were Miss Florence Deneen, his sister, and Mrs. Anna Rhodes, a maid. The other bomb, thrown from a black coupé at the home of Judge John A. Swanson, 7217 Crandon Avenue, landed in the driveway just as Judge Swanson was turning in from the street. It exploded three seconds before his car would have passed over it.

Senator Deneen ended his silence.

"The criminal element is trying to dominate Chicago by setting up a dictatorship in politics," he said.

Judge Swanson, who was the Deneen candidate for State's attorney, declared:

"The pineapple industry grew up under this administration."

United States Marshal Palmer Anderson in a message to Attorney General Sargent asked for five hundred deputy marshals to guard the polls.

Senator George W. Norris of Nebraska was suggesting that President Coolidge withdraw the Marines from Nicaragua and send them to Chicago.

Mayor Thompson, whose explanation of the bombs, like that of State's Attorney Crowe, was that "they were the work of the Deneen faction because they expect defeat in the primary," had a new theory as to Esposito's murder:

"They [the Deneen faction] sent prohibition agents here and then some of their own people ran to Joe for protection. He couldn't give it to them, and they wanted their money back. Those birds are tough. You can't take their money and the next minute double-cross them."

Which led the Deneenites to retort that Chief Hughes was still baffled as to the identities of the bombers of the mayor's cabinet family.

The mayor's reference to prohibition agents was caused by the activities of a special squad, which had arrived from Washington coincidentally with the appointment of George E. Q. Johnson, a Deneenite, as United States district attorney on March 30th. In a raid on a South Side saloon they had shot William Beatty, a municipal court bailiff, in the back. His story was that when they entered he thought they were holdups and started to run. Myron C. Caffey, accused of shooting him, testified that he drew a gun. A Federal grand jury promptly indicted him for resisting a Federal officer.

A tense situation developed. Chief Hughes demanded that Caffey be surrendered to the local authorities. George E. Golding, head of the special squad, told him it was none of his or the police department's business. The chief obtained a warrant and his men marched on the Federal building. Caffey was hidden away and Golding defied them.

"I will do all in my power to save Chicago citizens from any more suffering at the hands of the thugs and gunmen sent here by the Federal Government to further Deneen's political influence," said the mayor.

Sentiment was with him. Salvos of applause greeted his statement at a large South Side meeting that "Deneen is filling this town with dry agents from Washington, who run around like a lot of cowboys with revolvers and shotguns. Our opponents would have us

believe we don't know how to run our town. Vote for
the flag, the constitution, your freedom, your property,
as Abraham Lincoln and William Hale Thompson
would like to have you do."

In his denunciation of Golding's tactics, he said:

"We took out a warrant and we'll throw every damn
dry agent in jail."

The situation was relieved when Federal Judge
James H. Wilkerson ruled that Caffey should be surrendered to the police—but not until after the election.
Beatty's wound was not serious, and Caffey was not
prosecuted.

The mayor's stand was considered to have been sustained when Seymour Lowman, Assistant Secretary of
the Treasury, in charge of dry-law enforcement, issued
an order that "an officer shall not use his official authority or influence to coerce the political activity of any
person or body."

Chicago's choicest oases were mopped up by the
raiders. One of them was the Rainbo Gardens, owned
by Fred Mann, the mayor's intimate friend and a con-
tributor to his mayoralty campaign in 1927. After the
raid he went to Washington and protested to Secretary
of the Treasury Mellon, alleging political persecution. Secretary Mellon suavely agreed to "look into
the matter," but Mann's place was eventually padlocked.

The effect of these things was to thrust the prohibition problem and its corollaries into the forefront of
campaign issues.

Judge Swanson, arranging for a meeting in Elmwood

Park Grace Methodist Church, was informed by the pastor, the Rev. Thomas H. Nelson, that he would have to give his personal guarantee of reimbursement for damages on the event the church were bombed.

"We approached eight insurance companies for policies covering riot and civil commotion," explained the pastor, "and each company refused to write us coverage."

To such a pass had Chicago come in the spring of 1928. The whirlwind was gathering. Whether the onlooker sided with the Deneenites or the America Firsters, one fact was incontrovertible: vast destructive forces, set in motion through years of paltering with the underworld and its spawn by politicians; years of criminal-coddling and vote-exploitation, had suddenly got beyond control.

"It costs $243,000,000 to run Chicago and what are we getting?" asked Edward R. Litsinger, candidate for the Cook County board of review, addressing a noonday meeting in a Loop theater.

"Bombs!" cried the main floor.

"Pineapples!" yelled the gallery.

It was this incident that pegged the election as the Pineapple Primary.

State Senator Herman J. Haenisch, abjuring the America Firsters, now opposing the mayor in his own ward—the Forty-sixth—for Republican committeeman, notified the police of a letter warning him that his home would be bombed and his children kidnaped if he did not withdraw from the race.

All the elements of a *Comédie humaine* were in the

204

AL CAPONE

campaign—pathos, bathos. Here was John Dingbat
O'Berta, bantam sidekick of the behemoth, Saltis, the
beer peddler, announcing a double-barreled candidacy
—for Republican committeeman of the Thirteenth
Ward, and for the nomination for State senator from
the fourth district. Sponsoring him, speaking in his behalf, was Big Tim Murphy, recently of Leavenworth
Penitentiary, where he had been doing a stretch for
the Polk Street station $400,000 mail robbery. Big
Tim was to be machine-gunned soon and the Dingbat
was to marry his widow.

There were interludes—as when Milton Weil, com-
poser of "America First," and collaborator with Corporation Counsel Samuel A. Ettelson on "Big Bill the
Builder," was tendered a testimonial dinner and a
$5,500 Lincoln car at the Hotel Sherman. The mayor
was out of town, and Bernard P. Barasa represented
him, referring to Mr. Weil as "one of God's noblemen."
City Attorney William Saltiel described "Big Bill the
Builder" as "the most inspiring song ever written
about an individual."

Al Capone had expanded into legitimate business.
He had been taken into partnership by Morris Becker,
Chicago's largest individual dyer and cleaner, who had
been operating for forty-two years and had ten establishments on the South and North sides of the city.
Mr. Becker said that the Master Cleaners and Dyers
Association wanted to control the entire industry and
dictate prices and that "my places have been bombed
time and again; my employees slugged; robbed and
threatened; then without warning they were called out
on strike. Union officials told me I would have to see

Walter Crowley, manager of the Master Cleaners. Crowley said if I paid $5,000 and joined the association, everything would be okey."

Mr. Becker had bethought him of Capone, had made him an offer; he had accepted, and—

"Now I have no need of the State's attorney's office or the police department; I have the best protection in the world."

There were incidents apparently detached, unrelated, that yet had their place in the picture—component details of the general composition. Alderman Titus A. Haffa of the Forty-third Ward, the Gold Coast, an America First candidate for ward committeeman, and whom the reader may recall as having been a co-surety on a $10,000 bond for Dion O'Banion in a robbery case, was indicted by a Federal grand jury for conspiracy to violate the prohibition laws. The evidence revealed that he was head of a liquor syndicate with a business of $5,000,000 a year. He was eventually convicted, fined $11,000, and sentenced to serve two years in Leavenworth.

Haffa and his colleague, Alderman Arthur F. Albert, in the spring of 1926, sponsored the candidacy for Congress of Mrs. Bertha Baur, wealthy widow, of the Chicago social register. She sought to defeat the incumbent, Fred A. Britten, for the Republican nomination in the ninth district. Her campaign was sprightly and picturesque, the chief feature being an old-fashioned, horse-drawn beer truck, loaded with kegs, which paraded through the downtown streets. It bore a large sign, inscribed:

AL CAPONE

BEER AND LIGHT WINES
DELIVERED TO YOUR HOME
Vote for
BERTHA BAUR FOR CONGRESS

Mrs. Baur's candidacy, while unsuccessful, excited much comment, and the lager truck caused many demonstrations of popular approval, the crowds invariably acclaiming her as "Bertha Beer."

Up to within a fortnight of the primary, the Deneenites' cause seemed hopeless. They had suffered an irreparable loss in the death of Joseph F. Haas, county recorder, around whose office their organization had been built—with six hundred jobs for their adherents. These jobs, at Haas' death, had reverted to the America Firsters. Esposito's untimely demise was another reverse.

The America First machine was the most powerful ever developed in Chicago. Excepting Federal appointments, it controlled all the city, county, and State patronage—an army of something like 100,000 workers. And it was axiomatic that the machine had never been beaten in a primary election. Predictions were that it would win with majorities ranging from 90,000 to 150,000.

Admittedly, the ticket had encumbrances in Governor Small, seeking a third-term nomination, and Colonel Frank L. Smith, candidate for the United States Senate, but Mayor Thompson's generalship and proved campaigning ability were relied upon to carry them through.

The governor's record of pardons—more than 8,000 —was against him, and he had also been involved in the scandal of the diversion of State funds while State treasurer. He had been tried, after many delays and changes of venue, before Circuit Court Judge Claire C. Edwards, at Waukegan, Lake County, on a charge of embezzling $500,000, and had been acquitted.

Investigating charges of jury-bribing, a grand jury summoned Umbrella Mike Boyle, Chicago labor boss, and Ben Newmark, political protégé of Corporation Counsel Ettelson. They refused to testify and were sentenced to serve six months in jail for contempt. Governor Small commuted their sentences after they had served thirty days. Newmark in the interim had become an assistant State fire marshal. He was later murdered.

Two members of the Small jury were appointed State highway commissioners, a third an assistant State game warden, and Sheriff Elmer I. Green of Lake county, State superintendent of prisons. In a master-in-chancery suit, Governor Small was ordered to repay the State $650,000, which he did.

Colonel Smith, in November of 1926, had been elected United States Senator to succeed William B. McKinley, whose term expired March 4, 1927. Mr. McKinley died in December of 1926, and Governor Small appointed Colonel Smith to serve out his unexpired term in the Sixty-ninth Congress. He was not permitted to take his seat.

Appearing again at the opening of the Seventieth Congress, he was again excluded, and Vice President Dawes appointed a committee to investigate his campaign expenditures. Testimony revealed that he had spent $458,782, of which $203,000 had been contributed by public utilities magnates of Chicago, Samuel Insull's share being $158,000. This at the time when Colonel Smith was chairman of the Illinois Commerce Commission. He had given up his credentials in January of 1928 and was again submitting his case to the electorate.

Another disclosure was that Mr. Insull, through Attorney Daniel Schuyler, law partner of Corporation Counsel Ettelson, had advanced $35,000 to the Thompson organization. The Ettelson-Schuyler firm handled Mr. Insull's legal business.

For member of the Cook County board of review, the America Firsters were running Bernard P. Barasa, an assistant corporation counsel, against Litsinger, incumbent and Deneenite. For the state's attorneyship, Judge Swanson was opposing Robert E. Crowe, a man of brilliant intellect and promise, accounted the ablest prosecutor Cook County ever had, and considered by his friends to be headed for the governorship.

Mayor Thompson was seeking no office, except that of committeeman of the Forty-sixth Ward, his election to which was regarded as a foregone conclusion. His rôle was that of director general of the fight; commander-in-chief of the machine's city, county, and State forces.

As has been said, the Deneenites' cause seemed hopeless up to within a fortnight of the primary. They could not get going, while the America Firsters were steaming along at top speed, with Mayor Thompson vigorously prosecuting his "Draft Coolidge" movement, farm relief, waterways, anti-world court, and no entangling alliances—not overlooking, occasionally, His British Majesty.

"Bourbon has increased in price from $1.50 to $15 a bottle," he told an audience, "and King George's rum-running fleet, eight hundred miles long, lies twelve miles off our coast. So every time you take a drink, you say, 'Here's to the king!'"

Then occurred the bombing of Senator Deneen's home and the tossing of a bomb at Judge Swanson's car. A reaction set in, which was accelerated when the opposition ascribed both outrages to "the Deneenites themselves," as a maneuver for sympathy. The shift in public sentiment was self-evident, but not overwhelmingly pronounced. Its strength was undetermined, debatable. The moment was like that when one stands on the seashore at ebb, just before the turn.

The evening of Tuesday, April 3d, Mayor Thompson was speaking at Prudential Hall, North Avenue and Halsted Street, hard by the river, Goose Island, and the switch-yards, where the women folk wear cotton stockings and the men red flannel underwear.

"Litsinger," he shouted, "was brought up back of the gashouse, but it wasn't good enough for him, so he moved up to the North Side [the Gold Coast] and left his poor old mother behind. . . ."

There was an interruption. A woman in the audience had leaped to her feet.

"You're a liar, Mayor Thompson!" she screamed. "My mother died long before my brother moved."

She was Litsinger's sister.

The meeting ended in pandemonium.

In politics, as in war, apparent trifles often decide the outcome. The whole character of the campaign changed from that night. Litsinger, stung to the quick, lashed out with a fury unprecedented even in Chicago, where vituperation is accepted as a matter of course. He saw red.

"This low-down hound," he thundered the next day from the stage of the Olympic Theater, "who degrades himself and the city of which he is mayor, is guilty of as false and malicious a lie as was ever uttered in a political campaign. This man, who claims to possess the intelligence and instincts of a human being, digs down in a grave that was closed twenty years ago, and blasphemes the memory of my dear old German mother.

"Thompson knows that my dear old mother died twenty years ago, that she lived in my home up to the day of her death, and that from the time I was able to earn a dollar, she shared everything I had. For ten years, while I worked in an insurance office and studied law at night to become a lawyer, my mother and I lived on my salary of $70 a month.

"I did come from back of the gashouse, in Bridgeport, and from the bitterest kind of poverty. It's beyond politics. This is a question of ordinary human decency. When this befuddled big beast dares go back twenty years to desecrate my character as the faithful son of a poor old German mother, he should be tarred and feathered, and ridden out of town on a rail."

It was high irony and drama that the mayor and Litsinger should thus be juxtaposed. They had once been political bunkies. In the mayoralty campaign of

1919, Litsinger had been not only his supporter, but also his close adviser.

They were of and by Chicago—reared and bred to the environment—"talking the language"—adapted physically and mentally to its ebullient life, to the clamor of its growth. Each had a spacious animality of spirits—a gusto for the fustian and the hurlyburly; each was seasoned by many a campaign to the rough and tumble of the hustings.

For more than a decade—since his discovery by Fred Lundin as "presidential timber"—the mayor had been without a peer as a political speaker. His appeal to the crowd was irresistible, comparable to that of a Billy Sunday. He was a born showman. Consciously or unconsciously, he had dramatized himself. He was Big Bill Thompson—Big Bill the Builder. He was Chicago's platform champion, and none had successfully challenged him; no opponent had ever withstood his withering fire of sarcasm and invective.

Litsinger, in the public mind, had never been remotely associated with him as a rival. Litsinger was only another member of the board of review—no color there—no appeal—no chance of dramatization. Litsinger, anyway, had had his innings against Thompson; in the 1927 primaries he had contested for the Republican nomination for mayor and had been snowed under, Thompson getting 342,237 votes to his 161,947.

Therein lay the irony and the drama of their juxtaposition a week before the primary election. Blind to all issues, oblivious to the hokum of politics, Litsinger, a Stromboli of stentors, unpent his verbal lava, smoking hot. He was blighting, devastating:

"This man with the carcass of a rhinoceros and the brain of a baboon."

Again:

"Big Bill vilified my family and desecrated the memory of my mother. I have here," waving an envelope, "affidavits relating to the life of the big baboon. Shall I read them?"

"Go ahead!" yelled the gallery. "Give him both barrels!"

"No," cried a woman, "don't do that!"

"No," said Litsinger, whom the press had now tagged as the "Bridgeport Battler," "that old German mother of mine this man has struck at through me, is looking down on me from above, and may God strike me speechless if I ever descend to the level of Thompson."

It was not etiquette by the book; it was not cultured; not refined; not edifying; to the fastidious it would have smacked of the barroom—billingsgate. It was raw human stuff, distilled from the sweat and the soil of the Middle West. It was "the language," and the mass of the citizenry understood it, avidly devoured it, applauded it uproariously. Overflow houses greeted the Deneenites, where before there had been empty seats. Litsinger had broken the Thompson-crowd grip. A new platform champion had been acclaimed.

The psychological value was incalculable. Theretofore the stigma of "reformers," in itself sufficient to defeat any ticket in Chicago, had attached to the Deneenites and particularly to Judge Swanson. Litsinger counteracted it. He obtained a hearing for his side. His fulminations registered.

"You know the Three Musketeers," he roared.

"They are Big Bill, Len Small, and Frank L. Smith. The right way to pronounce it is the Three Must-Get-Theirs. Insull's shadow is over everything in the Small-Smith-Thompson combination."

Corporation Counsel Ettelson he described as "Insull's personal luggage." He said it was more than a coincidence that the America Firsters should choose for "one of the foremost places on their ticket, Barney Pineapple Barasa, who is president by proxy of the Unione Siclione, which he now calls, for political purposes, the Italo-American Union. It is more than a coincidence that Barasa is closely associated with Tony Lombardo, whose association with Al Capone is only too well known."

As to the bombings:

"All Big Bill has to do is to stop singing 'America First' long enough to call Barney Barasa, pal of Al Capone, into his private office at the Hotel Sherman, and say to him, 'Barney, who is responsible for these bombings? Did Al Capone plant those pineapples?' And Barney would be able to tell him. If it was not Capone, Bill could say, 'Well, who was it then?' And Barney would be able to tell him. In five minutes Bill could find out."

And Judge Swanson was voicing the question that was to dog State's Attorney Crowe to the end of his career:

"Who killed McSwiggin?"

There was no answer to that, and there was none to the assertion that Barasa was connected with the newly organized Italo-American Union. He admitted it.

State Senator Herman J. Haenisch, opposing the

mayor in his own ward for committeeman, was declaring that "the present Republican machine has exacted such tribute from gamblers and moonshine parlors that they have been forced to plunder their victims as never before in order to make payments of graft."

Indications that all was not well within the ranks of the America Firsters came two days after Litsinger went into action. As rumors persisted that leaders were selling out the ticket to have themselves elected ward committeemen, the mayor summoned the county central committee, and said:

"We have no place for trimmers and double-crossers. We are in this fight for the people, to protect them from the thugs brought here by Senator Deneen's friends under the guise of dry agents."

He then made two remarkable statements, which were widely quoted. One was:

"Should Deneen's candidate for State's attorney win next Tuesday, we will seriously consider resigning from office."

The other one had to do with Attorney General Oscar Carlstrom, who had intimated that he might call a special grand jury to investigate some of the mayor's associates.

"If Carlstrom attacks me, as I understand he threatens to do," he said, "I will resign and ask President Coolidge to turn the Federal patronage over to me. I will recommend a new United States district attorney and start something myself."

In the beginning, the campaign had been international in scope—anti-world court and no foreign entanglements; with a broad domestic program—Draft

Coolidge, farm relief, flood control, and waterways. Now, at the close, these had been shunted into the discard. The election was to pivot on the issues of the alliance between politics and crime; the City Hall and the Unione Sicilione; Al Capone; rule by the gun and the bomb.

Easter Sunday, two days before the primary, in a thousand and one churches throughout the city the clergy devoted the services to exhortation and prayer.

"We have a governor who ought to be in the penitentiary," said the Rev. Asa J. Ferry, standing among the Paschal lilies in the pulpit of the Edgewater Presbyterian Church.

"Ours is a government of bombs and bums, of grafters and corrupt politicians," said Louis L. Mann, rabbi of Sinai Congregation.

"O Lord! May there be an awakening of public spirit and consciousness," prayed the Rev. Charles W. Gilkey of the fashionable Hyde Park Baptist Church. "Grant that we may be awakened to a sense of our public shame."

"Chicago needs a cleaning. I hope every man and woman goes to the polls," said the Rev. Walter A. Morgan, D.D., of the New Congregational Church.

"Vote as a sacred Christian duty," urged the Rev. James S. Ainslie of the Argyle Community Church. His Easter-morn congregation was greeted with a placard bearing the inscription, "Bad officials are elected by citizens who do not vote."

Newspaper correspondents from the East, the West, the North, and the South, mobilized as on a battlefront. The London and the Paris press were represented by men from their New York City and Washington bureaus. The eyes of the world were on the Pineapple Primary.

"Will they get out and vote?" was the paramount question.

The registration in Chicago was 1,228,283. Based on past records, a percentage of 53.71 of the total vote was a fair average in a primary. The 1924 presidential primary had established that figure. The 1927 mayoralty primary vote, the highest to date, had been 668,511 or 58.48 per cent. The wiseacres were predicting something like that this time—around 695,000. Eliminating 165,000 of that as belonging to the Democratic party, in which there was no contest, the Republican vote would be 430,000.

The war correspondents had their fill of thrills. It was a day of sluggings, ballot-box stuffing by shotgun squads, and kidnapings, culminating in the murder of Octavius C. Granady, Negro attorney and ex-service man, and Deneen opponent of Morris Eller, America Firster, for Republican committeeman of the Bloody Twentieth Ward. Machine gunners pursued him through the streets, shooting him down after his car had crashed into a tree.

Capone, ostensibly in exile during the campaign, was a conspicuous figure, casting his vote in his home ward, the Eighth, and directing activities in Cicero.

Chicago, Cook County, and Illinois surpassed all expectations. For the governorship nomination, Louis L. Emmerson's plurality over Small was 439,792; he received 1,051,556 votes to Small's 611,764. Between them they had a total of 1,663,320, an all-time Republican record, exceeding the vote cast for Coolidge in the November election of 1924—1,453,321. Glenn for the United States Senate received 855,356 votes to 611,-879 for Smith.

Swanson's victory over Crowe for the State's attorneyship—focal point of the campaign in Chicago and Cook County—was equally decisive, his margin being 201,227. The complete vote was, Swanson, 466,-598; Crowe, 265,371. Crowe carried Cicero, receiving 5,180 votes to Swanson's 4,923.

In the privilege wards, where vice and gambling concessions were openly let, majorities were returned for the America First ticket—the First, where Big Jim Colosimo rose to power, and where Capone maintained his G. H. Q.; the Twenty-fifth, where Diamond Joe Esposito was murdered; the Forty-second, the late Dion O'Banion's bailiwick; Homer K. Galpin's ward, the Twenty-seventh; the Twentieth; the Second and Third, the Black Belt; and all wards where the foreign-born predominated.

As in the State, so in the city and county, the Republican vote smashed precedent—reaching nearly 800,000, confuting the wiseacres. How utter was the rout of the machine was indicated when the returns from the mayor's home ward, the Forty-sixth, disclosed that he had been beaten by State Senator Haenisch for committeeman. The administration's bond-issue program—thirty-one propositions, totaling $77,959,000 for public improvements—was rejected by a two-to-one vote.

It was a ballot rebellion and was so hailed by the

press of America and of Europe. To quote editorial comment:

Kansas City Star: "There is a God in Israel . . ."

Washington Post: "The primary brought results that are gratifying to the entire country. It was a mighty blow for the restoration of law and order in Chicago. The voters seem to have been aroused from their apathy."

St. Paul Pioneer Press: "The Republican voters of Illinois have cleaned house, unaided by the marines. . . ."

San Francisco Chronicle: "The objection to having Chicago elections dominated by bombs and its everyday affairs superintended by gunmen with machine guns was an important factor in the election."

New York Times: "The political revolution in Chicago came as a surprise to most political observers. They had thought that the city was disgraced, but not ashamed."

Louisville Courier Journal: "Chicago and Illinois have made a good job of it so far. It required a great deal to bring Chicago to its senses."

In London, the press was gleeful. To quote:

The Morning Post: "Evidently the self-respect of Chicago is tired of being made a byword and a laughing stock by its present mayor. It has told him in effect it is his own 'snoot' rather than King George's that needs to be kept out of the city."

Lord Beaverbrook's *Daily Express:* "Big Bill Thompson has been hit by his fellow citizens in Chicago in a place where it really hurts."

The Daily Telegraph: "A miracle has supervened, but whether he will resign as he vowed to do if beaten, is another matter."

Paris newspapers made a Roman holdiay of it:

"Eight Thousand Gendarmes Guard Polls in Chicago—Fusillades of Bombs—*Élections à l'Américaine!*" headlined the *Intransigeant.*

Le Journal gravely told its 2,000,000 readers how "the good city of Chicago, which formerly had the World's Fair, and enjoys a world-wide reputation as the great center of the meat industry, has developed a new form of slaughter, heretofore limited to the stockyards. It is human lives in which that world's sausage metropolis is now specializing."

In Chicago, the *Herald and Examiner,* a Hearst newspaper, which had championed the America First cause and supported the Thompson-Small ticket unconditionally, stated in its leading editorial two days after the election:

"The vote of Chicago in the primaries on Tuesday was a direct and tremendous expression of protest against the lawlessness and violence of booze runners, the gambling managers, the bombmen (sic) and the gunmen of Chicago. The situation had, to the minds of the citizens in general, got past bearing, and they freed their minds in the only way they could—at the polls."

Would the mayor resign?

"Let's analyze the situation," he said. "I haven't lost out so much in the election. I've got a majority of the ward committeemen, and the sanitary district trustees. You'd think I'd lost the whole fight. Why should I resign?"

. "But you said definitely you would get out if Swanson were nominated!"

"Well, I'll say definitely now that I'm not getting out."

There soon followed the decision of Judge Hugo M. Friend in the realty experts' fees case. It was that the mayor, Michael J. Faherty, president of the board of local improvements; George F. Harding, county treasurer; and Percy B. Coffin, public administrator, among others, were guilty of conspiracy and should make restitution to the city of $2,245,000. The decision set forth that when great sums were needed for political purposes in 1921, they had conceived a plan to pay "experts" some $3,000,000 to appraise improvements, the "experts" turning back most of it to the Thompson treasury.

Charles C. Fitzmorris abruptly quit as city controller. With special grand juries seeking sources of campaign contributions, Homer K. Galpin fled the city for the north woods, later resigning as chairman of the Republican Cook County central committee and sailing for Europe without returning to Chicago. County Treasurer Harding also left for Europe.

The mayor retired from political activities for several months, going into seclusion in the Eagle River country of Wisconsin. During most of the summer of 1928, Corporation Counsel Ettleson was acting mayor.

A pathetic incident occurred at the John B. Murphy Hospital, where Chief Michael Hughes was recovering from a tonsilectomy. Assistant Corporation Counsel James W. Breen visited his bedside with a typewritten letter of resignation, and had him sign it. Influential

friends of the mayor, including Corporation Counsel
Ettelson, counseling him on ways and means of salvaging
the wreck of his machine, had said that the place to
start was in the police department. It had been the
target of attack. It loomed in the public eye. And a
"police shake-up" was always good strategy. So Hughes
was sacrificed. His successor was William F. Russell,
like him risen from the ranks, a veteran of the old-
fashioned school.

Actually, in its much advertised primary Chicago had
achieved little more than a beginning. It had given itself
a pretty fair Saturday night bath, as it were.

The election had changed a few names. It had not
changed the system. The conditions upon which that
flourished still survived.

America First was sunk. Capone and America's
Thirst remained, in the city that votes five to one wet.

Russell was to be as helpless as Hughes to combat
gangster assassins and racketeer bombers. His régime
was to last exactly twenty-two months. He was to resign June 16, 1930, following the assassination of his
friend, Alfred J. Lingle, police reporter for the *Chicago
Tribune*. Lingle's death culminated the so-called
Slaughter Week, when eleven men were shot to death
in ten days by gangster gunmen.

John H. Alcock, another of those old-school policemen, was to succeed Russell, in the shuffle of personnel
resulting from Lingle's death, and Mayor Thompson
was to say to him, "Run the crooks and gangsters out
of Chicago." He had said that to Hughes in 1927. His
predecessor, Mayor Dever, had said it to Collins in
1925.

In the summer of 1928, however, it looked to the average man as if something akin to the millennium had arrived. The primary had solved everything. Civic righteousness had triumphed. A new deal was on.

Scarcely had Russell pinned on the gold badge of office, when Chicago and the world were horror-stricken by a crime that put murder on a quantity production basis—the Moran gang massacre.

PART FIVE

FATHER LOUIS GIAMBASTIANI was tacking a notice on the door of the church of San Filippo Benizi. September had come round again, bringing the joyous and hallowed festival of Our Lady of Loreto. It commemorates the legend of the holy house of Nazareth, in which Mary was born, received the annunciation, and lived during the childhood of Jesus. After His ascension, it was converted into a chapel by the apostles and used for worship until the fall of the kingdom of Jerusalem. Threatened by the Turks, it was carried by angels through the air and deposited on a hill at Tersatto, in Dalmatia. In 1294, the angels carried it across the Adriatic to a wood near Recanti, in the province of Ancona, Italy; either from this wood (lauretum) or from its proprietrix, Laureta, the chapel derives its name, *sacellum gloriosæ Virginis in Loreto*.

Such the legend. Annually, in the homeland, the time of the Nativity of the Virgin is an occasion of national observance. Thousands of pilgrims journey to Loreto, for devotion and to make their votive offerings. In America, September 8th is the Italians' biggest feast day. An entire week is set aside for celebration. Then the streets of Chicago's melting-pot burgeon with tinseled splendor—colored lanterns strung on arches; placards and banners fluttering in the breeze proclaiming the spirit of festa; bunting bedecking smoke-stained

224

fronts of tenements, stores, and shops; masque and har-
lequinade replacing the hard certitudes of life; the
city's pent-ups seeking escape from reality in illusion.

Camaraderie and worship commingle. No window so
humble that it does not boast its shrine of Mary and
the Child. No man of hands so calloused or clothes so
shabby that he does not visit his parish church. Evenings, families go strolling, the elders stopping to exchange greetings and choice tidbits of gossip, to indulge,
perchance, in folk-dancing; the youngsters to pirouette
to the organ grinders' music. Confetti men and hawkers
of fruits and sweetmeats come for blocks around. Car-
nivals and fortune tellers hold forth in vacant areaways.
And the red wine flows.

Father Giambastiani's flock was in the thick of
things—just east of the street of all nations, Halsted;
in that frayed heelpiece of the Gold Coast, back of the
water tower, where the Forty-second Ward slouches
down to meet the river and Goose Island.

Here once, in the endless shifting of the human tides,
the Swedish emigrants had come, had stayed a genera-
tion to rear families, and had passed on; then the Nor-
wegian; then the German; now the Sicilian. As had
their predecessors, these too had brought with them
their old-world customs and habits of thought, including allegiance to, or passive acquiescence in, the anti-
social principles of the Mafia—itself imbedded in
centuries of misgovernment and feudal oppression, and
whose oath of membership was to "resist law and defeat justice."

They had come direct from their tenantry of the soil
in the near-tropical island of the Mediterranean—chil-

dren of the sun—impulsive, unsophisticated in the American way, credulous, imaginative, naïve, needing in their new environment constructive guidance, readjustment, stimulus.

Something, possibly, of their attitude was expressed by Antonio Lombardo, when, having attained the summit of ambition, as he and his countrymen viewed it—presidency of the Unione Sicilione—he was moved to pen a brief autobiography. This, in part, is what he wrote:

Chicago owes much of its progress and its hope of future greatness to the intelligence and industry of its 200,000 Italians, whose rise in prestige and importance is one of the modern miracles of a great city.

No people have achieved so much from such small beginnings, or given so much for what they received in the land of promise to which many of them came penniless. Each life story is a romance, an epic of human accomplishment.

Antonio Lombardo is one of the most outstanding of these modern conquerors. . . . Mr. Lombardo came to America twenty-one years ago. He was one of hundreds who cheered joyously, when, from the deck of the steamer, they saw the Statue of Liberty, and the skyline of New York, their first sight of the fabled land, America. With his fellow countrymen he suffered the hardships and indignities to which the United States subjects its prospective citizens at Ellis Island without complaint, for in his heart was a great hope and a great ambition.

After he had landed, he paid his railroad fare to Chicago, and came here with just $12 as his initial capital. . . . Mr. Lombardo, however, accepted the hardships as part of the game, and with confidence in his own ability and assurance of unlimited opportunities, began his career. . . . He became an importer and exporter. . . . His political influence is due largely to his interest in civic affairs and his championship of measures for maintaining and improving standards of living, as well as his activity in the support of charities and benevolent institutions. Like most successful men, he has received much, but has given more to the community in which he lives. It is to such men that Chicago owes her greatness.

In the church of San Filippo Benizi at this festival time, the tapers burned before the image of the Virgin, and in a niche beside the altar was the replica of the Santa Casa of the legend. But no one occupied the pews. The place was empty. The buildings of Little Sicily were devoid of bunting, placards, or banners, and the streets were deserted.

Only Father Giambastiani was visible, standing in the entrance of his church. Sleeplessness had dulled the sparkle in his fine, kindly eyes; his ruddy features were wan and drawn, his shoulders stooped. He was a man bowed down by sorrow and despair. He bestowed a last look upon the notice he had tacked on the door, turned, slowly descended the flight of steps, and walked away. The notice, translated, read:

"Brothers! For the honor you owe to God, for the respect of your American country and humanity— pray that this ferocious manslaughter, which disgraces the Italian name before the civilized world, may come to an end."

His parish had been caught as in the jaws of a giant nutcracker, between the warring factions of the two great houses of the colony—the Lombardos and the Aiellos. A dozen of its menfolk had been killed within a year. Bombs had demolished $75,000 worth of property. Capone gunmen had routed Joseph Aiello, chief of the clan, but his followers had carried on against those of their countrymen aligned with Lombardo.

Alky-cooking was the *casus belli*. The system of home stills originated by the Gennas, and numbering under them one hundred, had been extended to include eighty per cent of the colony's families. There were now in operation 2,500, a still for each head of a household. Thus did these emigrants receive their tutoring in Americanism.

The Unione Sicilione had become a $10,000,000-a-year enterprise, supplying the basic ingredient for the synthetic Bourbon, rye, Scotch, brandy, rum, and gin marketed in and around Chicago, and controlling the sale of sugar to the affiliated distillers of the West Side Italian district: Melrose Park, Cicero, and Chicago Heights.

Lombardo, seated by Capone in November of 1925, ruled locally as a despot over some 15,000 Sicilians, and dominated the councils of the Unione's branches in St. Louis, Detroit, Pittsburgh, Cleveland, Philadelphia, and New York City. He was Capone's prime minister in the secret and largely alien organization—actually an invisible government—through which Capone was enabled to establish his gunman dictatorship of Chicago.

The "political influence" to which he referred in his autobiography was real. The Unione demanded and received its share of patronage in the City Hall. Carmen Vacco, city sealer in the Dever administration, had admitted at the O'Banion inquest that he was indebted to Mike Merlo, founder and first president, for the appointment. In the Thompson administration, Vacco had been succeeded by Daniel A. Serritella, personal friend of Capone, a visitor at his Florida villa, and the American First Republican committeeman of the First Ward. The Unione, renamed in the Pineapple Primary campaign the Italo-American Union, maintained headquarters in the Loop, at 8 South Dearborn Street, two blocks from the City Hall.

So powerful was Lombardo that all matters affecting the colony, even to breaches of the penal law, were submitted to him. His arbitrament was final. His word was life or death. The sinister workings of the Mafia were never better illustrated than in the case of ten-year-old William Ranieri, son of A. Frank Ranieri, a sewer contractor.

The boy had been kidnaped, and the ransom put at $60,000, with threats of torture and death if it were not forthcoming. Fiendishly prolonging the parents' agony, the kidnapers for three days had omitted to state where or how their agents could be approached to open negotiations. They had merely sent a daily letter by special delivery detailing the methods by which they proposed to kill the boy. The mother suffered a nervous breakdown, and was ordered to bed by a physician. The father was verging on collapse.

The morning of the fourth day—Thursday, September 6, 1928—Ranieri's telephone rang. An anonymous informant said, "See Lombardo," and hung up. Ranieri immediately went to the Unione's Loop headquarters, explained his mission to one of Lombardo's secretaries, and was told to return Friday evening, "The chief will have some word for you then." Hope came to him. He knew that whatever amount Lombardo set as the ransom, the kidnapers would have to accept. He could not raise $60,000 cash. His limit was $10,000. He had scraped that together after much borrowing from relatives and friends. The kidnapers had over-estimated his means.

Until then the public had been unaware of his plight. He had not informed the police. Fear of the Mafia had deterred him. He eventually got the boy back—safe and sound—but not through Lombardo. The press made such an uproar that the kidnapers were frightened into releasing him. The case has no relation to this story other than as a commentary on Lombardo's power and the attitude of citizens of Italian ancestry toward the invisible government he represented.

Ranieri did not get to see him that next evening. Lombardo had stepped out. He had left the Unione headquarters at 4:20 o'clock for a stroll around the Loop. With him were Joseph Lolordo and Joseph Ferraro, his bodyguards.

They had walked north on Dearborn, a half-block, to Madison, turning west on the south side of that swarming thoroughfare, which cleaves the geographical center of the city—Ferraro on Lombardo's left, Lolordo on his right, each of the three armed, and clasping the butt of his revolver where it rested in its specially constructed receptacle for street wear, in an outside coat pocket. A block from the intersection that Chicago calls the world's busiest corner, State and Madison, they passed a popular-priced restaurant.

It was the rush hour, when the downtown skyscrapers begin disgorging their 400,000 occupants; when streams of humanity sluice willy-nilly through the Loop—har-

ried commuters for suburban trains; fagged shoppers
with fretting children for elevated stations; pretty
typists and salesladies, fresh as daisies after their day's
work, bound for a dinner and a movie, maybe, or for
the four walls of a cheap room and a gas-plate snack,
maybe; sly-eyed fashion-plate loiterers and standees at
corners and in doorways, bound for nowhere and no
good, birds of prey and passage; respectable clerks,
brokers, professional men, and bankers hurrying to the
club or favorite speakeasy for an ante-prandial cocktail; newsies screeching their loudest; autos honking
their maddest; traffic coppers tootling their sharpest.
Babel and kaleidoscope.

As Lombardo and his bodyguard passed the restaurant entrance, two men detached themselves from the
sidewalk throng, and their hands too were in the side
pockets of their coats. They cast quick looks up and
down the street and then darted after the three. When
within arm's length they opened fire. Lombardo fell in
his tracks, two dumdum bullets in his brain, the third
president of the Unione Sicilione to die by the gun. Ferraro was struck in the spine and paralyzed in the legs.
He lay beside Lombardo, feebly waving his .45. Lolordo,
escaping injury, drew his revolver, and gave chase to
the assassins, who had run east on Madison and south
on Dearborn. Before he had gone thirty feet, he was
overtaken by Policeman John Marcusson, who disarmed him, and despite his protests backed him against
a building, thrust an automatic into the pit of his
stomach, and held him for the squad car in the belief
that he was one of the assassins. They escaped.

This might be said to be Chicago's most open gang-

ster killing. It could hardly have been more public if
the assassins had hired a hall. It was so conveniently
staged—so accessibly central—that one enterprising
newspaper, thanks to an agile photographer, was able
to present to its readers a picture of Lombardo and
Ferraro lying as they fell, with the crowds still milling .
about them on the sidewalk. Hundreds witnessed it.
Scores were ready with descriptions. But in the end, it
was written off in the familiar phraseology, "Slayers
not apprehended."

Lolordo saw them, knew them; in the first access of
rage, he pleaded wildly with Policeman Marcusson for
a chance to "get them." But at the inquest he didn't
remember; he hadn't recognized anybody; his mind was
a blank.

"Who shot you?" Assistant State's Attorney Samuel
Hoffman asked Ferraro.

Ferraro shook his head.

"You're going to die," Mr. Hoffman told him.

And so he did, two days later—by the code—mute
lipped.

That was how it was that Father Giambastiani on the
feast day of Our Lady of Loreto was tacking the notice
on the door of his church. The murder had been committed the preceding afternoon. He was a shepherd
without a flock. For two years his parishioners had
borne the brunt of the retaliatory terrorism in the
Lombardo-Aiello feud. Now fear had driven them from
the city. A thousand families, many of whom were
neutrals, had abandoned their tenement homes to go
into hiding in obscure villages of Wisconsin and Mich-

igan. All butcher shops, for some inexplicable reason, were closed. A check revealed four hundred fewer children in the Edward Jenner public school, and two hundred fewer in the St. Philip's parochial school.

The tragedy that had overtaken Father Giambastiani and his flock did not disturb Capone, sunning himself in the security of his Florida villa by the sea. These were only the little people—pawns of the game, cannon fodder in the bootleg war. Lombardo's death was something else. Capone, going unshaven as avouchment of his grief, hurriedly returned to Chicago, to supervise the funeral rites and matters of a practical nature appertaining to the Unione Sicilione.

The funeral was a success—seventeen carloads of flowers—a cortège two miles long—twelve pallbearers in tuxedoes—a silk American flag topped with a brass eagle; a silk Italian flag, topped with crown and cross; both furled over the bronze casket—a floral piece, suspended between two trees, bearing the name, "T. Lombardo," in pink and white carnations, the T standing for "Tony," his nickname.

In the backyard of the home, Capone himself, holding a reception, encircled by the bodyguard, including John Scalise and Albert Anselmi—the torpedo killers, who had helped put the Gennas on the spot; who were credited with a big hand in the O'Banion and Weiss jobs; who had knocked off two coppers and got away with it, Capone, shaking hands with the public, issuing orders to photographers—no trouble in taking pictures; no camera smashing if they just took crowd pictures; mustn't try to get any close-ups; some of the boys sensitive about that—assuring reporters he had no idea who shot Tony. Squads of police searching automobiles for machine guns, fanning mourners for revolvers.

The funeral rites had been scheduled for 10:30 in the morning, but Cardinal Mundelein had adhered to the policy established by him years ago of not allowing the bodies of slain gangsters to be taken into Catholic churches, and so, there being no church services, the procession to Mount Carmel Cemetery was postponed until the afternoon. The body was placed in a mausoleum, temporarily, pending the purchase of a burial plot, the cardinal's ban having excluded gangsters from consecrated ground. A civilian read a brief ritual in Italian, a male quartet sang "Nearer, My God, to Thee," and Tony Lombardo was laid to rest without benefit of clergy, but with the tribute of Capone as "an honored citizen."

Another kind of tribute was voiced by Frank J. Loesch, president of the Chicago Crime Commission, and in 1929 appointed a member of President Hoover's Law Enforcement Commission. Nine days after the funeral, with ten-year-old William Ranieri still missing and Judge Frank Comerford of the superior court caling for "annihilation of the Mafia," Mr. Loesch said:

"Judge Comerford has acted on a conviction that has been steadily growing among the people; that law enforcement has broken down completely when it comes to the arrest, prosecution, and attempt to convict such gang murderers as the Mafia gunmen. We cannot have law and order for ninety-nine per cent of the people, and anarchy for one per cent, when the anarchy is destructive of our peace, our security, our safety. . . . All three of the special grand juries have condemned the inefficiency of the police and their almost patent alliance with the criminals.

"And who are the gangsters seemingly tied up to this family tree? Scarface Al Capone, vice, gambling, and liquor king, and the recently murdered Tony Lombardo. Lombardo is dead, but his organization—the Mafia— the kidnapers of little Billy Ranieri—is still organized and ready to function uninterruptedly.

"Lombardo was actual master of the Unione Sicilione, which has become the Italo-American Union. . . . All the kidnapings, blackmail, terrorism, murders, and countless other crimes, committed in the name of the dread Mafia, sprang from the minds of Lombardo and the men who are now fighting to take the place vacated by his death.

"It was Lombardo who ruled the alcohol cookers. They bought their sugar from him or they died. The people paid him tribute on their cheese and their olive oil. And part of these spoils, the extortions from the fathers of kidnaped children, the profits of the alcohol sales, we hear, went into the political coffers. . . .

"Capone, partner of Lombardo, ruled in other ways. Through him the family tree spreads to take in the names of Jack Guzik and Ralph Capone. Guzik runs the brothels and the beer and booze syndicate; others, the dog-races and gambling—crooked races and crooked gambling. Ralph takes to moonshining. . . .

"The Mafia must be suppressed here as it was by Mussolini in Italy. The upper hand which the criminals are obtaining in this city by their alliance with politicians not only gives the city a bad reputation, but it will certainly end in anarchy if permitted to go on a few years longer."

The next to undertake the precarious incumbency of the Unione's presidency was Pasqualino Lolordo, elder brother of Joseph, the bodyguard; friend, confidant and business associate of Lombardo, and a staunch Capone man. He was inducted into office September 14th and managed to elude the coroner until January 8, 1929.

The manner of his passing was by way of being a unique contribution to what De Quincey described as "murder considered as one of the fine arts." It was different from anything Chicago had previously seen. It was a demonstration by bootleg killers in progressive ingenuity; an example of perfected technique, of definite sophistication of method, as contrasted with the crudity of the sawed-off shotgun ambuscade or motorized machine gunning.

The setting was the home, with the victim as host, the assassins as his guests—all the amenities of social intercourse obtaining: the afternoon call, the hospitable board, the clinking glass, the merry quip, the pledged toast; laughter, interrupted by the firing simultaneously of three revolvers. Sherlock Holmes would have fancied the case, if not Philo Vance.

Lolordo and his wife, Aleina, lived at 1921 West North Avenue, on the top floor of a three-story, two-flat building, owned by him, the street floor being rented for shops. The block is near Milwaukee Avenue, one of the city's major streets, on the Northwest Side. It is a good neighborhood, populated by substantial wage-earning citizens, many of them descendants of pioneer families. The Lolordos lived alone, except for a colored maid. They had one child, a boy, Vincent, eighteen years old, who was attending the University of Illinois.

They had been downtown shopping the morning of January 8th, returning to their home at 2:30 P. M. Awaiting them were two men, whom Mrs. Lolordo had seen frequently, she said, but whose names she did not know. They accompanied the Lolordos upstairs, chatted for a half-hour with Lolordo, and left.

They had not been gone five minutes when Mrs. Lolordo heard a knock at the door. She was in the kitchen with the maid, and her husband answered it. Three men entered. He welcomed them with jovial familiarity, ushered them into the living-room, and set chairs for them. Two heaping platters of sandwiches, relishes, and pastries and a box of cigars were placed before them, and Lolordo got out a decanter of Bourbon and four bottles of wine. Then, as was his custom, he closed the door.

Mrs. Lolordo, busied with housewifely duties here and there in the apartment, heard the resonant hum of their voices—noted the higher, heartier pitch and the louder, freer laughter as the liquor flowed. It was as if a group of cronies had gathered to relax in the lounge room of their club. An hour passed.

"Here's to Pasqualino!" someone shouted.

Chairs scraped across the oak floor as the company pushed them back to drink the health of the host. Then the shots.

Mrs. Lolordo ran down the hall. The door opened as she reached it, and the three guests shoved her aside in the hurry of their departure. Pasqualino was dead.

237

Sergeants Thomas Foley and Joseph Cullerton of the Racine Avenue station were there within thirty minutes. Foley picked up a .38 caliber revolver on the stairs and another of the same caliber in the living-room, six feet from the body.

On the table were three half-filled glasses, and in the ash-trays the stubs of the cigars. The box containing them was open, with the lid back toward Lolordo, indicating that he had passed them around. His right hand still clutched his glass, and from the position of the arm it was evident that he was standing with the glass just lifted to his lips when the assassins opened fire. Eleven bullets struck him, in the face, neck, and shoulders. Seven missed, lodging in the wall or caroming off the brick fireplace behind him. One chipped the top of his glass.

The place yielded no specific clues. In Lolordo's bedroom the police found a sawed-off shotgun, and the draft of a constitution for a Northwest Side branch of the Italo-American Union, reading, "to improve the education of its members, morally, economically and socially. . . ."

Mrs. Lolordo was a hindrance rather than a help to the police. She did not know the men. She was positive of but one thing, that they were not Italians, which only served to complicate the mystery. She was questioned not only by the detectives but also at headquarters by City Sealer Daniel A. Serritella.

"Slayers not apprehended," wrote the coroner.

Two key men in the Capone system had been killed within four months. What had happened?

AL CAPONE

Phantom-like, through this story, glides the figure of Francesco Uale, bracketing Chicago and New York City in gangs, crime, booze, and rackets. Frank Yale, as he was generally called, had been Capone's playmate in the Five Points days, and they had matriculated together in the school of Johnny Torrio, Gyp the Blood, Lefty Louie, and their breed. Capone had gone to Chicago when prohibition opportunity beckoned; Yale had remained in New York City, to become the big boss of the Italian colonies in the Borough Park section of Brooklyn, and in Mulberry Bend on the East Side; and to rule the Unione Sicilione, from which Capone recruited his eighteen-man bodyguard when the O'Banion musketeers in 1925 drove him to the cover of his portable fort.

Uale was in Chicago in 1920 when Colosimo was shot to death; he was identified, by description, as a suspect by Joe Gabreala, café porter. Gabreala, taken East by detectives to confront him, weakened in his presence, and refused to identify him. The police theory was that Torrio imported him for the job.

Uale was in Chicago the November day in 1924 when the torpedo killers bagged Dion O'Banion—and was nabbed at the La Salle Street station three minutes before train time.

"I came here for Mike Merlo's funeral," he said. "I don't know Torrio. Yes, I know Capone. I stayed over for a fine dinner that my friend Diamond Joe Esposito gave for me."

He had a revolver, as did his traveling companion, Sam Pollaccia.

"I have a permit from a Supreme Court justice of New York to carry it," he told the chief of police of that day, Morgan A. Collins. "I collect lots of money in New York."

He had an alibi, and the police had neither witnesses nor evidence—only "moral certainties." They let him go.

Ostensibly manager for a Brooklyn undertaking firm, and proprietor of a cigar factory manufacturing the "Frankie Yale" cigar, with his picture on the box, he was in reality an extortionist and an exploiter of his race. He exacted tribute from the rich in money and from the poor in toil. He organized the non-union bricklayers and the laundrymen, becoming their business agent and treasurer.

With the advent of prohibition, he turned to hijacking and bootlegging, using the Unione Sicilione to establish himself. He lacked Capone's, let us say, civic stature; he did not loom so compellingly in the public eye. But he was as much a symbol; he was armed violence, unrestrained, and enjoying the usual immunity. A long record of criminal charges was catalogued against him, ranging from robbery and assault to homicide, with only two convictions—one for disorderly conduct, one for violation of the Sullivan Act, which forbids the carrying of concealed weapons without a permit.

A showy dresser, he aped his friend Esposito in jewelry display—a three-carat diamond tie-pin, two solitaire rings, and a belt buckle like Joe's with his initials patterned in diamonds—seventy-five in all.

Enemies had made three attempts on his life—once his chauffeur had been killed while driving Mrs. Uale home from a wedding; once the top of the car had been almost blown off by shotgun slugs; once seventeen bullets had been fired into it as Uale was returning from Coney Island. He lived at 1402 Sixty-sixth Street, Brooklyn.

Capone, in the fall of 1926, had seen the necessity—and financial possibilities—of coördinating the rum-running activities of the nation, and had acted accordingly. His scheme contemplated a sort of benevolent monopoly; that is to say, the coöperation of gangster chiefs in the Middle West and lake ports with those of the principal cities of the Atlantic seaboard, with centralized control. The Unione Sicilione supplied him with a powerful nucleus, as well as a weapon, and gained respectful attention for his proposals.

The word "necessity" is used advisedly; the motivating factor in Capone's action was public demand. It requires a brief explanation: Synthetic liquor, or that made by the alky-cookers, is readily marketable for general consumption, but those of the wealthy class insist upon the bona fide stuff and are willing to pay for it. Before doing so, however, this discriminating trade has the liquor analyzed by chemists to determine its authenticity. In barkeep technology, it has to be the "pure quill."

Cellars stocked in 1917 and 1918 were beginning to get low in Chicago and its vicinity by 1926, particularly on the Gold Coast and in Lake Forest—the millionaire suburban colony. The replenishing process was causing famine prices to prevail. The situation set Capone to thinking. He concluded that the flow of imported liquor was not equably distributed, that, therefore, rum-running was not properly organized. So his action. The downright wets of Chicago invariably point to it with pride when extolling Capone as a public benefactor.

His affiliations already included Egan's Rats of St. Louis, the Purple Gang of Detroit, and Max Boo-Boo Hoff, Philadelphia's underworld boss, who controlled operations at Atlantic City and in New Jersey. Capone's own men were in charge in Florida and at New Orleans, inlet sources for Cuba and the Bahamas. Uale was to direct landings at Long Island points and guard shipments by truck from Brooklyn to Chicago. It was the boldest project yet to be conceived by the resourceful Capone, and if and when accomplished put him and his allies in command of more than 2,000 miles of coast line, and the Canadian border in the province of Ontario. One hesitates to speak of the value of the annual liquor traffic involved. An estimate by a Chicago prohibition official was $125,000,000.

Uale performed his part satisfactorily—the trucks coming through on time and unmolested—until late in the spring of 1927, when hijacking started, by whom nobody seemed to know, least of all Uale. As it continued Capone became suspicious. This was an old trick of the game. He assigned a trusted henchman, James De Amato, to spy on the Uale crowd. On July 1st, De Amato was shot to death in a Brooklyn street.

A year later, to the day, Uale was machine-gunned by four men in a black Nash sedan, who cruised alongside his new Lincoln and poured one hundred .45 caliber bullets at him as he was driving in Forty-fourth Street in the Homewood section of Brooklyn. The police found him, diamonds and all, slumped over the wheel, his .32 caliber revolver, which he had been unable to draw, in the right outside coat pocket.

He had double-crossed Capone. A kinsman of the Aiellos, he had aligned himself with them in their feud with Lombardo, lending them support and men to prosecute the campaign of terrorism that had desolated Father Giambastiani's parish. His followers, from whom so many killers had been recruited in the bootleg war, vowed to avenge him. A crew slipped out of Brooklyn for Chicago, awaited its opportunity, and got it two months later—September 7, 1928—in the Loop, when Lombardo was assassinated. From that day on, Capone did not sleep so well. The Pole, the Irish, the German, even the Neapolitan, may forget—may be placated by money and a new deal; the Sicilian, never.

Uale's death gave the New York City police an interesting case and the citizens a new shiver. It marked the introduction of the Chicago method. It was the first time Thompson sub-machine guns had been used there. As a study in criminology it was of profound significance, because its ramifications not only led to the origins of gang killings, but also set the stage, in a sense, for the Moran gang massacre.

The murder car, abandoned in the outskirts of Brooklyn, was recovered a couple of days later. Investigation disclosed that it had been sold originally by the Nash agency of Knoxville, Tennessee, to John McGhee, a resident of that city. Mr. McGhee had turned it in for resale, and two strangers, one giving the name of Charles Cox, had bought it, paying $1,050 cash. They had immediately driven away and Knoxville had never seen them again.

An automatic revolver and a sawed-off shotgun left in the car were identified by the police as belonging to

Capone, having been bought for him prior to the murder by Parker Henderson, Jr., son of a former mayor of Miami. Henderson, testifying before a King's County grand jury, admitted the purchase.

One of the machine guns (two were used, it eventually developed) was traced through its secret number to Peter Von Frantzius, sporting goods dealer, of 608 Diversey Parkway, Chicago. Sale of such firearms is not illegal in Illinois. Von Frantzius said that he had sold several over the counter to Frank Thompson, roustabout mystery man of Elgin, a suburb west of Chicago and Cicero. Thompson in turn had sold them to city gangsters, one of his best customers being James Bozo Shupe, ex-convict, since killed. Shupe, apparently, was the real go-between, for sub-machine guns bought by him turned up in the hands of Fred Burke, of the notorious Egan's Rats. Remember him, reader.

Capone, subpœnaed, had a personal alibi. He had not been away from his Florida villa. That was not what Inspector John J. Sullivan, of the New York City police department, wanted to know. This was his theory:

"The murder was committed by a New York gunman and three Chicago gunmen, who four days previously were visiting with Capone. They left Miami presumably for Chicago, but somewhere along the line transferred and picked up the Nash sedan bought in Knoxville."

Disclaiming any knowledge of a plot against Uale, Capone informed County Solicitor R. R. Taylor of Miami that the three guests at the villa on Friday, June 29th (the murder was committed Monday, July 1st) were "Chicago fellows, and they went home. They don't know who killed Uale."

They were Jack Guzik and Charles Fiaschetti, Capone lieutenants, and City Sealer Daniel A. Serritella.

Here, temporarily, the story leaves Uale. District Attorney Charles A. Dodd of Brooklyn officially closed the case in the grand jury rooms. It yielded no prosecution, but it was prolific of echoes. A year afterward when Frankie Marlow, the racketeer and Uale's buddy, was killed because he "owed $250,000 to gangland bankers and welched," Police Commissioner Grover A. Whalen publicly declared:

"The evidence gathered by Inspector Sullivan was not only sufficient for Capone's indictment, but, I believe, sufficient to convict the Chicago gangster of murder."

In their feud with Lombardo, the Aiellos had the help of the O'Banions, whose enmity toward Torrio and Capone was traditional. The treacherous killing of their three-gun florist leader had engendered a venomous hatred that resisted time and peace conferences. They were but a gang remnant, outnumbered and outmaneuvered, but while Earl Hymie Weiss lived their spirit was unyielding, invincible. Like Spike O'Donnell they seemed not to know when they were licked.

"They're poison to Johnny and Al," Old Shoes had said.

Their audacious exploits had put fear in both men's hearts—the daylight bombardment of the Cicero headquarters; the three hell-bent musketeers' ride to Fifty-fifth and State streets, to riddle Capone's sedan with slugs and bullets; the shooting down of Torrio in front of his home. These things rankled with the Scarface. They were "unfinished business."

George Bugs Moran, who succeeded to the leadership with the machine-gunning of Weiss, had his full quota of intestinal fortitude, but otherwise did not measure up to his predecessors as a genus Big Shot. He had not their arrogant self-confidence, their frank criminality, their knack of political bigwiggery. He was a lurker in the shadows, secretive, furtive, seldom seen, masking his activities, steering shy of the cops and the public generally. Withal, he was typical of the class that has capitalized its talents through prohibition. His record:

Sent to the penitentiary for robbery September 17, 1910, under the name of George Miller; paroled June 18, 1912.

Sent to the penitentiary from McLean County October 3, 1913, for burglary and larceny.

Forfeited bonds in a robbery case December 19, 1917; case subsequently stricken off by the court.

Sent to the penitentiary for robbery May 24, 1918; paroled February 1, 1923.

A roll-call of his buzzards' nest would have discovered Willie Marks, his bodyguard and second in command; Ted Newberry, his whiskey peddler; the Gusenberg brothers, Frank and Pete—Frank, burglar, robber and stick-up; Pete, who had served in Leavenworth for the Polk Street station $400,000 mail robbery; John May, safe-blower and the father of seven children; Albert R. Weinshank, speakeasy proprietor; James Clark, brother-in-law of Moran, bank robber suspect and crack rifle and pistol shot; Adam Heyer of the three aliases, owner of the S. M. C. Cartage Company at 2122 North

Clark Street, the gang's booze depot, where it also kept its trucks and cars; Dr. Reinhardt H. Schwimmer, a young optometrist, just starting to "play around" with gangsters, who lived at the Parkway Hotel, 2100 Lincoln Park West, a hotel referred to by the society editors as "fashionable," where the O'Banion crowd strutted under assumed names and assumed respectability.

Unfinished business. Uale's men had bumped off Lombardo, but the Morans had got Lolordo. "They were not Italians," Mrs. Lolordo had cried. The pipe-line word was that the killers were the Gusenbergs and Clark, who had established friendly relations with Lolordo by consenting to let him operate a still in their territory for a stipulated amount—$1,500 down and $500 a month; that on the day of the murder they had visited him on pretense of collecting the initial payment. Lolordo had drawn $1,500 from the bank in the morning while in the Loop with Mrs. Lolordo.

Unfinished business. While Capone was in Florida, superintending a new dog-track venture, the Morans and Aiellos had horned in on the alky-cooking, beer, and booze game in one of the richest areas of his domain —the Twentieth Ward. The pipe-line word was that they had also hijacked a dozen trucks that the Purple outfit in Detroit was running into Chicago for Capone. Incidentally, in the Twentieth Ward, an aldermanic fight was raging, with the Capones supporting State Representative William V. Pacelli, who had entered the race at the behest of City Sealer Daniel A. Serritella.

The gangster was emerging as an entity in the city's economic life. Rule by the gun and the bomb was being extended from bootlegging into legitimate business, and into the affairs of the workingman and the budget of the home. It was to result in much bloodshed.

George Red Barker, pal of the West Side O'Donnells, ex-convict, twice paroled, who already had throttled the garage industry, was to seize control of the Coal Teamsters, Chauffeurs and Helpers Union, after shooting James Lefty Lynch, its business agent. During the Christmas holidays of 1929 he threatened to call a strike of Local No. 704, which delivers fuel to the downtown district, if a pay increase were not granted by the dealers. Every skyscraper, office building, bank, hotel, shop, store, and theater in the Loop would have been affected. The dealers capitulated.

William Three-Fingered Jack White, safe-blower, once sentenced to life imprisonment for killing a policeman, was to run the Coal Hikers Union, Jack McGurn the Bill Posters and Billers Union. Three hoodlums, headed by Dickey Quan, were to try to extort $10,000 from M. J. Powers, president of the Tire and Rubber Workers Union, as the price of his retention of his office —and good health; and—Powers notified the police, they were to shoot it out with them, killing all three.

It was a situation that was to prompt the statement by Col. Robert Isham Randolph, president of the Chicago Association of Commerce, in February of 1930, after a member of the association had been shot while directing a construction job on the University of Chicago campus:

"There is not a business, not an industry, in Chicago, that is not paying tribute directly or indirectly to racketeers and gangsters."

In the same month of that year, former Chief of Po-

GUNS ROAR IN GANGLAND

AND Bugs Moran's hardboiled gunmen cease to threaten Capone supremacy. Here we see them being hauled away after the St. Valentine's Day massacre.

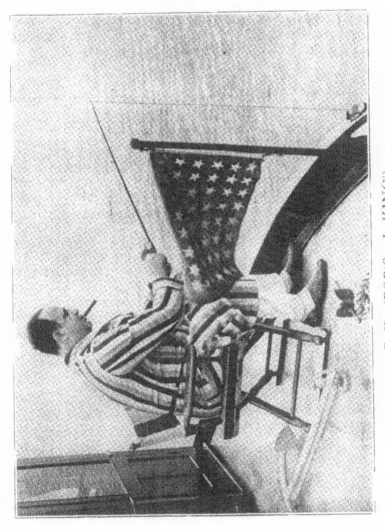

THE SPORT OF KINGS

Waire death stalks through Chicago The Big Shot fishes
from a palatial acht off his Miami estate.

lice Morgan A. Collins, and a member of the department for thirty-seven years, was to appear before the House judiciary committee at Washington, in its prohibition hearing, and say:

"The men who took money from bootleggers for overlooking violations of the Volstead Act were incapacitated from arresting them for any other crime. They had to stand for murder, robbery and many other crimes."

Since 1928, Collins had been traveling about the United States, studying conditions, and "conditions in Chicago are only typical of those throughout the country."

The Morans, like Capone, had entered the $35,000,-000-a-year clothes-cleaning industry, and the causes leading thereto provide something of an explanatory picture of the development of racketeering.

Originally, the industry was a monopoly run by the Master Cleaners and Dyers Association, which owned all the cleaning and dyeing plants. It functioned in conjunction with two subsidiaries, the Retail Cleaners and Dyers Union, and the Laundry and Dyehouse Chauffeurs Union. The founder and secretary-treasurer of the latter was John G. Clay, who in seventeen years had seen it grow from a handful of men to the strongest union in the city, with a treasury fund—for defense purposes and strikes—of $300,000.

In between the Masters and the unions were the small shopkeepers or tailoring establishments, helpless, forced through intimidation to accept the dictates of the Masters. These finally boosted prices so outrageously high that the public instituted a tacit boycott, giving what work could not be done at home to independents in the suburbs. The chief sufferers from the sharp decline in business were the small shopkeepers. They had to pay inside help and drivers the same wages, and contribute the same subsidy to the Masters. Conditions were unbearable. The result was a revolt.

One hundred shopkeepers on the North and Northwest sides withdrew from the monopoly and organized an independent coöperative plant under the name of the Central Cleaning Company, with one Ben Kornick as president. But the Masters had their gunmen, sluggers, and bombers, and to protect themselves, Kornick and his associates hired Moran at $1,800 a week, as Morris Becker, fighting the Masters on the South Side, had retained the services of Capone. It will be obvious to the reader that this is an instance where greed created a so-called racketeering situation.

Becker never had occasion to regret his move. Not so Kornick. He was dealing with a different kind of fellow. Willie Marks and James Clark were installed as vice presidents of his concern. Within six weeks Kornick was convinced that the Morans were trying to muscle him out.

He was in a dilemma. He faced the prospect of being hoist by his own petard, as it were. He and his associates decided that the only way to rid themselves of the Morans was to reaffiliate with the Masters. But to do that they would have to unionize their help. The man to see, then, was John G. Clay, who had a reputation for honesty and square dealing.

The Morans learned of Kornick's intention. They did not propose to be ousted. They had larger ideas by now. Willie Marks hastened to see Clay; he told him he could unionize the Central company's drivers. Clay asked him to show his authority from the company—meaning from Kornick—to negotiate and sign an agreement. Marks had none. Clay refused to talk to him. The Morans tried to bully him. They couldn't. What they were aiming at was to get into his good graces, then muscle him out as they were doing with Kornick, and seize his drivers' union and its $300,000 treasury.

Big Tim Murphy had tried to do that and had died. Clay, fifty-nine years old, a veteran of the labor game, was wise to the Morans before they started. He gave Willie Marks the air and went about his business.

The third Thursday of each month the stewards met at Clay's union headquarters, 629 South Ashland Avenue, a remodeled residence. Clay's desk was in the front room. He was sitting at it the night of November 16, 1928. Two men stepped from an automobile and walked up the short flight of steps to the stone landing, One fired a revolver, the other a sawed-off double-barreled shotgun, through the window. Clay fell dead, with six bullets and two charges of slugs in his head and body. The men escaped. The Morans did not muscle in on Clay's union. Organized labor was so enraged that the gang "went in a hole" for a while. But later it ousted Kornick as president of the Central Cleaning Company, and installed in his stead Albert R. Weinshank.

All of which was more Unfinished Business—in a new quarter, where, for once, the police couldn't laugh it off by pointing a smug finger at Capone.

Moran maintained headquarters at Heyer's garage, 2122 North Clark Street. Late on Wednesday evening,

February 13, 1929, he received a telephone call, informing him that a truckload of liquor, "right off the river," en route from Detroit to Chicago, had been hijacked, and could be had at a reasonable figure; that the hijacker was giving him "the break" on it. Evidently Moran knew his man and trusted him, because he wasted no words in palaver.

"How much?" he asked.

"Fifty-seven dollars the case."

"Okey; deliver it to the garage."

"When?"

"By ten-thirty tomorrow morning. All the boys will be here; we're short and they'll want a cut."

It was a ruse. How many bargain cargoes the pretended hijacker had delivered to Moran to worm his way into his confidence, to outsmart him at his own stuff; how long he and his co-conspirators had bided the opportune moment; how often they had drilled and rehearsed to perfect themselves in the rôles for the five minutes' use they were to make of it—all this only they will ever know.

The forces that in the spring primary campaign of 1928 had risen to flout authority—to cow a mayor, his cabinet, and his chief of police—to dragoon and slay at the polls—to bomb Swanson into the State's attorneyship—were rising to smite again, this time with a savagery that was to faze even the gorillas of gangland.

A light snow was falling the morning of St. Valentine's Day, the thermometer registering 18 above zero, with a westerly wind nipping ears and noses. Spindrifts of clouds intermittently veiled the sun. Pedestrian and motor traffic was at its minimum for the year.

In Clark Street, though, there is hardly ever a lull, even in midwinter. It is a basic artery of surface-car transportation, and its nine angling miles, north from the Loop to the city limits, are lined with groceries, restaurants, pharmacies, movie theaters, garages, flats, secondary hotels, corner cigar stands, banks, stores, etc. Its life is an unending clangor and clatter. It is a succession of neighborhood communities—a continuous Main Street—and historic. Its genesis antedates Chicago. The red men trod it as the Green Bay Trail when State and Madison was a sandspit. The stagecoach to Milwaukee rumbled over it in the thirties when the swamp by the lake numbered four thousand souls. It grew with the city. It is desultory, sprawling, indiscriminate; plain, friendly, unassuming. The rugged simplicity of the prairie sits upon it.

In the twenty-one-hundred block on this day, a stranger would have noted nothing unusual. The peaceful humdrum of existence was monotonous in its sameness. Sam Schneider, the tailor, and his wife were pressing and sewing in their shop at 2124, next door north of Heyer's garage. Sam was on the first floor of a three-story flat building, remodeled for rooming and light housekeeping. The landlady, Mrs. Jeanette Landesman, was sweeping, dusting, and making the beds. Directly across the street, at 2125, lived Mrs. Alphonsine Morin, who also kept roomers.

They entertained no suspicions regarding the squat brick structure with the uninteresting name—the S.M.C. Cartage Company—wedged in so inconspicuously between its taller neighbors. They accepted it at its face value: It was another furniture moving concern.

253

The garage, one story in height, was forty feet wide and one hundred and fifty feet long. Although it fronted on Clark, its vehicular entrance was in the rear, on the alley. The front was so contrived as to conceal the interior. It had a large plate-glass window, but the passerby could see no farther than an office partition. A door opened into the garage beyond the window. Entering it, one passed for twenty feet through a narrow passageway, formed by the end of the office partition and the north wall of the garage.

Seated in chairs in the northwest, or alley, corner at 10:30 o'clock on St. Valentine's morning were the Gusenbergs, Frank and Pete; John May, the safeblower; Al Weinshank, the speakeasy proprietor; James Clark, bank robber suspect; Adam Heyer of the three aliases; and young Dr. Schwimmer, the optometrist; each a gangster model of upkeep and dress—shave, hair trim, manicure; the silk shirt, the flashy tie; here and there, a diamond stick-pin and ring; in Dr. Schwimmer's case a carnation boutonnière; fedoras with brims slanted down over the right eyes; spats; tailored suits and overcoats; each with the customary roll—Heyer, $1,135; Weinshank, $1,250; May, $1,200, and so on; each armed.

They were waiting for George Bugs Moran, Willie Marks, and Ted Newberry, who were late. The load of hijacked liquor should be along any moment, too. Heyer's police dog would growl the alarm when it drove up. He was chained to one of the seven trucks in the garage. It was going to be a busy day for the Morans. At noon, led by the Gusenbergs, and joined by the Aiellos, they were to start for Detroit, on the biggest rum-running expedition they had undertaken since Capone went away. They were to utilize all seven trucks and three automobiles, which, freshly oiled, greased, and gassed, were ready for George Bugs' "Let's go."

Lucky George Bugs! He and Marks and Newberry, coming south on Clark Street, toward the garage, had seen a Cadillac touring car, with curtains drawn—such as the detective bureau squads use—stop at the curb, two doors north of the garage; had seen five men alight —three in police uniforms, two in civilian clothes—and walk to the door and enter. "Coppers," they figured, and decided to keep strolling around till "the heat" was off. The decision saved their lives. The reader may judge from this incident, hitherto unpublished, how close the Moran gang massacre came to being a ten-man instead of a seven-man affair.

Sam Schneider, in shirtsleeves, spectacles low on his nose, beads of perspiration on his honest brow, was pushing his gas iron up and down a pair of trousers when his wife exclaimed:

"What's that?"

Sam set the iron in its holder. He had heard it, thought it a truck back-firing—but it was too sustained for that, too insistently rhythmical, a steady metallic rat-a-tat-tat, prolonged only for seconds, then two heavy detonations, which came to them through the brick walls deadened, as when dynamite is exploded underground. They ran to the window and saw the Cadillac touring car.

"A police raid, I guess," said Sam.

The sharper women's ears of Mrs. Landesman and Mrs. Morin had heard the noises. They were more

255

curious. Keeping watch at a third-floor window, Mrs. Morin saw:

"Two men coming out of the garage, with their hands high above their heads. Behind them were three other men in what looked like police uniforms. They had guns on the first two men. They were walking slow, easy-like. I thought an arrest had been made. I watched them get into the squad car."

Mrs. Landesman reached a window in time to see the Cadillac driving south on Clark Street. She ran downstairs and tried to open the front door. It was jammed. Then:

"I called to C. L. McAllister, a roomer. He tried the door, and when it still stuck, he forced it open. He went out and into the garage. He came running back and said the place was full of dead men. I called the police."

He saw seven men lying on the concrete floor, with their faces upturned as they had fallen backward from the brick wall against which they were executed. They had died with their slant-brimmed fedoras on. Heyer's police dog lunged and howled under its beer truck. In his excitement McAllister failed to notice that one of the men was squirming—desperately mustering his strength in a last dying effort to evade the hated coppers, who would soon be there. He was Frank Gusenberg. Sergeant Thomas Loftus of the Hudson Avenue station, arriving fifteen minutes later, had him taken to the Alexian Brothers' Hospital. Sergeant Clarence Sweeney was detailed at his bedside.

"Who shot you, Frank?" he asked him.

"No one—nobody shot me," he whispered. He was too far gone to talk out loud.

AL CAPONE

Frank could have spilled a lot. He and Pete were along the afternoon Capone's Cicero abode was bombarded, and the evening McGurn was shot while in a cigar-store 'phone booth of the McCormick Hotel; they had toasted the health of Pasqualino Lolordo with eighteen bullets; the police had questioned them in the John Clay killing.

"Which gang was it?" asked the sergeant.

No answer.

"Want a preacher, Frank?"

Getting weaker now. The lips twitched, but Sweeney had to bend over to catch the reply. It was, "No."

He died at 1:30 P. M., the gangster way, unshriven, not squawking.

If the Lolordo murder was sophistication of method, the Moran job was precision engineering. The five assassins might have been robots, wound up and synchronized, every movement clicking concurrently and reciprocally. As reconstructed from examination of the scene, and from piecing together the stories of the Schneiders, Mrs. Landesman, Mrs. Morin, and others, it was evident that the two or three men (the number has never been definitely established) in police uniforms first entered the garage. They were officers; they had orders to search everybody, to question the inmates. This was no new experience for the Morans; they were used to it. The official version read:

"Two of the crew were in police uniforms and the seven victims, thinking it was only another routine raid —with perhaps an arrest—and a quick release on bonds —readily yielded to disarming and obeying the command to stand in a row, fifty feet from the Clark Street door, facing the north wall. It was a clever trick. Otherwise, the Morans would have sold their lives dearly."

The whole success of the plot, then, devolved on the men in uniforms, who performed faultlessly. While they did, the real executioners, in civilian clothes, remained in the passageway. One carried a Thompson sub-machine gun, with a drum of one hundred .45 caliber cartridges; the other a twelve gauge, double-barreled, sawed-off shotgun. Coming from the car to the garage, these had been concealed under their overcoats.

As soon as the Morans had been disarmed and stood up against the wall, the machine gunner stepped forth. East to west, his victims were Schwimmer, May, Clark, Heyer, Weinshank, Pete and Frank Gusenberg. Presumably the gun was adjusted for rapid fire. If so, the job was completed in ten seconds.

The executioner was cool and expert. The post-mortem showed that the line of fire had not deviated; that it had been accurately sprayed "between the ears and thighs; all were wounded in the head and vital organs." The shotgun was another indication of the assassins' thoroughness. It was for emergencies, to finish off. Apparently Clark and May were considered tough to kill, for they received its two charges of buckshot. These were the sounds that came through the brick walls to Schneider and his wife.

Having done their work, the assassins again had recourse to the police camouflage to accomplish their getaway. Its purpose was to allay suspicion and the reader has seen how successful it was; how the two men in civilian clothes marched out of the garage with hands in air, their uniformed companions behind them with guns drawn; how they walked, "not too fast," to the pseudo-squad-car, climbed in and were gone.

On that same St. Valentine's Day, three murderers, sentenced to die in the electric chair, were getting reprieves, due to petitions filed by their attorneys for reviews of their cases by the State supreme court. Two of them had shot down a policeman, Arthur Esau, when he walked into a drugstore they were robbing.

Clues developed slowly in the massacre case. Nearly three weeks elapsed before the authorities, on March 4th, named three men as having actually participated in it. They were Joseph Lolordo, brother of Pasqualino, Fred Burke, and James Ray, these two of Egan's Rats, St. Louis.

Burke was, and is, a much-wanted man, a fugitive from justice since April of 1925. His specialty is robbing banks, and for that he is wanted in Kentucky, Indiana, and Wisconsin. Ohio wants him for killing a policeman, and the United States Government for a national-bank robbery. Ray was said to have been his confederate in a holdup at Jefferson, Wisconsin, in which bonds worth $350,000 were taken.

The plot called for men unknown to the Morans to pose as policemen, and Burke and Ray were chosen for the rôles. Assistant State's Attorney David Stansbury further announced that Jack McGurn had paid them $10,000 each for their services. Another Capone henchman, Jack Guzik, as telephone records subpœnaed from the Congress Hotel showed, had been holding daily long-distance conversations with Capone at his

Florida villa up to within three days of the massacre. Then they had ceased, to be resumed again February 18th.

Joseph Lolordo had been in the army with a machine-gun detachment. He knew his typewriters and ukelele music. He was rated "a natural" with a Thompson sub-machine gun. He was eager to avenge his brother's death. To Joe, therefore, went the trigger honors. Albert Anselmi was also suspected of having had a hand in it, according to the announcement from the State's attorney's office, but the evidence against him was not strong enough to warrant an arrest. John Scalise was involved, and witnesses had identified him.

Lolordo had disappeared. McGurn and Scalise, already in custody, were indicted on seven charges of first-degree murder, their bonds being put at $50,000 each. These were duly forthcoming and they were released. McGurn's surety was hotel property at Sixty-fourth Street and Cottage Grove Avenue, on the South Side, valued at $1,300,000, scheduled by Harold C. Hayes, proprietor of the Metropole, Capone's G.H.Q. in Michigan Avenue.

Gangland justice unexpectedly disposed of Scalise, which left McGurn to face the charges alone, and undergo a series of queer adventures with the law. The four-term statute in Illinois provides that if a defendant demands trial at four terms of court and the State is not prepared to prosecute, the State must enter a nolle prosequi.

McGurn appeared for trial May 28th. The State requested a continuance to July 8th. McGurn appeared again on that date, his attorneys demanding immediate trial, but the State asked and received another continuance, to August 15th. The State was still not ready then, and once more the case was continued, to September 23d, when McGurn's attorneys made their fourth demand for trial. But Assistant State's Attorney Harry S. Ditchburne informed the court.

"The State must ask for another continuance. We are still investigating."

McGurn's next appearance was October 28th.

"The State is not ready to go to trial," said Mr. Ditchburne. "We desire another continuance."

"The indictment was voted last March," interposed James McDermott of counsel for McGurn. "We have made repeated demands for trial of this case."

"If you haven't the evidence," tartly remarked Judge George Fred Rush to Mr. Ditchburne, "you should not take advantage simply because this happens to be a notorious case."

He granted a continuance, however, to December 2d, with the stipulation:

"The State must be prepared to go to trial on that date. If it is not I will discharge the defendant."

On December 2d, Mr. Ditchburne advised the court:

"We are forced at this time to nolle prosse the case against McGurn."

Jack went free. So far as prosecution goes, his adventures represent the sole accomplishment to date by the authorities in the matter of the Moran gang massacre.

The case has another phase, which challenges interest and speculation in the future of crime detection. It introduces the exact methods of science—forensic ballistics and the microscope—the fingerprinting, one might say, of shells and bullets, and the identification of firearms. Every gun has individual peculiarities—the grooves and lands of the bore, which put distinctive striations on the bullets; and the breech block and firing pin, which imprint their telltale hieroglyphics on the shells and primers. No two guns produce the same markings.

Already, in his laboratory, Colonel Calvin C. Goddard, formerly of New York City, has supplied a thrilling sequel to the Uale killing and the massacre. The long arm of coincidence helped him. "Stranger than fiction," one is tempted to write.

In the little city of St. Joe, Michigan, one hundred miles around the lake from Chicago, on the afternoon of Saturday, December 14, 1929, a traffic dispute occurred. One motorist had hit another. Patrolman Charles Skelly, asked to intercede, approached the offending motorist with a request that he accompany him to the station to file a report. The man drew a gun and shot Skelly dead, then sped away. The car's license number had been copied. It was traced to one Fred Dane, a resident of St. Joe for six months. He was buying a home there. The St. Joe police hurriedly visited it. He was gone, but a search disclosed numerous revolvers, two Thompson sub-machine guns, a case of ammunition—and a library of dime-novel police tales. Dane was Fred Burke, under cover in a hideout. The car he was driving, and which he wrecked and abandoned in his flight, had been bought in Cicero.

Colonel Goddard had previously studied and indexed the massacre shells and bullets. Burke's machine guns were turned over to him, and after conducting firing tests, he reported that one of them was the weapon with which the Morans were executed. Within three weeks, following studies of bullets extracted from the body of Uale, he identified the same weapon as having been used in his assassination.

In Colonel Goddard's quietly consummated labors, the drama of the laboratory is presented. A man is killed in a residential street of Brooklyn in July of 1928. A thousand miles away, in an obscure Chicago garage, seven men are killed, months later. Well nigh a year passes, and a motorist shoots a patrolman. The keenest lay mind could not connect the three occurrences on the known facts. The scientist, peering through his microscope, reading the hieroglyphics of the shells and bullets, correlates them and says, "This happened; that is so." The foundation is laid for police work that may yet result in a complete solution of the Uale and Moran gang cases.

Some day the Chicago Historical Society may be minded to erect a tablet at 2122 North Clark Street, and posterity will read:

"Here Ended the Bootleg Battle of the Marne."

And how!

George Bugs, last of the O'Banions, was a leader without a gang.

General Al the Scarface had won the war to make the world safe for public demand—in and around Chicago.

PART SIX

INTERLUDE:

Momentarily, Tony Steger's clumping feet were idle, and his strident basso profundo stilled. Which was to say that momentarily the flow of the night's news had ceased.

A man of parts in the local room drama, Tony's stellar rôle is that of engineer of a funny little oblong contraption on the starboard side the city desk. It has 24 red and black levers and 24 pea-sized red bulbs. A bell rings; a bulb glows; Tony shifts a lever, says, "Hello," and listens.

It may be a stickup, a murder; Dr. Stork with twins or triplets; an elopement, a divorce, a golden wedding anniversary; another nameless floater in the river; the obituary of a prominent citizen; a 13 suit hand in bridge; the last bird in Chicago wearing a straw katy in the fall, or the first robin of spring in Oak Park. Whatever it is, Tony listens, and then his basso profundo booms above the chattering telegraph keys, the fretting typewriters of earnest fingered reporters, and the infernal popping brass tube delivering its pouches from the City News Bureau:

"A story on five, Fitz."

The item has landed with the rewrite, and the situation is well in hand.

Tony is the ear of the local room. He is successor to

that late James Aloysius Durkin, world's greatest
office boy of the world's greatest newspaper. Durkin, in
shirtsleeves, the twinkle in his blue Irish eyes un-
dimmed, gazes serenely down upon Tony from the east
wall—a Tribune tradition, now—just as when he used
to crack his gum, catch the number ticked off by the
fire alarm buzzer, maintain a telephone conversation,
and handle a piece of copy—all at one and the same
time.

The hour was 11 P. M. The deadline was nearing.
Soon editors and copy readers would rise en masse to
start the march downstairs to the composing room to
put the paper to bed for the home edition. Soon the
clicking of more than 60 linotypes would give way to
the roar of the mighty Goss presses, and in circulation
alley the waiting trucks would begin receiving their con-
signments of 800,000 newspapers.

Sir Arthur Conan Doyle had died. The cables from
England, as well as press wires about the United States,
had been glutted with tales of séances, astral contacts,
psychic manifestations, communications from the spirit
world—even messages from Sir Arthur. Perhaps these
had had their effect upon Tony. Perhaps the unseen, un-
fathomable forces of the universe were exerting their
spell upon him. He ended a pensive silence with:

"It's about time for Jake to call."

Three weeks had passed since the morning of June 10,
1930, when the Tribune, under an eight column banner
line, had carried a story:

Alfred J. Lingle, better known in his world of newspaper
work as Jake Lingle, and for the last 18 years a reporter on the
Tribune, was shot to death yesterday in the Illinois Central

subway at the east side of Michigan boulevard, at Randolph street.

The Tribune offers $25,000 as a reward for information which will lead to the conviction of the slayer or slayers.

An additional reward of $5,000 was announced by the Chicago Evening Post, making a total of $30,000.

(The next day the Chicago Herald & Examiner, Hearst morning paper, also offered a $25,000 reward, bringing the total up to $55,000.)

An organized gang planned and executed the murder of Lingle, and at least six gunmen of the band are believed to have been nearby at 1:25 o'clock yesterday afternoon when one of them crept behind the newspaperman, lifted a stubby .38 caliber revolver, and fired a single shot through the back of his head. Lingle was killed instantly.

Tony nodded at Eddie Johnson, boss of the night cameramen:

"He'd call in and ask, 'Anything doin', Tony?'"

"Say," from Eddie, "I met Paddy Walsh at the wake. Jake was best man at his wedding. He and Jake went to Niagara Falls once on an $8 excursion—that was years ago before Jake was married. They were ready to return. Paddy had $2 and Jake had $2. Jake spent $1.50 for a pennant for his girl—the one he finally married—the only one he ever went with. Paddy held out on Jake. He put a dollar of his two in his shoe, and told Jake he only had one. So Jake had to get by on fifty cents. Paddy remembered it at the wake. It bothered him. . . . God, Jake was a big hearted guy."

A fellow newspaperman's wife had died—a newspaperman whose work is notable for diligence and conscientiousness—but whose salary was inadequate to defray both hospital and funeral expenses. Somebody recalled how Jake had forced $300 on him.

"There was a south side policeman named Reynolds, who had killed eight holdup men," spoke up a police reporter. "I told Jake about it, and Russell (commissioner of police) called Reynolds right in and made him a sergeant."

The talk rambled on, but I could not rid my mind of Tony's saying:

"It's about time for Jake to call."

Only in fictional narrative, of course, and through some such imaginative genius as an Edgar Allan Poe or an Ambrose Bierce, could the theme of Lingle still alive be maintained. Yet as the days and weeks and months have passed, I have frequently surprised myself fancying that Lingle is out there somewhere busy on his last and biggest, his supreme assignment; busy despite himself—counter to himself—his city editor, destiny—with a gangster bullet—rousing a community and a nation to the menace of gang anarchy to urban civilization.

Who was Lingle? A prize specimen of the era. A $65 a week man, posthumously revealed as having had an income of $60,000 a year; who admitted he had "fixed the price of beer" in Chicago; who was labeled the "Unofficial Chief of Police"; who drove a Lincoln car, with a chauffeur; plunged on the stock market and on the races; lived at the best hotels; owned, or was buying, an $18,000 summer home in the Michigan Riviera, at Long Beach, Indiana; hobnobbed with millionaires; with the governor of Illinois, the attorney general of the State; with judges and county and city officials; golfed and vacationed with the commissioner of police, and speculated with him—and wore, even as Esposito and Uale, what has come to be regarded as the gangster emblem, a diamond studded belt buckle given to him by Capone:

"A Christmas present," said Al. "Jake was a dear friend of mine."

His education was limited to an elementary public school, the Calhoun, at 2850 West Jackson Boulevard. His post-graduate course was vacant lot baseball; thence, a semi-professional team. His first job was as office boy in a surgical supply house. He quit there to go to the Tribune in the same capacity in 1912. He was a typical product of the sidewalks of Chicago. He had no inclination for books or the thing called culture. They comprised an alien world to him. He was engrossed in the knockabout life of the streets. He never wrote a line for his paper. He never tried to write a line. He had no inclination for it.

In that early knockabout life of the streets, an incident occurred that was to shape his career. Quoting again from the Tribune story of June 10:

Twenty years ago, when Jake was a stripling, he met Bill Russell, a patrolman, traveling a beat in uniform. Jake was playing semi-professional baseball with William Niesen's team. He and the patrolman took a liking to each other, and together they would patrol Russell's beat, talking the while. . . . . So Lingle came to know the glamour of police work.

With Russell he learned to develop an easy attitude toward policemen and police characters, and in later years, this penchant developed, until he came to know their life and haunts as few men outside those worlds have ever known them.

When his friend Russell began to climb toward higher posts in the police department, Lingle continued and ripened their friendship. First, a sergeantcy, then a lieutenancy, then a captaincy, and then a deputy commissionership. Lingle shared with his friend the pleasure the promotions gave, and when at last Russell was appointed commissioner, Lingle gloried, not with any hope of sharing in the power of the office, but solely with the personal zeal with which he had followed his friend's rise.

When the commissioner was ailing, it was always Lingle who came to offer him cheerful solace. They played golf together, and went about to the theaters and to visit mutual friends.

I first met Lingle in 1918. I was a rewrite man on the Tribune. He was a police reporter. He had been with the paper six years. Occasionally I would be sent out on stories with him. Generally, our objective would be a police station. If it wasn't, and there was one anywhere in the neighborhood, Jake would suggest we drop in for a visit. I used to enjoy the experience. I was new to Chicago—I had been here only three years—and these expeditions afforded me opportunity for observation.

Wherever the station—north, west or south—Lingle would know patrolmen, sergeants, lieutenants and captains. It was obvious to me that he not only was popular with them, but that he had their confidence. The greeting invariably would be:

"Hello, Jake."

And:

"Hello, Mike," or Sam, John, Bill, Jack; Tom, Dick or Harry.

Lingle's right hand would go up to the left breast pocket of his coat for a cigar. There was a cigar for every greeting. I never knew him to meet the newest rookie policeman that he didn't tender a cigar. They were a two-for-a nickel brand and Lingle smoked them himself then.

He knew all the coppers by their first names. He spent his spare time among them. He played penny-ante with them. He went to their wakes and funerals; their weddings and christenings. They were his heroes. A lawyer explained him:

"As a kid he was cop struck, as another kid might be stage struck."

The police station was his prep school and college. He matured, and his point of view developed, in the stodgy, fetid atmosphere of the cell block and the squad room. Chicago's 41 police stations are vile places, considered either æsthetically or hygienically. I doubt if a modern farmer would use the majority of them for cow sheds. Yet the civic patriots put their fledgling blue-coats in them, and expect them to preserve their self-respect and departmental morale.

In this prep school-college, Lingle learned a great deal the ordinary citizen may, or may not, suspect. He learned that sergeants, lieutenants and captains know every handbook, every gambling den, every dive, every beer flat and saloon in their districts—that that is part of the routine—that not to know them is to admit in-competency—that a word from the captain, when "the heat is on," will close any district tighter than a Scotch-

man's pocket in five minutes. He learned that they
know which joint owners have "a friend in the hall or
county," and which haven't. Few haven't. He learned
that the Chicago police department is politics ridden;
that the average chief is a stuffed shirt.

In ratio as his intimacy with members of the department deepened, his acquaintance broadened in
that nether stratum of society, the underworld. He
learned that it, too, is caste conscious, with rigid social
and professional distinctions. The best jackroller is
beneath the contempt of a pickpocket. A pickpocket
is only to be tolerated by a successful stickup man.
No safecracker would be seen in the company of a
porch climber. He learned that some criminals have
drag and quick habeas corpus service—the big dealers; that some have no drag and can be tossed in
the can with impunity; these are the punks. He
learned to despise the punks. He learned to talk the
argot. A $5 bill was a fin; a $10 bill, a sawbuck; and,
later, a $100 bill was a C; a $1,000 bill a gran'; a
holdup or a hijacking was a h'ist; a man shadowed
was tailed or cased; a hoodlum was a hood, the oo
pronounced as in fool; a pretty woman was a swell
broad; an indictment or complaint was a rap; a revolver was a heater; a policeman was The Law;
victuals were groceries; one who talked too freely
was a squawker; if a criminal confessed, he sang.
These are but random selections from the vocabulary
of the new Americanese that would cause Noah Webster to play leapfrog in his grave.

An occurrence of which I have personal knowledge
will illustrate how thoroughly Lingle knew his under-

world. He was escorting his fiancée home. They had boarded a crowded street car. A seemingly accidental jostling caused Lingle to feel in his right hip pocket, where he carried his wallet. It was gone. He scanned the passengers, recognizing a face. Saying nothing to the girl, he continued on to her home. After leaving her he hurried to a bar and poolroom in West Madison Street. There, as he knew he would be, was the pickpocket. Lingle demanded his wallet back and got it. He never wrote a line, but in his casual manner he could give a Bertillon of any criminal in the country, and rattle off inside information on the toughest cases —whether murders, bank robberies or big time confidence games. I refer particularly here to the Lingle I knew in 1918.

The police environment stamps a man with definite characteristics. His working hours are spent with the mentally deficient, the so-called scum of the city, and he has contact with graft and corruption. His sensibilities harden; his sympathies diminish; his judgment warps. Toward his clientele he is apt to assume a domineering, superior attitude, and a sneering cynicism. I never detected any traces of a superior attitude in Lingle. I think he was as incapable of a superior attitude as a frolicsome colt. He did develop a pose of cynicism. And with the happy-go-lucky Lingle this pose sat as with the youngster in the nursery rhyme who "stuck in a thumb, pulled out a plum, and said, 'What a big boy am I!' "

Lingle was 38 years old; married; the father of two children; he had his Lincoln car; owned his $18,-000 summer home on the Michigan lake shore, and lived in Chicago at the Stevens Hotel. Yet I never heard him addressed as "Mr. Lingle." He was "Jake" to everybody. I cannot conceive of a headwaiter at the Blackstone addressing him as "Mr. Lingle" and getting away with it. He would have called him out of the left corner of his mouth—the ever present cigar being in the right corner—with:

"Aw, g'wan; tryin' to make a big dealer out of me."

I see him now as he strolled into the local room of the Tribune a few nights before his death—his round, beaming, full moonish face, with its inevitable quizzical grin and its inevitable cigar. He was smoking three-for-a-half-dollar cigars, then. I suppose the grin was as susceptible of as many interpretations as there are personal reactions, but to me it was always the grin of a mischievous, likable kid, who has just tiptoed out to the pantry and is wondering if there is any jam on his lips. A tiny cleft in his chin enhanced this impression of boyishness. His hair was short, sparse and curly; complexion, dark; rosy cheeks; smooth shaven; of medium height; chunky shouldered; thick barreled; solid underpinning.

His eyes belied his grin. They were bland as a Chinaman's—and as cryptic; a little tired. The cynicism he had acquired in the police environment looked out from them. He had a trick of dropping the eyelids half down, when engaged in interviewing, and the eyes then became as cold as interplanetary space. Then, too, the left corner of the mouth would curl upward into a sinister crescent, and out of it, in a long, harsh drawl of rising inflection. would issue:

"Y-e-a-h?"

AL CAPONE

It had the sting of a whip lash.

Strolling into the local room he would join in the current reportorial debate—if interested—or stop for a bit of chaffing with one of the older men. For these men he would have dug in his pocket for his last dime. He was conspicuous amongst them by reason of his sartorial ensemble; always newly tailored, manicured, barbered, shined and polished. He was vaguely embarrassed about the newness of his clothes; never entirely at ease in them; he seemed to be expecting his shoes to squeak. He was midwest—Chicago. No cane for him; no spats; no yellow chamois or doeskin gloves; none of that "rose-in-the-buttonhole-stuff" his friend Capone affected. And he never packed a heater, as do many Chicago police reporters. He was abstemious. A glass of beer was his limit.

Gambling was a consuming fever with him. It debilitated his moral being. It enslaved him like a drug. His craving for it was insatiable. It finally ruined him. Truly, he was a gambling fool. The race track was Seventh Heaven. He never bet less than $100 on a horse and often $1,000. There is a challenge to the individual as well as to the community in Lingle. He is terrific drama in the sense expressed by Dean Shailer Mathews of the divinity school of the University of Chicago:

"Lingle's killing was the apex of a pyramid (of crime and its hookups), ninety per cent of which is still underground."

Today he would be broke, borrowing right and left; nobody exempt from a touch; approaching even office boys. Tomorrow, back "in the bucks"; strutting;

274

brandishing his roll; wisecracking about it. Stege noosed that phase of him in a five-word sentence:

"Jake was a Pittsburgh Phil."

The reader may recall that Pittsburgh Phil, operating largely in Philadelphia, become famous for his bankroll and the display he made of it. It might contain only $50, but Phil would have $40 of it changed into $1 bills, put the $10 on top, snap a rubber band around it, and flash it everywhere. Therein lies the origin of the phrase, "a Philadelphia bankroll."

"Jake couldn't help showing his roll," said Stege.

He was a fire fan. He and the immortal Durkin were the only men I have ever known who could cock an ear at the signal box in the Tribune local room as it buzzed its numbers and instantly give the location from which the alarm had been turned in. He never missed a fire. His varied acquaintanceship included all the division marshals, the battalion chiefs, the company captains and many members of the crews of the Chicago fire department.

Further evidence of that varied acquaintanceship was had at his funeral. Police Commissioner William F. Russell headed the active pallbearers. Among those attending were: Deputy Police Commissioners Thomas Wolfe, Martin Mullen and Stege, who was also chief of detectives; Deputy Chief of Detectives John Egan; Police Captains Daniel Gilbert, William Schoemaker, Michael Grady and Daniel Lynch; West Parks Police Captain William Schramm; County Coroner Herman N. Bundesen; County Judge Edmund K. Jarecki; County Assessor Charles Krutckoff; County Clerk Robert M. Sweitzer; State's Attorney John A. Swanson; Municipal Judges Francis B. Allegretti, William R. Fetzer and Edgar A. Jonas; Alderman John B. McDonough.

I have sometimes thought of this story of Capone as the Uncle Tom's Cabin of prohibition. On that basis Lingle was a Topsy. He just grew up. He grew up from the knockabout hurly-burly of the streets into the police station environment, thence into the insane era of the Volstead gold rush.

As I view the pattern of his life, in so far as it has been posthumously revealed, I see two profoundly significant moments—the first when he met Bill Russell, the patrolman, in 1910; the second when he met Al Capone, the Torrio handy man at the Four Deuces, in 1920. Parenthetically, the reader who may be superstitious will note the decade element in his life—1910, Russell; 1920, Capone; 1930, Death. As I progress thus far in the writing of the Lingle chapter, I realize the irony of it. Here is Lingle, living, whose business was solving mysteries, who probably had worked on more crime cases than any other Chicago police reporter; here is Lingle, dead, bequeathing to the world the greatest mystery of all—the mystery of Lingle. Some of the material used in this biography was obtained from Lingle. And witness: Lingle himself now provides the dénouement; his murder caps the apex of that pyramid of crime and its hookups. It matches the insane pattern of the story.

The popular inference regarding Lingle's friendship with Capone is that it was financially advantageous to Lingle. I shall speak of that later. I wish to advert briefly to 1921. In that year, from Lingle's lips, I heard that his father, dead some years, had left him $50,000, principally in west side real estate in Chicago. He said a parcel of it consisted of a three-story flat building.

Lingle in 1921 had displayed unexpected affluence. He had made a trip to Cuba, and had returned with what was literally a treasure trove of gifts. These included egrets, coveted by women for hats. They had to be smuggled in. I question whether he was earning $65 a week then; probably around $50. His friends naturally commented on his lavish expenditures, but it never occurred to them to suspect him. He was at my home for dinner, immediately following his return, and I recall I thought little of it when he mentioned his father's $50,000 estate. The value of this estate—as disclosed by an examination of the probate court records, in June of 1930—was five hundred dollars.

In perspective he emerges as a split personality: naïve and juvenile; crafty and secretive.

The record, then, shows that in 1921 Lingle began living a lie, leading a dual life—deceiving his associates, betraying his newspaper trust. In the local room he was still Jake, the grinning office boy who became a police reporter. Outside . . . What was he outside? What had happened? Whence the source of the income that had corrupted this boy? Was it Capone? I think not. Capone wasn't established. Maybe some other in the Torrio outfit. Maybe police graft. Maybe the slot machine racket, or gambling rakeoff in one form or another. Whatever the source, Lingle in 1921 was sufficiently "in the take," to quote the argot, that he felt impelled to concoct an alibi for himself in a mythical estate. And "the take" increased to such an extent that he concocted another alibi—a double one—that of a couple of rich uncles.

Much discussion has transpired as to how Lingle could have so completely duped his office. I can best answer that with a story. Rare Frank Carson, who knew Chicago newspapermen like a big brother, was for years day city editor of the Tribune. In 1919, if memory serves aright, he resigned to go to the Chicago Herald & Examiner, as city editor. In 1923, when he was managing editor, I went to work for him. On an afternoon either in the fall of 1924 or the spring of 1925, Lingle telephoned he was coming to see me. He came. He wanted a job. He had had a fight with the day desk of the Tribune, he said. Carson was not in the office. I located him at the Congress Hotel, and told him what had happened.

"Keep him there," he said. "I'll hop a cab and be right over. We'll sign him to a contract before he snaps out of it."

Lingle was pretty nervous, walking up and down and chewing his cigar. I managed to keep him for about a half hour. Then he said he guessed he would walk around the block. Two minutes after he had left, Carson arrived. His cab had been caught in a traffic jam. Lingle never came back. Carson was chagrined at losing "a chance to grab Jake." I cite the incident to show the professional esteem in which Lingle was held and the lack of suspicion concerning him. The fellows used to joke him:

"Jake, if it hadn't been for a tardy taxi, you would have been a Hearst man now."

AL CAPONE

For nine years this singular figure moved through that segment of the Chicago scene composed of the police stations and their headquarters; the haunts of gangdom, and the blatant, trivial world of the politician. The axis, so to speak, of this world, is in the loop; specifically, around Randolph and Clark streets, where the historic Sherman Hotel faces the city hall and county building.

Lingle was as familiar to the habitués of the Randolph Street Rialto as was that landmark, the blind newsboy, in front of the old Ashland drugstore, where the Broadway surface car owl, in charge of Ike, the Jewish conductor, was wont to pick up Mike Mowschine of George Cohan's orchestra, and others of the night life fusileers and fuseloilers.

Save for the police department, the segment of the Chicago scene through which Lingle moved is but an infinitesimal and ignoble part of the real Chicago—but it is one that has received endless notoriety. I mention this, in passing, to set the reader right and to place Lingle in his proper relationship to the Chicago that is. I quote from the Illinois Crime Survey:

Chicago is a city of marvelous paradoxes. It is a city of 1,060 churches, and of numerous other religious organizations. It is a city of universities and of theological institutions. It is a city of libraries, parks and playgrounds. It is a city of magnificent altruism. Its chief defect has been in its very energy, its very industry and its democracy. It has welcomed to its streets the people of every community, and it has sought to provide for them on a large scale.

As in all new cities its industries and its industrial development have been absorbing. Its business men have furnished

279

employment to millions, and have established institutions for the culture of millions, but they have had little time for the engrossing world of politics.

They are charitable toward the people of the slums, but they do not understand them, nor the problems that are theirs. They have left these people to the control of the often corrupt politician. They have had too much of the usual and sublime American optimism; too much of the feeling that all is well with the world. They have been engrossed in everything but in government. While they have given millions for education and charity, they have failed to provide for their own police department. . . . London with its homogeneous population has one policeman for every 175 people. . . . Rome has a policeman on every corner. . . . Chicago, however, has only one policeman for every 900 people."

One remembers the futile premonitory cry of Chief Hughes, at Silas H. Strawn's town meeting, "Give me three thousand more policemen."

As Lingle's world was but a fraction of Chicago's industrial, financial and cultural totality, so Lingle, in the larger editorial aspect of the Tribune, was inconsequential. His obscurity was such that Colonel Robert R. McCormick, editor and publisher, was unaware of his identity. A Tribune man had been killed and he was putting the vast resources of the Tribune into action not only to solve the murder, but to expose to public view that pyramid of crime and its hookup mentioned by Dean Mathews. Lingle, however, he did not know. He mistook him for another reporter, with whom he had had contact. Nearly 4,000 persons are employed on the Tribune.

LINGLE'S SLAYER?

NINE witnesses swore that they saw Leo ("Buster")
Brothers run through the crowd and disappear after the shooting. No one saw the
shot fired.

THE CAPONE VILLA

Down in sunny Florida far from the rat-tat-tat of gangland guns
lies the million dollar estate of the king of racketeers.

AL CAPONE

Lingle, his quizzical grin and his three-for-a-half cigar. They might be dropping in on a municipal, circuit or superior court judge, in chambers; or visiting at the home of Joy Morton, the capitalist, or at the country estate of Arthur Cutten, the millionaire broker; or in the private office of the commissioner of police, whose race-track pass Lingle used and whose official car he sometimes drove—the greeting there would be, "Hello, Jake," and, "Hello, Bill." They might be chinning with Governor Louis L. Emmerson; they might be attending a gangster funeral; they might be sauntering through the city hall, or calling on State's Attorney John A. Swanson; they might be in conference with a hood, hard by the cigar store on that corner of the Rialto known as Racketeers' Roost; they might be just standing and looking at a good 4-11 fire; they might be talking turkey with an applicant for a privilege concession, as with John J. McLaughlin, former State senator, who wanted to open a gambling place at 606 West Madison Street—Capone territory. Did open it. The police raided it. He protested to Commissioner Russell. He said State's Attorney Swanson had granted him permission to open it. His next action strikingly illustrates the unique status of the $65 a week reporter. He telephoned to Lingle; appealed to him as to an arbiter, judging from the conversation. He repeated to Lingle that Swanson had granted him permission to open.

"I don't believe it," replied Lingle, "but if it is true, you get Swanson to write a letter to Russell notifying him it is all right for you to run."

This conversation, mind you, reader, is the record.

"Do you think Swanson's crazy?" asked McLaughlin. "He wouldn't write such a letter."

"Well," ruled Lingle, "Russell can't let you run then; that's final."

Swanson denied he had ever granted McLaughlin permission to open. McLaughlin was not involved in the Lingle killing. He was questioned and released. But the incident is revealing. It brings out in bolder relief the apex of the pyramid. The Tribune, by the way, in March of 1928, had listed 215 gambling houses in Chicago with an estimated daily business of $2,500,-000.

Lingle as arbiter or dictator, unofficial chief of police or whatever the rôle he played in that twilight zone between crime and respectability, appears to have been at his best in the headquarters on the twenty-seventh floor of the Stevens Hotel, 720 South Michigan Avenue, fourteen blocks north of the present Capone G.H.Q. at the Lexington Hotel, 2135 South Michigan Avenue. The picture of him there I can only present through another's eyes—those of John T. Rogers, staff correspondent of the St. Louis Post-Dispatch. I quote from one of a series of articles Mr. Rogers wrote for his newspaper:

It was not Lingle's career as a reporter on which the searchlight of investigation has been focused, for his newspaper achievements could hardly be called a career. He was only a leg man (a reporter who does not write) on a salary of $65 a week in an institution that boasts the highest paid men in the world.

It was his life of ease, enjoyment and plenty, and the power he wielded in police affairs, that has aroused the curiosity not only of the new police commissioner, but of the Tribune itself, and turned the inquiry for the moment on the man and the mysterious sources of the large sums of money that passed with regularity through his bank account.

If Lingle had any legitimate income beyond his $65 a week as a reporter it has not been discovered. There is no record of an inheritance to explain his affluence. But it is known that he received from unknown sources payments by the week that would aggregate possibly $40,000 a year. Most of this he seems to have disbursed as mysteriously as he received it, but no record of the beneficiaries has been found, or if it has it is being suppressed.

This $65 a week reporter lived at one of the best hotels in Chicago. Although employed by a morning paper, which usually requires the services of a routine man in the afternoon, Lingle spent nearly all his afternoons at race tracks and some of his winters at Miami or on the Gulf Coast.

A day with Lingle is hardly the day of the average police reporter in any city.

To begin with, police reporters, especially veterans like Lingle—he was 38 years old and had been with the Tribune 18 years—live modestly. Not so Lingle. His life was that of a gentleman of leisure. At 10: 30 or 11 o'clock he rose and breakfasted, after which he would take the air along Michigan boulevard or chat with friends in the hotel lounge. The early afternoon would find him during the season, off for the races in his chauffeur driven automobile, to make his play from the clubhouse.

But duty called after the races, and he would be driven to the Tribune Tower. Sauntering into the city room, he would take his envelope of assignments, if any, or inquire what was doing. If there was nothing special for his attention he would be off.

Then to dinner at his hotel, usually with a certain police

captain; a stroll about town; to the theater or a speakeasy and then to bed.

There he was not disturbed unless for weighty matters. The hotel management saw to that, for Lingle was on the "private register." His room was No. 2706, and you could not call it, unless your name had been designated by Lingle as a favored one. He had lived there alone for six months prior to the day he was murdered.

The writer inquired of an assistant manager of the hotel what was meant by "private register."

"That is for persons who do not wish to be disturbed by telephone or otherwise except on important matters," he explained. "I cannot tell you that Mr. Lingle was on the private register. We have been instructed to refer all queries concerning Mr. Lingle to the house officer."

That dignitary was summoned.

"Sure, he was on the private register," the house officer said. "How could he get any sleep if he wasn't? His telephone would be going all night. He would get in around 2 or 3 and wanted rest."

"Who would be telephoning him at that hour?" the writer inquired. This question seemed to amaze the house officer.

"Why!" he exclaimed, "policemen calling up to have Jake get them transferred or promoted, or politicians wanting the 'fix' put in for somebody. Jake could do it. He had a lot of power. I've known him twenty years. He was up there among the big boys and had a lot of responsibilities. A big man like that needs rest."

The load he carried proved too heavy at times. The naïve and juvenile in him overmastered the crafty and secretive. He had to unburden himself. At least, that is the only explanation I can imagine for the admission of his activity in the beer racket quoted in the beginning of this chapter. I learned of it a few days after his death. Lingle was motoring in the early morning, after the home edition had gone to press. The streets were deserted, or as nearly so as they ever are. The city slept. Only here and there, those skyscrapers, whose names Lingle knew by heart, winked at the starry sky—yellow squares of light, showing the scrubwomen were at their tasks. Perhaps the brooding hush of the hour and the tranquillity influenced him. Without preliminary he ended a reflective silence:

"You know I fixed the price of beer in this town."

That was all. He closed up.

He could have fixed the price of beer for but one man—Capone. The Capone monopoly controlled the traffic in that commodity as it controlled vice and gambling. The price was $55 a barrel, although in the Loop it had been advanced to $60, thereby exciting bitter, if cautious, mutterings, amongst the prudent speakeasy proprietors.

The reasonable assumption is that Lingle's multifarious activities included the post of liaison man for Capone, as well as privilege concessionaire. He seems, besides, to have been a sort of unofficial mayor of the Loop, or the first police district, the richest booze and gambling territory in Chicago.

As one may infer from half revealed facts something of the nature of the Lingle-Capone business relationship, so with the personal relationship. It obviously transcended that of reporter and client. The diamond studded belt buckle indicates that. Lingle must have known that acceptance of such a gift constituted a violation of the ethics and a breach of trust with his newspaper, for the record is that he evaded direct

285

answering of questions as to its source. Capone and Lingle seem almost to provide Volstead's perfect *folie-à-deux*.

Lingle had entrée at all times with Capone, whether at the Palm Island, Florida, estate, or in Chicago. In December of 1927, when Capone was traveling the country in quest of a city to allow him shelter, and when Los Angeles' chief of police had given him his famous bum's rush, Capone boarded a train for Chicago —rather for Joliet, a suburb 40 miles west. Lingle was the only reporter Capone would have around him. He rode in Capone's compartment, whilst other reporters cooled their heels in the train vestibule.

An incident, once unremarked, now assumes peculiar meaning. Lingle fell down on his greatest Capone assignment. He had been sent to Philadelphia in March of 1930 to establish contact with Capone when Capone should be released from Eastern penitentiary—to interview—possibly to accompany—General Al the Scarface on his Return from Elba. The press of the nation had mobilized its correspondents at the gates of Eastern penitentiary. Lingle missed Capone, he reported to his office, and gave out that he was, "sore; through with him."

Capone, rid of the newshounds, kept his peripatetic whereabouts secret for four days, until he popped up in Chicago.

The anti-climax of this incident came four months later—after Lingle's death. Henry T. Brundidge, staff correspondent of the St. Louis Star, interviewed Capone at his Palm Island home. Quoting from the interview:

Then the writer, said, "Was Jake your friend?"

"Yes, up to the very day he died."

"Did you have a row with him?"

"Absolutely not."

"If you did not have a row with Lingle, why did you refuse to see him upon your release from the workhouse in Philadelphia?"

"Who said I didn't see him?"

"The Chicago newspapers, the files of which, including his own, the Tribune, set forth the facts."

"Well—if Jake failed to say I saw him—then I didn't see him."

Capone in that interview was also quoted by Mr. Brundidge as saying, "The Chicago police know who killed Lingle." That was July 18, 1930. I doubt if the police knew—then. But I venture the opinion as I write these lines, in mid-August, that Capone now knows who killed his friend. And Capone's loyalty is such that I should not be surprised, if and when the history of the case is compiled, to read that the agencies working on it had received aid from an unexpected quarter; that Capone had aligned himself on the side of the law. And again, maybe I'm wrong.

"Policemen calling up to have Jake get them transferred or promoted, or politicians wanting the fix put in," the Stevens Hotel house officer had said. Investigators checking outgoing telephone calls from Lingle's suite discovered, it was published in the press, that they were mainly to officials in the Federal building, county building and city hall.

Lingle as a possible tieup between the underworld and the world of politics, interested Attorney Donald

R. Richberg, author, and student of political economy. Speaking at the City Club, he said:

"The close relationship between Jake Lingle and the police department has been published in the Chicago papers. Out of town newspapers describe Lingle even more bluntly as having been, 'the unofficial chief of police.' But Lingle was also strangely intimate with Al Capone, our most notorious gangster.

"Surely, all Chicago knows that Samuel A. Ettelson, Mr. Insull's political lawyer, who is corporation counsel for Chicago, is also chief operator of the city government. Thompson is only a figurehead. Are we to believe that there existed an unofficial chief of police associating with the most vicious gang in Chicago, without the knowledge of Mr. Ettelson—who is neither deaf nor blind, but on the contrary has a reputation for knowing everything worth knowing about city hall affairs?"

Mr. Ettelson was silent.

Whether or not Lingle, somebody had to function as the tieup with the administration, and as Capone liaison man; somebody had to let the privileges. The system couldn't operate otherwise. Its scope is too vast; its revenues too enormous.

"Federal officials," reported the Tribune, five days after Lingle's death, "estimate that there are 10,000 speakeasies in Chicago, which buy six barrels of beer at $55 a barrel each week. This would mean a weekly revenue for the gangs of $3,500,000. In addition to this, the speakeasies buy approximately two cases of booze a week at $90 a case, bringing in $1,800,000 more a week for the gangs. The beer costs about $4 a barrel to make, and the booze about $20 a case."

The Chicago Daily News put the number of speak-easies at 6,000 and the number of handbooks—for horse-race betting—at 2,000—and the total revenue, along with that from vice and rackets, at $6,260,000 a week. Elsewhere, I have estimated the number of speakeasies in Chicago at 20,000. The disparity lies in the fact that the newspapers have not listed the drug stores and cigar stores peddling gin and Bourbon, and the beer flats. These I included under the general heading of speakeasies.

Of the more than 500 gangster slayings in Chicago since the beginning of the Volstead bootleg war in 1923, none roused the public and the press like that of Lingle. It centered world-wide attention on Chicago. Only two others have so dramatized organized crime and its hookups. The one is that of Assistant State's Attorney William H. McSwiggin in April of 1926, and the other that of Gerald E. Buckley in Detroit, July 23d of 1930. Buckley, announcer for radio station WMBC, and who played a leading part in the election recalling Mayor Charles Bowles, was shot down a few hours after he had announced the result of the election.

In Chicago, the old question, never answered, "Who killed McSwiggin?" was supplanted by, "Who killed Lingle and why?" None was more determined to get at the answer than Colonel Robert R. McCormick. He took command of the local room and within four hours had offered a reward of $25,000. I shall not forget a Sunday afternoon when he summoned the members of the entire news staff, and talked for 45 minutes. I feel I am not at liberty to discuss what he said. He minced no words. When he had finished we knew what he meant. We knew the search for Lingle's slayers never would abate. We knew that the investigation of the Lingle case would explore all ramifications, wherever they might lead, and pitilessly reveal them. This meeting was but one of the incidents back of the scenes, back of the Front Page, as someone described it, of which the public was unaware. I believe Colonel McCormick unhesitatingly would spend a million dollars to solve the Lingle case and another million to expose and rid Chicago of the conditions underlying it.

I have said Lingle was terrific drama. The fact that he was a nonentity in the larger editorial aspect of the Tribune intensifies him as such. He had never had a byline in his newspaper. His name was unknown to its readers in Chicagoland and the five Middle West states in which it circulates. He was, of course, unknown to his office associates in the rôle posthumously revealed. With his death, he dominated Page One news and topped the editorial columns. He caused the ouster of a police commissioner and a chief of detectives. Two days after his murder, the Tribune's leading editorial, entitled The Challenge, read in part:

Alfred J. Lingle, a reporter for the Tribune, was murdered Monday afternoon in the Illinois Central subway at Randolph street and Michigan avenue. He was passing through to take a train. Many people were in the passageway. Thousands were nearby. The murderer escaped in the crowds. The indications are that he had accomplices, one probably close at hand, and several others on the scene.

The meaning of this murder is plain. It was committed in reprisal and in attempt at intimidation. Mr. Lingle was a police reporter and an exceptionally well informed one. His personal friendships included the highest police officials and the contacts of his work had made him familiar to most of the big and little fellows of gangland. What made him valuable to his newspaper marked him as dangerous to the killers.

It was very foolish ever to think that assassination would be confined to the gangs which have fought each other for the profits of crime in Chicago. The immunity from punishment after gang murders would be assumed to cover the committing of others. Citizens who interfered with the criminals were no better protected than the gangmen who fought each other for the revenue from liquor selling, coercion of labor and trade, brothel house keeping and gambling.

There have been eleven gang murders in ten days. That has become the accepted course of crime in its natural stride, but to the list of Colosimo, O'Banion, the Gennas, Murphy, Weiss, Lombardo, Esposito, the seven who were killed in the St. Valentine's day massacre, the name is added of a man whose business was to expose the work of the killers.

The Tribune accepts this challenge. It is war. There will be casualties, but that is to be expected, it being war. The Tribune has the support of all the other Chicago newspapers. . . . The challenge of crime to the community must be accepted. It has been given with bravado. It is accepted, and we'll see what the consequences are to be. Justice will make a fight of it or it will abdicate.

June 18th, the Tribune carried an editorial, The Lingle Investigation Goes On. It stated in part that while the Tribune did "not know why its reporter was killed," it was engaged in finding out, "and expects to be successful. It may take time; the quicker, the better, but this enlistment is for duration. It may require

long, patient efforts, but the Tribune is prepared for
that, and hopes that some lasting results will be obtained which will stamp justice on the face of the
crime."

At the masthead of its editorial page, the Tribune,
had long had a "platform for Chicagoland," consisting
of five planks. June 20, it added a sixth, End the Reign
of Gangdom.

"Little need be added," it stated in a supplemental
editorial, "by way of explanation. The killers, the
racketeers who exact tribute from business men and
union labor, the politicians who use and shield the
racketeers, the policemen and judges who have been
prostituted by the politicians, all must go."

The investigation went on, and June 30th, in a column and a half editorial entitled, The Lingle Murder,
the Tribune said, in part:

When Alfred Lingle was murdered the motive seemed to be
apparent. He was a Tribune police reporter and when, in the
Illinois Central subway at Randolph Street, he was shot, his
newspaper saw no other explanation than that his killers either
thought he was close to information dangerous to them or intended the murder as notice given the newspapers that crime
was ruler in Chicago. It could be both, a murder to prevent
a disclosure and to give warning against attempts at others.

It had been expected that in due time the reprisals which
have killed gangster after gangster in the city would be attempted against any other persons or agencies which under-
took to interfere with the incredibly profitable criminality. No
one had been punished for any of these murders. They have
been bizarre beyond belief, and, being undetected, have been
assumed, not the least by their perpetrators, to be undetectable
—at least not to be punishable.

AL CAPONE

When, then, Lingle was shot by an assassin the Tribune assumed that the criminals had taken the next logical step and were beginning their attack upon newspaper exposure. The Herald and Examiner and the Chicago Evening Post joined the Tribune in offering rewards for evidence which would lead to conviction of the murderers. The newspaper publishers met and made a common cause against the new tactics of gangland. The preliminary investigation has modified some of the first assumptions, although it has not given the situation a different essence.

Alfred Lingle now takes a different character, one in which he was unknown to the management of the Tribune when he was alive. He is dead and cannot defend himself, but many facts now revealed must be accepted as eloquent against him. He was not, and he could not have been, a great reporter. His ability did not contain these possibilities. He did not write stories, but he could get information in police circles. He was not and he could not be influential in the acts of his newspaper, but he could be useful and honest, and that is what the Tribune management took him to be. His salary was commensurate with his work. The reasonable appearance against Lingle now is that he was accepted in the world of politics and crime for something undreamed of in his office, and that he used this in undertakings which made him money and brought him to his death. . . .

There are weak men on other newspapers and in other professions, in positions of trust and responsibility greater than that of Alfred Lingle, The Tribune, although naturally disturbed by the discovery that this reporter was engaged in practices contrary to the code of its honest reporters and abhorred by the policy of the newspaper, does not find that the main objectives of the inquiry have been much altered. The crime and the criminals remain, and they are the concern of the Tribune as they are of the decent elements in Chicago. . . .

If the Tribune was concerned when it thought that an attack had been made upon it because it was inimical to crime, it is doubly concerned if it be the fact that crime had made a connection in its own office. Some time ago a criminal use was made of a Tribune want ad. A Negro by means of it raped a girl nurse in a north shore household and escaped. His crime was atrocious and his escape might have been successful, but the Tribune regarded it as one which could not go unpunished. It therefore put its own men on the work and at the end of five months the criminal was taken, convicted and sent to the penitentiary. He might have remained immune if the ordinary processes of law had been used, because they are not equipped for these particular efforts. . . . The police would have hunted for this rapist until other and newer criminals required their efforts. Thereafter he would have been only a man wanted. To particular efforts he was a man wanted until he was had.

The Tribune trusts that it will be the same with the murderers of Alfred Lingle in the search in which it is engaged. That he is not a soldier dead in the discharge of duty is unfortunate considering that he is dead. It is of no consequence to an inquiry determined to discover why he was killed, by whom killed and with what attendant circumstances. Tribune readers may be assured that their newspaper has no intention of concealing the least fact of this murder and its consequences and meanings. The purpose is to catch the murderers. . . .

The murder of this reporter, even for racketeering reasons, as the evidence indicates it may have been, made a breach in the wall which criminality has so long maintained about its operations here. Some time, some where, there will be a hole found or made and the Lingle murder may prove to be it. The Tribune will work at its case upon this presumption and with this hope. It has gone into the cause in this fashion and its notice to gangland is that it is in for duration. Kismet.

The investigation by June 30th had uncovered some of Lingle's financial transactions—as many as were conducted through one bank, the Lake Shore Trust and Savings—and all of his stock market transactions. The bank account inquiry included the period from January 1, 1928, to June 9, 1930, the day of his death. It showed that in 1928, Lingle had deposited $26,500; in 1929, $25,100; in the six months of 1930, $12,300. That the bank account was an incomplete record was indicated to the investigators in the matter of the Long Beach, Indiana, summer home. The bank checks showed he had paid only $6,000 toward the purchase price, whereas he actually had paid $16,000. The additional $10,000 was said to have been paid in cash.

"Where he obtained the funds, with which to make these payments," the official report read; "except insofar as they are covered by the checks above referred to, we have thus far been unable to ascertain.

"We have heard from sources fairly reliable that the night before Lingle was murdered he had as much as $9,000 in cash in his possession. The source of this also remains a mystery at the present time."

Elsewhere:

"At the time of the murder, when the coroner made a search of the body, only $65 in money was found. But it later developed that a reporter on the Tribune had taken $1,400 in bills of $100 denomination from one of Lingle's pockets. This sum was turned over to Mrs. Lingle by a representative of the Tribune."

The investigators found evidence that Lingle in March of 1930 had paid insurance premiums on jewelry valued at $12,000, but they were unable to locate it.

Evidently for betting purposes, Lingle drew out in

1928 on race-track checks, $8,000, and on dog-track checks, $2,300; in 1929, $5,300 race track and $200 dog track; in the six months of 1930, $1,500 race track, and $100 dog track. In March of 1929 he made a $2,000 initial payment on his Lincoln car.

In his stock market speculations, Lingle operated through five accounts. In one of these, his partner was Police Commissioner Russell. It was started in November of 1928 with a $20,000 deposit. The official report read:

"This account appears to have been carried anonymously on the broker's books as Number 49 Account. However, our information is that it was an account in which equal interests were shared by Lingle and William F. Russell, who was then commissioner of police. . . . We have advised with experts, and they give us the date of September 20, 1929, as the peak date (preceding the stock market crash in October of 1929) as far as paper profits were concerned. . . .

"Using that date the . . . account showed a paper profit of $23,696.84, if it had been closed out on that date. After the stock market crash, these stocks went down and on June 26, 1930 (when the official report was written), the condition of this account showed a loss of $50,850.09."

Lingle's total paper profits, in all five accounts, at the peak date, September 20, 1929, were $85,000. With the crash they vanished and he incurred a loss of $75,000. Russell's loss was variously reported as $50,000, $100,000 and $250,000.

"As to the source of the moneys put up by Lingle in these stock accounts, and deposited by him in his bank account," the report reads, "we have thus far been able to come to no conclusion except as indicated in the accounts."

The investigation showed Lingle had borrowed extensively from gamblers, politicians and others. One loan, of $2,000, was from James V. (Jimmy) Mondi, once a Mont Tennes handbook man, who was with Capone in Cicero and is now a Capone Loop gambling operator.

"Lingle," the report read, "has not yet paid Mondi."

One loan, of $5,000, was from Alderman Berthold A. Cronson, nephew of Corporation Counsel Samuel A. Ettelson, and "he states," the report read, "that the loan was a pure friendship proposition. . . ." The loan was made in August of 1929 and was not repaid.

The investigators were informed that Corporation Counsel Ettelson had let Lingle have $5,000. "Mr. Ettelson," the report read, "could not be reached personally, but persons apparently authorized to speak for him have denied to us that he ever loaned Lingle anything any time, but that he had a custom of giving Lingle some small remembrance at Christmas time, like a box of cigars. . . ."

One loan of $2,500 was from Major Carlos Ames, president of the civil service commission. "Major Ames states," the report read, "that this loan was a purely personal affair, and that Lingle's excuse for borrowing from him was that he was being pressed because of market losses and needed it to cover transactions upon the market."

One loan of $300 was from Police Lieutenant Thomas McFarland. "Lieutenant McFarland insists," the report read, "this loan was a purely personal affair, he having been a close personal friend of Lingle's for many years."

A check for $500, payable to cash, drawn by Lingle, bore the endorsement of Police Captain Daniel Gilbert, in command of the first district. "Captain Gilbert states," the report read, "that during a conversation with another friend and Lingle, who were complaining of the market conditions, he, Gilbert mentioned he was unable to pay an insurance premium then due, and that Lingle insisted upon loaning him the $500. Gilbert used it to pay the insurance."

Rumor had it that Sam Hare, roadhouse and gambling joint owner, had loaned Lingle $20,000. Hare denied it.

The murder investigation was conducted with a minimum of publicity, clues and new avenues of information being withheld. The policy was the reverse of that previously employed in gangster killings in Chicago, and the purpose was to develop evidence that would produce convictions. The Lingle case was a fight to the finish, between justice and organized crime.

The odds overwhelmingly favored organized crime. In Cook County since 1923 there had been more than 500 gangster killings, with not a single conviction. I doubt if in all its long career the Tribune had ever tackled an undertaking of such magnitude as when it enlisted with the state's attorney's office to send Lingle's murderer or murderers to the electric chair. The wondering looker-on could be pardoned an involuntary gasp. David had challenged Goliath.

While officially no announcement was forthcoming,

there were developments that high-lighted basic elements of the investigation and emphasized its trend. Two theories were widely discussed. Both cast Lingle in the rôle of privilege concessionaire. Significantly enough both pointed to Capone's enemies—the Moran gang and the Aiellos, who had affiliated and were referred to as the North Side Mob. As by-products of these theories the investigators studied rumors that certain members of the Morans, notably Ted Newberry and Frank Foster, had deserted to set up in business for themselves, under the all-mighty Capone ægis.

The first theory, predicated on the maze of reports emanating from the underworld following Lingle's death, was that he had been paid $50,000 to put the fix in for an indoor dog track on the west side; that he had failed, but had kept the money. The second, and which was considered more plausible in the light of subsequent happenings, was that he had demanded a fifty per cent rakeoff from the ritzy Sheridan Wave Tournament Club at 621 Waveland Avenue, on the near north side, and that when the management refused to comply he sicked the police on the place. Among those sought or questioned in the investigation were:

Jack Zuta, vice monger, general utility racketeer, and brains of the North Side Mob, whom the reader has met before in the pages of this book; Zuta was believed to have had knowledge of the plot to kill Lingle, if not to have planned it.

Frank Foster, an original O'Banionite, brother of John Citro, who once was an intimate of Sam Samoots

Amatuna; indictment for murder voted against him in 1924, but stricken off; the revolver with which Lingle was killed, a snub barreled .38 Colt, known as a belly gun, was traced to Foster. It was one of a dozen he had bought from Peter Von Frantzius, sporting goods dealer, at 608 Diversey Parkway. Von Frantzius is the same who sold machine guns used in the Moran gang massacre. Foster, captured in Los Angeles July 1st, was indicted for complicity in the murder; extradited to Chicago, and as this is written is awaiting trial.

Ted Newberry, Moran whiskey peddler, said to have been with Foster when Foster bought the dozen revolvers. Newberry was with Moran and Willie Marks, both of whom by the way have been strangely missing for weeks, when on February 14, 1929, the three nearly walked into the North Clark Street garage to make the massacre a ten- instead of a seven-man affair.

James Red Forsyth, described in reports as the actual killer; an associate of Simon J. Gorman, former labor official and owner of a trucking company, and of Frank Noonan, both of whom also are sought; Forsyth, arrested once in a police raid on the Loop headquarters of the Morans, was released when he was discovered to be on the payroll of Corporation Counsel Samuel A. Ettelson.

Grover C. Dullard, attaché of the Sheridan Wave, once chauffeur and bodyguard for Terry Druggan. Dullard, who lived in Lingle's old neighborhood, had known him since boyhood.

Joey Josephs, professional gambler, and Julian Potatoes Kaufman, owners, along with Moran, of the Sheridan Wave. Kaufman, son of a wealthy commission merchant, is listed in the Who's Who of Organized Crime in Chicago, as having been "associated with important gangsters, notably those of the old O'Banion gang, as a receiver of stolen property, and has been mentioned frequently after murders charged to O'Banion gangsters." Lingle had known Kaufman for at least six years.

Fred Burke, America's most wanted man, and its most dangerous criminal; for whose apprehension rewards totaling $75,000 have been posted in Kentucky, Indiana and Wisconsin for bank robberies and by the United States Government for a national bank robbery, wanted in Ohio for the murder of a policeman; in Michigan for the same crime; in St. Joe, of the latter state, December 14, 1929, he shot down Patrolman Charles Skelly in cold blood, when Skelly sought to adjust a traffic argument with him; Burke, formerly of Egan's Rats, St. Louis, is a professional killer, whose services are for hire to the highest bidder; notorious for his disguises; in the Moran gang massacre he wore a policeman's uniform; in the Lingle killing he posed as a priest, it is believed.

Of these, Zuta, a Jew, was the first questioned. The vice monger was a softie. He lacked the stamina to withstand the ordeal of a session with the police. He always sang. Gangland had him pegged as yellow and a squawker. But he was necessary. He had a shrewder mind than the run of the mill criminals.

Held for 24 hours at the detective bureau, 1121 South State Street, Zuta was released on bond at 10:25 o'clock Tuesday night, July 1st. In Los Angeles the

morning of the same day, Frank Foster had been arrested. Either the coincidence or his conscience—maybe
both—terrorized Zuta. Lieutenant George Barker of
the bureau, off duty, was leaving for his home. Zuta
accosted him in the lobby:

"Lieutenant, I'll be killed if I go through the Loop.
When you arrested me, you took me from a place of
safety and you ought to return me to a place of safety."

Barker replied half jestingly:

"Run along."

Zuta's teeth were chattering:

"Lieutenant, I got a woman with me. You'd do that
much for a woman, wouldn't you?"

"All right," said Barker. "You're entitled to safe
conduct. Climb in."

In they climbed into Barker's own car, a Pontiac
sedan. Besides the woman, a Miss Leona Bernstein,
Zuta had two male companions, Solly Vision and Albert Bratz. Vision sat with Barker in the front seat.
Zuta, between Bratz and the Bernstein woman, in the
rear.

The bureau is six blocks south of Van Buren Street,
which is the southern boundary of the Loop. From
Van Buren to Lake Street is seven blocks. Barker's
objective was Lake Street, where Zuta and his party
were to board an elevated train. Barker thus had 13
blocks to go—north in State Street. He drove slowly—
15 miles an hour. Entering the Loop at Van Buren
he was behind a surface car.

State Street, a White Way, since its $1,000,000 light-
ing system was installed, was bright as day, and
thronged with after talkie theater patrons, sauntering

groups of window shoppers, and motorists enjoying an evening spin. The Pontiac had passed Quincy, and was within two blocks of the World's Busiest Corner, Madison and State, when Zuta yelled:

"They're after us."

Solly Vision rolled over the back of the front seat and hugged the floor in the rear of the tonneau.

A blue sedan with two men in the rear seat had slipped up behind them. It swung to the right, to nose through traffic and get between them and the curb. As it accomplished the maneuver, one of the men stepped on the left running board, yanked a .45 caliber automatic from an armpit holster and emptied a 7-cartridge clip at the Pontiac. His fellow gunman opened fire through the left rear window, and the driver, gears shifted into neutral and engine idling, joined them.

Now Barker, 33 years old, youngest lieutenant on the force, was with the United States Marines in the world war. He was one of eight survivors of a company of 250 that fought at Château Thierry, Soissons and St. Mihiel. He was twice wounded. He has received 15 creditable mentions since becoming a policeman. Barker slapped back his emergency brake, and hopped out, his revolver going as he hopped. The occupants of the sedan had either reloaded or grabbed other guns. They were blazing away again. Barker traded shot for shot with them.

A northbound State Street surface car behind Barker was forced to stop because the Pontiac was in the car tracks. The motorman was Elbert Lusader, 38 years old, 7643 Berwyn Avenue, father of three children. As he stood on the glass enclosed front platform, fumbling with the controls and still wondering, perhaps, what it was all about, a .45 caliber bullet pierced his throat. He died 12 hours later. Olaf Svenste, 69 years old, 1519 North Avers Avenue, a night watchman, plodding to work, was wounded in the right arm. It was the wildest shooting in the Loop since the killing of Lombardo.

Waving his revolver at Barker, Policeman William Smith came galloping on the scene. He thought it was a gangster mêlée. He was set to shoot Barker, who was in civilian clothes, when Barker called to him he was a police officer and showed his star.

The gunmen apparently had exhausted their ammunition. They ceased fire and headed north in State Street. Barker, with Policeman Smith as a reinforcement, jumped in the Pontiac. Zuta and his party had ducked. They were nowhere to be seen, although the battle had not lasted more than a minute. Barker shifted gears and started after the sedan. As he did an astounding thing happened. A black curtain materialized before him, completely blocking his view—a gigantic black curtain stretching from side to side of State Street, and rising high as the cornices of the buildings. Gangland was using its newest device to baffle pursuit. The driver of the sedan had pressed a plunger near the accelerator and from the exhaust poured a smoke screen dense as any belched by United States naval destroyers. It is much used in bringing truckloads of booze in from Canada.

Barker wasn't deterred. The Pontiac snorted through it at 50 miles an hour. He sighted the sedan at Madison

Street. It turned east for a block to go north again in Wabash Avenue. Barker was 50 yards behind it and rapidly overhauling it, when his car abruptly stopped. He couldn't start it. He decided he was out of gas. He was, but he didn't learn the real reason until the next day, when examination showed a bullet had perforated the tank.

"If we can learn from Zuta who was shooting at him, we may have the solution of the Lingle murder," said Chief Investigator Pat Roche of the State's Attorney's office. It was the clearest indication of the trend of the investigation yet revealed.

Zuta had ducked; fled Chicago; gone in a hole. Roche didn't find him; neither did the police; gangland caught up with him a month later to the day—August 1st—in a summer resort dancehall on Upper Nemahbin, 25 miles west of Milwaukee. Zuta must have figured he was safely hidden. He was putting a nickel in the mechanical piano. A dozen couples were dancing.

Five men entered, single file. One carried a machine gun; one, a rifle; two, sawed-off shotguns; one, a pistol. Zuta's back was toward them. He was still fiddling with the nickel. He just had time to turn, when all five opened fire, putting 16 slugs and bullets into him.

What did Zuta know? Too much.

Death couldn't silence this squawker. His tongue wagged from the grave; wagged of things gangland's chieftains and the politicians would have paid a fancy price to suppress; quite the best job of squawking he had ever done. Zuta, the Jew, was scrupulous in his bookkeeping and punctilious as to personal data. He hoarded his memoranda. He was a Shylock Pepys. The memoranda were discovered by investigators in four Loop safety deposit boxes. Included were balance sheets, described as revealing "for the first time in the history of gangdom the operations of a mob."

Each sheet, presumably, represented one week's transactions of the Zuta-Moran-Aiellos in gambling and bootlegging. The average weekly receipts were $429,000, from cafés and roadhouses, slot machines and the Fairview Kennel dog tracks—and yet the beggared Zuta and his mob, kicked around by the Capone monopoly, were but a Lazarus crew snatching at crumbs from the rich man's table.

Under disbursements was an item, "East Chicago, $3,500," believed to refer to East Chicago avenue police station, whose district comprises the Forty-second ward, in which Zuta operated many handbooks, brothels and beer flats.

Canceled checks, notes and various documents supplied evidence of the entente cordiale with city and county officialdom. The ledger showed payments of as high as $108,469 a week to one, M. K., believed to be Matt Kolb, ward heeler and gambling operative, according to the investigators. He apparently distributed the protection bribes to police and city and county officials. These aggregated never less than $100,000 a month. The Zuta agenda showed he had divided the county into districts for slot machine privileges and booze, alky and beer sales, and had listed the political leaders of each district.

Some of those revealed as receiving checks from Zuta or giving notes to him, with the amounts, were:

Judge Joseph W. Schulman of the Municipal court, $5,000.

Emmanuel Eller, former judge of the Municipal, Superior and Criminal courts, son of Morris Eller, boss of the Bloody Twentieth ward, $250.

Nate De Lue, assistant business manager of the Board of Education, $150.

P. W. Rothenberg, former chief deputy coroner of Cook County, Republican committeeman of the Twenty-fourth ward, $500.

Attorney Louis I. Fisher, brother of Judge Harry M. Fisher of the Circuit court, $600.

Illinois State Senator Harry W. Starr, former assistant to Corporation Counsel Samuel A. Ettelson, $400. He said the checks were in payment of legal services.

Former Illinois State Senator George Van Lent, $600.

There was a check for $500 payable to the Regular Republican Club of Cook county. It was signed by Zuta and bore the rubber stamp endorsement of Charles V. Barrett, mayoralty aspirant, member of the Cook County board of review, and former treasurer of the Republican county central committee.

There was a card issued in 1927 by former Sheriff Charles E. Graydon of Cook County, reading, "the bearer, J. Zuta, is extended the courtesies of all departments." Another souvenir was, "Membership Card No. 772—Jack Zuta—William Hale Thompson Republican Club—America First—Farm Relief—Inland Waterways—Flood Control. Homer K. Galpin, chairman." Galpin then was chairman of the Republican county central committee.

AL CAPONE

There was a letter from Chief of Police William O. Freeman of Evanston, churchly suburb of 65,000 souls, adjoining Chicago on the north, and whose foremost citizen is Charles G. Dawes, United States ambassador to Great Britain. The letter, handwritten, in pen and ink, was on the official stationery of the Evanston police department. It read:

"Dear Jack: I am temporarily in need of four C's ($400) for a couple of months. Can you let me have it? The bearer does not know what it is, so put it in envelope, and seal it, and address it to me. Your Old Pal, Bill Freeman. P.S. Will let you know the night of the party, so be sure and come."

Freeman, a former member of the Chicago police department, acknowledged the handwriting. He enjoyed the warm friendship of Mr. Dawes and was expecting through his influence to be appointed chief of police of the Chicago World's Fair in 1933.

No plaguy tidbit was overlooked by this Shylock Pepys. Here were two picture postcards from the genial Alderman George M. Maypole. They had been mailed from Hot Springs, Arkansas, where the Maypoles were vacationing in February of 1926, and were addressed to "Mr. Jack Zuta." One, on the bridle path, bore a photograph of the alderman, his wife and daughter, and read, "Regards from the Maypoles." Another read, "I hope when this reaches you, you will be feeling much better."

Ghosts of gangland promenaded. Here was the card of

AL CAPONE

Frank Yale

Yale
Cigar M'f'g Co., Inc.

Factory
6309–11 New Utrecht Ave.
Brooklyn, N. Y.
Tel. Utrecht 10281.

That same Francesco Yale, long since slain. Here was a check for $500 to Camille Lombardo, widow of Antonio Lombardo, Capone head of the Unione Sicilione; another for $560 to Anthony Mops Volpe; yeoman of the Capone bodyguard in 1927 and for whom Diamond Joe Esposito had obtained a special deputy sheriff's badge. And, too, there was a check for $1,000 to Diamond Joe himself, former Republican committeeman of the Twenty-fifth ward, political lieutenant of Deneen, the dry United States senator.

No such insight had ever before been vouchsafed into the labyrinth of gangland. Louis La Cava, who in 1924 had negotiated for the Capone-Torrio invasion of Cicero, had lost favor with the Scarface and been exiled. In June of 1927, from his hideout in New York City, he was writing to Zuta to organize against Capone. If "Dear Jack," would only consent, "I'd help you organize a strong business organization capable of coping with theirs in Cicero. You know you have lots of virgin territory on the north side limits border line, and they are going to try and prevent me from lining up with you and thereby keep starving me out, until I go back to them, begging for mercy." And in another letter, "I have heard the Big Boy (Capone, apparently) is stopping my brothers from making a living. . . ."

One of the four safety deposit boxes yielded a suppressed police document—the confession of a 19-year-old girl that she had been hired as a decoy to lure Zuta to a spot where he could be kidnaped and held for $50,000 ransom. She named Mops Volpe and Joe Genaro. The confession was dated June 16, 1927. It was not only suppressed but was delivered into Zuta's keeping, supposedly by friendly police officials.

As voluminous as were these revelations, they represented but a small part of the evidence amassed by the relentless Roche, chief investigator of the state's attorney's office. That which had a direct bearing on the Lingle case was withheld from the public. That which was revealed, however, was sufficient to elicit the observation from Roche:

"A lot of men will be leaving town."

McCutcheon, dean of cartoonists, hailed the evidence as, "At Last a Breach In the Walls," and the Tribune editorialized:

. . . Progress has been made in solving the murder of Al Lingle, the Tribune reporter. Foster has been indicted for the murder. The business records of Jack Zuta, the murdered racketeer, have been located, and the prosecuting authorities are examining them in detail . . . they provide evidence for the first time of the relations of gangdom with politics and the police. This is a tremendous advance over anything that has been accomplished hitherto in any American city toward the suppression of the universal threat to society. The Zuta journals may throw light on the Lingle murderers, and, more than that, they promise exposure and prosecution of gangsters and their allies who have hitherto enjoyed immunity. . . . Chicago is on the way to becoming the first great city in America to rid itself of gangster influence and gangster assassination. The energy and resourcefulness which uncovered the Zuta papers will follow through. The day of reckoning is measurably nearer.

Zuta was the second squawker to die in 1930, the other being Julius Rosenheim, professional stool pigeon for the police and a paid informant of the Chicago Daily News. He was killed February 1st. Leland H. Reese, the News' crime reporter, who was at the Washington Park track the day Lingle was killed and asked for a bodyguard, stated in a signed article that he had been informed by "a man who has reason to know," that Rosenheim had been killed by the Capone gang in an effort to frighten the News from its campaign to halt the Capone gang's beer selling activities in the Loop.

The State Street shooting and Zuta's subsequent assassination show the desperate lengths to which gangland will go when cornered, as it appears to have been at that juncture. Again, the authorities were hot on the trail of Fred Burke. Charles Bonner, a minor racketeer, in July of 1930, had discovered Burke's hideout, in northern Michigan, in a secluded cottage 40 miles north of Grand Rapids, and near the town of Newaygo and Hess' Lake. Anxious to get the $75,000 rewards, Bonner tipped off the police that Burke occasionally visited a pharmacy in Chicago at 501 West 79th Street. Bonner arranged with the police to trap Burke. Burke was expected to visit the pharmacy either Wednesday, July 9th, or Saturday, July 12th. Burke did not visit the pharmacy, but—

Soon after midnight of Wednesday, the 9th, two men walked into Bonner's home at 7353 Yale Avenue. He and Mrs. Bonner—she with her five months' old son, Bobbie, in her arms—were alone. Mrs. Bonner stepped out of the room, thinking they were to talk over some kind of business matters. She heard her husband say, "You've got me wrong on that, pal." Then shots. She rushed into the room. Bonner was dead. The two men were leisurely taking their departure. She described one of them as "a blond haired man, who was drunk and held his gun in his left hand." Significant words. The other she identified as Burke, referring to him as "that arch fiend."

Zuta's killing and that of Bonner somehow remind me of the comment of Edgar Wallace, the English playwright and author of crime stories:

"The big gang leaders who did not connive the murder will take action and the murderer will be 'put on the spot,' at the earliest opportunity, and with him the man or men who organized Lingle's murder. Gangland is making a last desperate effort to keep the hold which venal lawyers and politicians have secured for it."

That latter in turn reminds me of a remark by Capone:

"There is one thing worse than a crook, and that is a crooked man in a big political job. A man that pretends he is enforcing the law and is really taking 'dough' out of somebody breaking it—even a self respecting hood hasn't any use for that kind of fellow. He buys them like he would any other article necessary in his trade, but he hates them in his heart."

The spring and summer of 1930 had been comparatively uneventful. There had been no worthwhile coroner's inquests except that of John The Dingbat O'Berta, and the only other good shooting was that of Julius Rosenheim. The lull ended with a bang Saturday, May 31st. Peter Gnolfo of the defunct Gennas, now with the Aiellos, fell dead with 18 sawed-off shot-gun slugs in his body. It was charged to the Druggan-Lake outfit.

The Sabbath morn was ushered in with a triple slay-ing at Fox Lake, Illinois, a summer resort 50 miles northwest of Chicago. The dead were Sam Pellar, elec-tion terrorist of the Bloody Twentieth Ward, and who was with Hymie Weiss when Weiss was machine gunned; Michael Quirk, labor racketeer and bootleg-ger; and Joseph Bertsche, brother of Barney, gunman and safe-blower, who since his release from the Federal penitentiary at Atlanta, Georgia, had nested with the Frankie Lake and Terry Druggan crowd—Capone al-lies. The wounded were George Druggan, brother of Terry, and Mrs. Vivian Ponic McGinnis, wife of a Chicago attorney.

These five were drinking at a table on the glassed in porch of a small hotel on Piskatee Lake. Out of the night a hundred machine-gun bullets crashed through the windows, and the assassins drove off in their car. The Druggans, rumor had it, had been muscling in on Fox Lake beer selling, to the exclusion of breweries favored by the Morans and Aiellos.

Tuesday, June 3d, the body of Thomas Somnerio was found in an alley back of 831 West Harrison Street. His wrists were bound with wire. A welt around his neck indicated he had been garrotted, the wire being pulled tighter as his captors tried to make him sing. Reprisals by the Druggan-Lake crowd, said the police.

Then Saturday of that week in the drainage canal at Summit, on the southwest side of the city, a passing tugboat churned up the body of Eugene Red Mc-

Laughlin. His wrists were bound with telephone wire, and his body weighted with 75 pounds of angle iron. He had been shot twice through the head. McLaughlin, friendly with the Druggan-Lake crowd, had been accused of four murders, and twice identified by victims of diamond robberies. But he had never served time.

The body lay at the county morgue, unidentified, until the arrival of his brother, Robert McLaughlin, president of the Chicago Checker Cab Company. He had succeeded Joseph Wokral to the presidency. Wokral, shot in the head while seeking reëlection, on his death-bed had named Red McLaughlin as his slayer.

"He had been missing two weeks," said Robert McLaughlin. "A better kid never lived . . . I put up $20,000 reward for information leading to finding him, dead or alive, just among my friends . . . I don't know . . . I don't know . . . He was friendly with them—the west side outfit . . . the north side boys . . . the bunch on the south side. . . . Yes, he knew Al Capone . . . was friendly with him, too."

Lingle was much interested in this case; speculated quite a bit about it. He knew both Red McLaughlin and Robert well.

New Milford is an Illinois village 90 miles northwest of Chicago, in Winnebago County, near Rockford. Sunday night a man drove his car into the only garage, stumbled out of it, fell to the floor, said to the attendant, "Get a doctor."

He was Frank R. Thompson, the roustabout mystery man who had bought machine guns that had found their way to Fred Burke, and were used, the science of ballistics revealed, in the Moran gang massacre and the killing in Brooklyn of Frank Yale. Thompson, severely wounded, was removed to a hospital at Rockford. There he was visited by Sheriff Harry Baldwin of Winnebago County, who had known him for ten years. He tried to question Thompson.

"Listen, Harry," said Thompson. "I've seen everything, done everything, and got everything, and you're smart enough to know I won't talk. Go to Hell."

In the foregoing, the reader will note the enlarged scope of operations in the bootleg war. In the beginning, 1923, and for many years after, gangland in its shootings had confined itself solely to Chicago. In 1930 it had overrun the entire countryside of the central west; its battlegrounds and hideouts including the choicest sections of the playground states of Wisconsin and Michigan, and Illinois counties far removed from Chicago.

The morning of Monday, June 9th, dawned joyously for two winsome children—Alfred Lingle, Jr., six years old, and his sister, Dolores, five. Only their parents didn't call them by those names. They called them Buddy and Pansy. Trunks were packed; suitcases were waiting, in the home of their grandparents at 125 North Austin Boulevard. Tomorrow they would leave for the new summer home in the country, by the lake, that their father had bought for them.

Their father himself was in an expectant mood. He was going to Homewood, in the afternoon, for the race program at Washington Park, but today another event divided interest with the track. In the evening he would attend the dinner of 2,500 grain traders at the

Stevens Hotel, to celebrate the opening of Chicago's
new $22,000,000 Board of Trade, and the christening,
as it were, of a new member of Chicago's skyscraper
family. Attorney Silas H. Strawn was to speak. Jake's
friend, Arthur Cutten, would be there. He would sit
beside him.

Then there was still another event. It had been ad-
vertised with a flourish in a New York sports paper.
It concerned the butter and eggy Sheridan Wave
Tournament Club, and read:

"Joey Josephs is set to go in Chicago, beginning the
night of June 9."

The club had had an extraordinary history. It had
been the object of a court injunction, issued in June of
1928, and enjoining, "Michael Hughes, commissioner
of police of Chicago, his servants, agents and solicitors
from annoying, molesting or in any manner interfering
with the complainant in its lawful conduct of its members."

Here again we step into that twilight zone of Lingle unknown to his office. Fact becomes rumor, hear-
say. I shall quote from a résumé story published in the
Tribune of July 1, 1930:

Another theory advanced places the blame for the Lingle
murder in connection with a gambling resort at 621 Waveland
avenue, known as the Sheridan Wave club. As the story goes,
this place in the winter of 1928–29 was one of the most fashionable and prosperous gambling places in the city.

A lookout's most rigid inspection through a slot in the outside door preceded the players' admission. Once admitted the
guest was not permitted to purchase food or drink. If he wanted
a highball, it was served him free. If his tastes ran to cham-

pagne he got champagne. Liveried lackeys served trays of food.

The play ran high, many thousands of dollars being passed across its tables every night. It was generally known in gambling circles that the place was operated for the profit of the Moran gang.

With the massacre and disintegration of the Moran gang, the place was closed, but ever since that time, for a year and a half, according to reports, strenuous efforts have been made by Moran gangsters to obtain official permission to reopen.

Recent reports have drawn Lingle into the negotiations for the reopening of the gambling resort. The place had been in charge of Joey Josephs, a well-known gambler, and Julian Potatoes Kaufman. The latter has been known as a long time acquaintance or friend of Lingle, and is reported by the Chicago Daily News to have approached Lingle in the hope of obtaining permission from the police to relaunch the Sheridan Wave club.

According to one report in the Daily News, Boss McLaughlin, previously mentioned as having threatened Lingle for the latter's refusal to intercede with the police in getting an okey on another gambling place, had been engaged by the Moran gang to make a satisfactory contact with the state's attorney's office.

Then, as this Daily News report has it, Josephs and Kaufman, went to a police official, whose name is withheld, and said:

"We have the O.K. from the west side. How about you?"

"It's all right if Lingle is cut in," was the reply, if this published report is authentic.

Then, so the rumor runs, Lingle is supposed to have called upon Josephs and Kaufman and demanded 50 per cent of the profits, Kaufman violently refused, the report has it, and the place was not opened.

According to another report, this in the Chicago Herald &

Examiner, Lingle demanded $15,000 in cash from the two gambler promoters, and when this supposed demand was refused, Lingle is reported in this rumor to have replied that, "if this joint is opened up, you'll see more squad cars in front ready to raid it, than you ever saw in your life before."

The grand opening of the Sheridan Wave club had been extensively advertised, in sporting circles, as to take place the night of June 9, Lingle was murdered that day. The place did not open on that night.

Three days before the murder, according to the Herald & Examiner, the detectives on the staff of State's Attorney Swanson, at the direction of Investigator Roche, had raided the Biltmore Athletic Club, 2021 West Division street, another supposed gambling house. (Author's Note: This address is in Aiello territory.)

Within an hour after the raid, Lingle was seeking frantically to talk with Roche over the telephone. Roche refused to talk with Lingle, it is said, and the reporter met Roche the next day.

"You have put me in a terrible jam," Lingle told Roche, it is said. "I told that outfit they could run, but I didn't know they were going to go with such a bang."

Lingle knew he had enemies. Attorney Louis B. Piquett, former city prosecutor, related an incident that occurred Sunday, June 8th, twenty-four hours preceding the murder. Mr. Piquett said:

"As has been a habit with me, I came down to the Loop Sunday morning. While walking down Randolph Street, going east, I met Lingle, whom I know well. We talked of the murder of Eugene Red McLaughlin, whose body had been taken from the drainage canal on Saturday.

"Lingle was telling me his theory concerning the

slaying when a blue sedan with two men in it stopped at the curb alongside us. Lingle stopped in the middle of a sentence, looked up at the two men in a startled way and they looked back at him.

"He apparently had forgotten what he had been saying, for he turned suddenly, walked back the way he had come, hurriedly said 'Good-bye,' and entered a store as quickly as he could."

Leaving the Stevens Hotel about 10:30 Monday morning, June 9th, Lingle went first to Tribune Tower, chatted awhile with the boys in the local room, then departed to stroll Loopward. He dropped into a State Street department store and bought some haberdashery and a pair of shoes for the Board of Trade dinner. He had luncheon in the coffee shop of the Sherman Hotel, at Clark and Randolph streets. He had been eating there for years. Finished with his meal, he strolled into the lobby. He met Sergeant Thomas Alcock of the detective bureau, and said to him:

"I'm being tailed."

Unaccompanied, he left the Sherman, after buying a pocketful of cigars, about 1:10 P. M. He had twenty minutes to catch his train for the Washington Park track, it being scheduled to leave at 1:30. Heading east in Randolph Street, he began the four block walk to Michigan Avenue, a north and south thoroughfare. On the southwest corner of the avenue, in the lee of the Chicago Public Library, he would enter the pedestrian subway, and cross through it to the Illinois Central suburban electric railroad on the east side of the avenue, in Grant Park. This subway is about 100 feet long and 20 feet wide. Steps lead down into it at the west entrance, but at the east where Lingle would emerge, it slopes upward, ramp fashion, giving on to a sidewalk that extends to the station.

The humor or whatever it is that guides gangland in selecting its execution sites is ghastly beyond words. Here was one nearly as public as that chosen for the assassination of Lombardo. Here the in and outgoing currents of traffic bottleneck; surge, and eddy in near confluence as they pursue their opposite courses. At high tide, in rush hours it is a series of human whirlpools and maelstroms. It was, relatively, as if the assassins had picked Times Square subway station.

Death was close to Jake now as the next second, Zuta, or whoever had planned the job of rubbing him out, had planned it cunningly. Whoever it was had to know Lingle; had to know his habits and way of thought; had to know enough to outsmart him; to frame a trap he would walk into. For here was one to whom killers' tricks were only another yawn.

Six, possibly nine, even a dozen men may have participated. Through the stories of witnesses one can partly reconstruct their rôles. A lookout lounged at the east exit. Two or three, idlers to the casual eye, walked post near the Illinois Central station. These probably knew the city's plainclothes men on sight. Across the avenue, on the west, the trap called for three men in a roadster. In the subway, after the killing, was one in the vestments of a priest. What was his rôle? Overseer?

Somewhere, between the Sherman and Michigan Avenue, two of the death crew—or so they seem to have been—hailed the victim. They were walking with him when he arrived at the west entrance of the subway. One of these wore a sailor straw hat, and a medium shade gray suit. He was five feet, ten inches in height; weight, 160 pounds; age 27 to 32 years; blond hair. And later he dropped, in his flight, a silk glove for the left hand, a precaution evidently against fingerprints on the gun he threw away. One remembers Mrs. Bonner's words, "A blond haired man, who was drunk and held his gun in his left hand." The other was five feet, eight inches in height; weight, 150 pounds; age 35 years. He wore a dark blue suit and had dark hair.

Lingle walks between these two. Arrived at the entrance he buys a Racing Form. A roadster darts up to the curb, on the south side of Randolph Street, in front of the public library steps. Its horn is blowing to attract Lingle's attention. That much was seen by Armour Lapansee, a superintendent for the Yellow Cab company. He told the police:

"Three men were in the roadster. Two other men apparently were with Lingle. One of the men in the roadster called to Lingle:

" 'Play Hy Schneider in the third!'

"Lingle waved his hand and grinned, and replied, 'I've got him.'

" 'He walked down the steps into the subway. A few seconds later I heard the shot."

Play Hy Schneider!

Was that "the finger"? Or was it a signal to the death crew, that Lingle was alone; no friends near?

Mechanically puffing his cigar, holding the Racing Form outspread, Lingle entered the subway. He walked slowly, oblivious to people. Dr. Joseph Springer, a former coroner's physician and a friend of long standing, passed him. He was headed west. Lingle didn't see him.

"He was reading the race information," said Dr. Springer. "He was holding it before him with both hands and smoking a cigar."

Lingle was almost out of the subway. He had passed under the avenue, and was within 25 feet of the east exit. There is, as one approaches the exit, a stairway from the right side of the subway up to the sidewalk on the east side of the avenue. At the foot of the stairway is a news stand. As Lingle came abreast of, and passed this news stand, the dark man with him stopped as if to buy a newspaper. As he did, the blond man dropped behind Lingle; his left hand, holding the .38 snub-barreled Colt shot forward, and as the muzzle grazed the back of Lingle's neck, he fired a single bullet. It ranged upward, into the brain to come out the forehead. Lingle pitched forward on his face— his half smoked cigar between his teeth, the Racing Form clutched in his hands. Death was instantaneous.

The blond killer first ran west, then doubled back, past Lingle's body, and ran out through the east exit. He hurdled a fence, and again doubled his course to return to Michigan Avenue. He crossed it, ran west in Randolph Street to an alley that angles into Wabash Avenue. He turned into this alley, and was soon lost in the Wabash Avenue crowds. Traffic Policeman Anthony Ruthy, stationed at Randolph and Michigan, responding to a woman's cry of, "Get that man," pursued him to Wabash Avenue, but was outdistanced. The left handed glove discarded in the alley was picked up by Harry Komen, 1506 South 60th Street.

In the subway immediately after assassination, Patrick Campbell of 6840 Essex Avenue saw the dark haired man running toward the west entrance, and strangely enough, as Campbell involuntarily quickened his own pace, "a priest bumped into me. I asked him, 'What's the matter?' and he answered, 'I think some one has been shot, and I am going to get out of here.' "

"No," said Lieutenant William Cusack of the detective bureau, "he was no priest. A priest would never do that. He would have gone to the side of the stricken person."

The gods were kind to Jake. He died as he had lived —on the sidewalks of Chicago. The end of the trail was the end of the Rialto he had strolled for 20 years. In his ears was the roar of the Loop. About him the milling crowds. Above him his old buddies, the skyscrapers.

End of the trail? Or is it the beginning? Is it that he is out there, somewhere, on that assignment—the embers of the cigar glowing—becoming brighter—brighter—illuminating dark places—shining—gleaming—a beacon—until some night, as editors and copy readers go marching down to put the home edition to bed, the city desk phone will ring, and Tony Steger shall answer it? And a voice shall ask:

"Anything doin', Tony?"

And Tony, sitting there under the serene gaze of

Durkin—Tribune tradition—will lift his strident basso profundo to a pitch to be heard from all the housetops:

"Okey, Jake."

PART SEVEN

"**D**URING the last two years I've been trying to get out, but once in the racket you're always in. The parasites trail you wherever you go, begging for favors and money, and you can never get away from them—no matter where you go.

"You fear death every moment. Worse than death, you fear the rats of the game, who would run and tell the police if you didn't constantly satisfy them with favors. I never was able to leave my home without a bodyguard."

General Al the Scarface, puffing away at a fat cigar, was sitting in the office of Major Lemuel B. Schofield, director of public safety of Philadelphia, relating the success story of a gangster. It was midnight of May 16, 1929. He and his bodyguard, Slippery Frank Rio, stealthy visitors in Boo-Boo Hoff's home town, had been pinched for gun-toting as they left a movie theater. They were to be sentenced to serve a year in prison, but they did not know that yet.

"I haven't had peace of mind in years," Capone was saying. "I never know when I'm going to get it. Even when I'm on a peace errand, I take a chance on the light going suddenly out. I must hide from the rest of the racketeers to the point of concealing my identity under an assumed name, in hotels and elsewhere, when traveling.

325

"I have a wife and an eleven-year-old boy I idolize, at Palm Island, Florida. If I could go there and forget it all, I would be the happiest man in the world. I want peace, and I'm willing to live and let live. I'm tired of gang murders and gang shootings."

For a week he had been sequestered at the President Hotel, Atlantic City, talking shop with other Chicago gangsters. There had been, at his suggestion, a new truce, a disarmament conference. There was to be no more bloodshed, no more machine gunning. All the delegates had "signed on the dotted line" in a defensive alliance against their common enemies, the stool pigeons and the police.

Apparently, after nearly three years, Maxie Eisen's sage wisecrack, "We're a bunch of saps killing each other, and giving the cops a laugh," had penetrated.

Corporation efficiency methods were to be applied to the industry of booze, rackets, vice, and gambling. An executive council had been organized, with Johnny Torrio as chairman of the board.

"What are you doing now, Al?" queried Major Schofield.

"I'm retired."

He meant he was trying to retire.

"I asked him," said the major, "if there was any connection between the Philadelphia and Chicago liquor rings, and he answered smilingly, 'Well, there are connections, of course. The situation as revealed by the grand jury of this city [Philadelphia], bad as it was, was nothing to compare to Chicago.'"

Capone's presence in Philadelphia has never been satisfactorily explained. So far as Chicago was concerned he had been A.W.O.L. for ten days, had dropped from sight as completely as if the earth had yawned and swallowed him.

"Three of my friends have been bumped off in the last two weeks," he told Major Schofield.

"From reports I received," said Mayor Harry A. Mackey of Philadelphia, "Capone was running away from a gang which was out to kill him."

Al, his bodyguard, and his $50,000 eleven and one-half carat diamond ring spent the night under lock and key, to breakfast the next morning on boloney, dry bread, and coffee; then to appear at the detective bureau for scrutiny and questioning by Captain Andrew Emanuel and his squad.

"You are charged with being a suspicious character and with carrying concealed deadly weapons," said Captain Emanuel. "What have you to say?"

"Oh, nothing, nothing," and Al laughed.

"Were you ever arrested before?"

"Once before."

"For what?"

"For carrying concealed weapons, in Joliet, Illinois. I was discharged."

"Do any time?"

"No."

"Weren't you arrested in New York?"

"Yes, eighteen years ago—pardon me; I'm a little twisted. I guess I'm not fully awake. I was arrested in New York about three or four years ago. I was picked up there on suspicion of murder, but I was discharged. I was also arrested in Olean, New York, on a disorderly conduct charge, but I was discharged."

"You have never done any time, anywhere?"

"No, not a minute."

Within sixteen and a half hours after their arrest, Capone and Rio were on their way to begin serving their year's prison term—Capone to become No. 90725 at Holmesburg County jail and later No. 5527-C at Eastern Penitentiary. He and his counsel had not reckoned on the ideas of magisterial duty of Judge John E. Walsh of the criminal division of the municipal court. They had entered pleas of guilty to the gun-toting charge with the expectation of a three months' sentence. Capone was astounded.

Back in Chicago, Police Commissioner William F. Russell (the title of chief had been abolished) was grinning as broadly as if he had made the hole-in-one club.

"That's certainly great news," he was telling everybody.

John Stege, his able deputy commissioner, was explaining a fundamental reason for the helplessness of the police against gangsters with political drags and money to retain high-pressure lawyers:

"I've arrested Capone a half-dozen times, and each time found guns on him. The same goes for a hundred other gangsters around town. But what happens?

"The minute you get them before a municipal court judge, the defense attorney makes a motion to suppress the evidence. The policeman is cross-examined, and if he admits he didn't have a warrant for the man's arrest on a charge of carrying concealed weapons, the judge declares the arrest illegal and the hoodlum is discharged.

"The law should be changed so that a policeman won't have to have a warrant—which would be so radical an innovation as to be practically impossible—to arrest notorious gangsters who infest the city's streets with their guns in armpit holsters or side pockets, ready to shoot at the slightest provocation."

Much had happened since Capone had gone A.W.O.L. Gangland justice, swift, merciless, but retributive, had rid the State's attorney's docket of the Scalise indictment in the Moran case—seven charges of murder—by ridding the world of Scalise, and of Albert Anselmi and Joseph Guinta at the same time.

The farewell to arms of this trio of inseparables was lurid melodrama. They were put on the spot by their own crowd at a private dinner presumably given in their honor, if the story the underworld pipe-line finally delivered is reliable, and it generally is. The means they had so often employed with their victims was used against them—the simulated brotherly love, the unctuous guile of the smiling lip and lying tongue.

The reader is sufficiently acquainted with Scalise and Anselmi, dubbed the Homicide Squad. He has seen them taking the unsuspecting Mike Genna for a ride, battling the police, killing Officers Harold F. Olson and Charles B. Walsh. He has heard them named in the O'Banion, Weiss, and Moran cases.

Guinta, like them a torpedo, was a Brooklynite, a Uale man, in 1925, when Antonio Lombardo brought him to Chicago to help run the Unione Sicilione. Lombardo had not yet quarreled with the Aiellos, and Capone was still friendly with Uale. Guinta was to promote good-will for the new president and keep the home stills burning. He made himself indispensable to Lombardo and popular with the Sicilians. Sharp-witted, glib, ingratiating, he was an easy mixer in the social and business life of the colony.

His jaunty temerity pleased the men, and his smirking flattery the women. He was single and twenty-two. An unappeasable yen for dancing possessed him. The confraternity marveled that his feet did not blister. He was jazz mad. His elegant little person, compact of gimp and muscle, was, when inspirited by the grape and the ululating saxophone, motion lyricized. His zeal was dionysiac. He was bacchanalian. Few were the evenings he was not stepping in tuxedo and pumps at cabaret or night club—unless the Sicilians happened to be giving an affair. The underworld called him the "Hop Toad."

His following was so strong by 1929 that when Pasqualino Lolordo was killed in January of that year, he succeeded him—the fifth president of the Unione since Mike Merlo's death in 1924. For Guinta, as for his predecessors, the office represented the fulfillment of ambition—the reward of years of plotting, bickering, and intriguing. For him, as for the others, the fact that occupancy of it was about as safe as sitting on a keg of gunpowder with a lighted fuse attached made no difference.

The bullet-plugged bodies of Scalise, Anselmi, and Guinta were found early Wednesday morning, May 8, 1929, twenty miles southeast of the Loop, across the Illinois State line, in Indiana, near Wolf Lake, in the town of Hammond. Those of Scalise and Guinta were in the rear seat of an abandoned car, which had been nosed into a ditch. That of Anselmi lay twenty feet away. Each had been severely beaten before being shot.

Surmise dallied for weeks with this case, which, as the reader will note, was outside the jurisdiction of the Chicago and Cook County authorities. The pipe-line story was that the three had been guilty of treachery; that they had conspired to seize control of the $60,000,-000-a-year liquor monopoly, and, with Guinta bossing the Unione, rule as a triumvirate; that Scalise had offered a Capone gunman $50,000 to kill the Scarface.

Rash Scalise. Better punks than he had incurred inquests trying that.

Gangland's humor is ghastly and sardonic. No truer example of it can be cited than the seating of the scheming torpedoes as guests of honor at what was to be their last meal on earth. The dinner was said to have been held in a Torrio roadhouse, near Hammond, and to have been allowed to proceed to a bibulous and roistering end before the toastmaster rose, bowed to the guests, and said:

"This is the way we deal with traitors "

In one-two-three order, Scalise, Anselmi, and Guinta were bludgeoned with what is described as a sawed-off baseball bat, and then shot to death as they sat in their chairs.

Dr. Eli S. Jones, conducting a post-mortem for the Lake County coroner, partly confirmed the story in his report that "the three men apparently were seated at a table when their killers surprised them. Scalise threw up his hand to cover his face and a bullet cut off his little finger, crashing into his eye. Another bullet crashed into his jaw and he fell from his chair.

"Meanwhile, the other killers—there must have been three or four—had fired on Guinta and Anselmi, disabling them. Anselmi's right arm was broken by a bullet. When their victims fell to the floor, their assailants stood over them and fired several shots into their backs."

No indictments were ever voted in this case.

"You can figure out gangdom's murders and attempted murders with pencil and paper, but not with a judge and jury," observed Deputy Commissioner Stege.

The bodies of Scalise and Anselmi were shipped to Sicily, but Guinta was buried in Mount Carmel Cemetery, in his tuxedo and dancing pumps.

The police theory is that Capone in Philadelphia was fleeing Sicilian vengeance, which coincides with the information received by Mayor Mackey of that city that he "was running away from a gang that was out to kill him." He was eager to save his skin; to "go in a hole" for a while; otherwise he would have fought the gun-toting charge. He had been advised that the best strategy was to "take a rap," but, as one of his associates remarked after Judge Walsh had imposed sentence:

"Al figured on taking a rap and he took a kayo."

The benign providence that had fostered the Capone career from the bouncer days of the Four Deuces exerted its ubiquitous influence in prison. He and Rio were soon transferred from the Holmesburg jail, which has a reputation for rigorous discipline, to Eastern Penitentiary, where Al had his own cell and was permitted to make long-distance telephone calls and to use the warden's office for transacting business with his attorneys, Bernard Lemisch and Congressman Benjamin M. Golder of Philadelphia.

Regular trips East to confer with them were made by his chief aides—Jack Guzik, Frank Nitti, Mike Carozza of the Street Cleaners' Union, and Al's brother, Ralph Bottles Capone. The conferences were held sometimes in Mr. Lemisch's offices, sometimes at Atlantic City. Johnny Torrio commuted by plane twice a month to Chicago from Brooklyn, in which latter city he had settled permanently, finding its climate more salubrious than that of Chicago.

Al's status in the commonwealth was attested by his counsel in the efforts to regain his freedom. Only the most expensive Latin words and phrases—like "prothonotary" and "coram nobis"—were used in the petitions, something no lawyer does unless the fee is proper and the client important.

Al's geniality, his boundless sympathy for the unfortunate and the under-dog, and his Uncle Bim munificence, won the instant esteem of the penitentiary inmates. His first act was to buy $1,000 worth of their handiwork—inlaid boxes, ship models, cigarette cases, figurines, and other such trinkets. These he mailed to acquaintances about the country. Someone told him of a Philadelphia orphanage in rather straitened circumstances, and he sent it $1,200. At Christmas time he was the life of the party for the gray-clad humans who are no longer men, but numbers.

Yes, Al made friends, among them Dr. Herbert M.

Goddard of the Pennsylvania State Board of prison inspectors, who removed his tonsils and operated on his nose.

"I can't believe all they say of him," declared the doctor, a few days before Capone's release. "In my seven years' experience, I have never seen a prisoner so kind, cheery, and accommodating. He does his work—that of file clerk—faithfully and with a high degree of intelligence. He has brains. He would have made good anywhere, at anything.

"He has been an ideal prisoner. I cannot estimate the money he has given away. Of course, we cannot inquire where he gets it. He's in the racket. He admits it.

"But you can't tell me he's all bad, after I have seen him many times a week for ten months, and seen him with his wife and his boy and mother."

Perhaps a sociologist of speculative bent would apply the Dr. Jekyll-Mr. Hyde parallel to Capone—only in the objective instead of the subjective sense; that is to say, he might conceive of a personal Capone, and a police Capone, "and never the twain shall meet." He would find in the personal Capone a man much maligned—a wholly delightful fellow, who could talk interestingly of many things, not the least of them grand opera; whose heart is as big as all outdoors; whose way through life has been strewn with deeds of kindness for the sick and needy.

Be that as it may, Al's stay in Eastern Penitentiary, whether or not he realized it, was the happiest period of his career. In the circumscribed world of its stone walls, in his convict's garb, he won the freedom he had so long desired—freedom from fear of "the light's going suddenly out." He had peace of mind. He could sleep nights.

A statement he made to an official has a bearing on this story. It was that he had established connection with booze-running rings in Philadelphia, Atlantic City, and New York City, to interlink with his Chicago and Detroit organizations. The reader will recall that this project was outlined in the description of Francesco Uale.

A further substantiation of it came from former Police Commissioner Richard E. Enright of New York City, in a reference during his campaign for mayor in the fall of 1929.

"The principal Capone lieutenant here," he said, "operates five trucks, nine limousines, and two boats in bootlegging activities. In some instances, police ride the beer trucks to protect them from hijackers."

The one prominent captain of industry who not only has no press agent, but shrinks from publicity as diffidently as the violet by its mossy stone, Al, even in prison, was denied the boon of remaining half hidden from the eye. The pitiless spot was kept turned full upon him, whenever possible. Thus:

"CAPONE GAINS ELEVEN POUNDS"

"CAPONE RESIGNED: WON'T ASK PARDON"

"CAPONE READS LIFE OF NAPOLEON"

"CAPONE DOESN'T GO TO CHURCH ON SUNDAY"

"CAPONE PICKS CUBS TO WIN 1930 FLAG"

A newspaper sent a reporter to investigate an exclusive tip that he had bought a second-hand ship from the Government, paying $150,000 cash; that he was having it remodeled and refitted as a seagoing restaurant and cabaret, to be anchored off the Florida coast, beyond the twelve-mile limit; that he had retained the "best chef" in Philadelphia; and that he would have two seaplanes to carry cash customers from prohibition to champagne dinners in two minutes. The reporter couldn't verify it.

"Too beautiful to be true, anyway," commented the philosophical editor.

The hoodlum of 1920 had become page-one news, copy for the magazines, material for talkie plots and vaudeville gags. Jack Dempsey had shaken hands with him. McCutcheon had cartooned him.

Chicago's Exhibit A had become America's Exhibit A. Al had grown from civic to national stature. He was an institution. He had been put in the family album of notabilia, with its diversified Americana:

Will Rogers.
Henry Ford.
Rin Tin Tin.
Childs.
One-Eyed Connolly.
Jimmy Walker.
Mabel Willebrandt.
Babe Ruth.
O. O. McIntyre.
Senator Heflin.
Farm Relief.
Arthur Brisbane.
California Climate.
Blood Pressure.
The 4 Marxes.

Lindbergh.
Doug and Mary.
Congress.
Tex Guinan.
Forty-second and Broadway.
Cal.
White Rock.
Bromo Seltzer and The Specialist.
Al Smith.

Al had outlasted four chiefs of police, two municipal administrations, three United States district attorneys, and a regiment of Federal prohibition agents; he had survived innumerable crime drives, grand jury investigations, reform crusades, clean-up election campaigns, police shake-ups, and Congressional inquiries and debates. He was like the man in the repetitive poem:

> The battle of the Nile,
> I was there all the while,
> I was there all the while,
> At the battle of the Nile,
> The battle of the Nile,
> I was there all the while,
> I was . . .

His truce and disarmament conference did not function as advertised. There were some thirty gangster killings in 1929, and in the spring of 1930, John Dingbat O'Berta, bantam pal of Polack Joe Saltis, rounded out his little crowded hour. Once again the former Mrs. Big Tim was in mourning, the crape band on her bonnet signifying her second service-stripe in the bootleg-racketeer war.

For the genesis of his passing we must visit the German Deaconess Hospital, where, on the night of February 24th, in a flower-banked room, lay Frank McErlane, recovering from a fracture of the right leg, caused by a bullet above the knee. He had been there since January 28th. The leg, suspended in midair by weights and pulleys, was encased in a plaster cast.

McErlane, rated a dangerous gunman, has been named nine times by the coroner in gangster killings. He was tried for murder in Indiana, and acquitted. He was indicted in the George Spot Bucher-Georgia Meeghan double killing, but the charges were dismissed. He was originally allied with Saltis in that Balkans of prohibition Chicago, the back of the yards district, but they quarreled over profits and became bitter enemies, McErlane enlisting with the South Side O'Donnells— or what was left of them.

On this February night, about 10:30 o'clock, while his nurse was absent from the room, which is on the second floor, two men entered and opened fire. McErlane, bound rigidly to the bed as in a vise, drew a .38 from under his pillow and replied with five bullets, splintering a panel of the door. The intruders emptied their revolvers at him and fled. Their aim was poor. They scored only three hits, wounding him painfully, but not fatally.

"Who were they?" McErlane was asked.

"Shoo, shoo! Just say the war's on again. It's been brewing since last November. You'll know all about it in two weeks."

Ten days, to be exact. The Dingbat and his chauffeur, Sam Malaga, were taken for a ride in his own Lincoln

sedan the night of Wednesday, March 5th. The killers
—three, apparently—had posed as friends, sitting in the
rear seat. They had used a sawed-off shotgun and revolvers with soft-nosed bullets.

The Dingbat had gone to his death fighting. He had
not had a chance to draw his .45 automatic, which,
cocked but with the safety set, and a clip of seven cartridges in the magazine, was found in his right outside
overcoat pocket. He had let the assassins have three
slugs, however, from his belly-gun, before he dropped.
This weapon was a .38, with the barrel sawed down
to one-inch length, and its purpose explains its name.
It was for thrusting into a foeman's abdomen quietly
and unobtrusively when occasion demanded. He carried it in a trick holder, inside his left sleeve, for a
lightning draw.

Fifteen thousand back-of-the-yards folks attended
the Dingbat's two-day wake—and a grand one it was—
and followed his casket to Holy Sepulchre Cemetery,
where the stately, blonde, and dimpled Widow Murphy-
O'Berta had it placed next the grave of her six-foot-four
Big Tim. She and the Dingbat had first met in June of
1928, when he was a pallbearer at Big Tim's funeral.
The two men sleep side by side, in the hands of each his
rosary.

"They were good men," said the Widow Murphy-
O'Berta.

Hustling papers when he was eight to support his
widowed mother; soaking up guttersnipe wisdom; learning the law of the street and the alley, that might with
the fist makes right; fifteen when the United States
entered the World War; eighteen when back of the

yards began buzzing with talk of the new big dough racket—a cinch—just peddling beer to neighborhood saloons. About that time he met Joe Saltis.

As a specimen of the bootleg clinic, the Dingbat was a rara avis. Chicago will not look upon his busy like again. In his multifarious activities, we see him as honorary member of Post No. 1489 of the Veterans of Foreign Wars—"a testimonial banquet to Comrade O'Berta."

We see him as the rising young politician, entertaining, with that large flourish peculiar to him, the constituency at outdoor parties at Justice Park—free hot dogs, free drinks, free everything—another "testimonial picnic to our leading citizen, the People's Candidate."

We see him as the civic patriot, earnestly haranguing the Stockyards' Business Men's Association at a noonday luncheon, urging the need for public improvements of the district, assuring them, "I will see that Ashland Avenue is widened."

We see him in riding togs on the bridle paths of Hot Springs, Arkansas; in plus fours and Scotch tweed cap on the links around Chicago—golf clubs slung over shoulder, belly-gun handy in its trick holder in the left sleeve.

We see him thrown in the can time and again by the cops as hoodlum and thug; we see him running for State senator, for alderman, for Republican committeeman of the Thirteenth Ward—he would have run for mayor if he had felt that way.

The Dingbat was gorgeous satire, caricature, burlesque. All the futility of life's fret and strut was in him.

In the Pineapple Primary campaign of April, 1928, he was elected ward committeeman, his principal opponent being Hugh Norris, America First candidate. He served until a few days before his death, when a court decision, sustaining charges of polls terrorism and fraudulent voting, awarded the office to Norris.

For almost a year, though, the Dingbat sat with his peers on the Cook County Republican central committee—sat with him, but not as one of them. He was snubbed, ostracized, ignored. The pious brethren—the majority of them Homer K. Galpin's old mates—were distressed and scandalized and pained beyond measure that this gangster person should have been admitted to their councils. They drew in the skirts of their garments and passed him with averted eyes. It was a contretemps for François Villon's pen.

Joe Saltis was absent from the city when the Dingbat was killed. Deputy Commissioner Stege had "put the heat" on for him. Could he come back?

"I want to go to his funeral. I picked O'Berta up as a newsboy and made a man of him."

"You'll have to report to me if you do," was Stege's ultimatum. "I want to talk with you."

Stege decided that the moment was opportune to talk also with George Bugs Moran and Spike O'Donnell —to hold a reunion, as it were, of the Veterans of Local Wars.

Wherefore, on Monday, March 10th, Stege drew up chairs for the Messrs. Saltis, Moran, and O'Donnell.

Said Polack Joe:

"I got a fine country home and farm at Saltisville, on Barker Lake, Wisconsin. I'm out of the racket. I got mine all in a pile and I got $100,000 sunk in my farm—a nine-hole golf course, a clubhouse that sleeps twenty-six people, ponies, deer, plenty of fishing."

"How come the place is named Saltisville?" queried Stege.

"I named it," explained Joe. "It's honorary now, but we're going to make it stick. You see, there are only sixty-two voters in the township, and I got twenty-six of them working for me. I'm going to hire five more, which will give me majority control. At the election this spring when we ballot on it, I'll have enough to put it across. What I want is for my kids to be able to look in the United States Postal Guide and see their town, Saltisville. Okey, chief?"

Okey. Joe was one up on Capone. Miami hadn't even named a street for Al.

George Bugs' turn next. Said he:

"I'm in the cleaning and dyeing business. I've got $125,000 invested. I've been made president of the Central Cleaners and Dyers Association."

Straight as a poker for all his years, Spike O'Donnell then spoke his piece—Spike, for whom six State senators, five State representatives, and a judge of the criminal court of Cook County had interceded with a governor for a parole. Said he:

"Don't you know, chief? I'm in the fuel business now. I got $50,000 sunk in it. Why, I deliver coal right here to the detective bureau and to the City Hall and the County Building."

The reunion adjourned sine die.

Certain other oddities, ironies, irrelevancies—call

them what you will—divert the looker-on in prohibition Chicago:

Mrs. Eleanor Weber, filing suit for divorce against State Representative Charles H. Weber of the sixth district, on the Northwest Side, the city, listing as assets:

1 brewery at 2922 Southport Avenue.
1 gambling house at 2924 Southport Avenue.
1 speakeasy at 2924 Southport Avenue.
1 roadhouse in Irving Park Boulevard.
1 Rolls-Royce automobile.
1 Minerva automobile.
1 yacht valued at $65,000.
1 speedboat valued at $25,000.
1 speedboat valued at $16,000.

Mrs. Myrtle Tanner Blacklidge, collector of internal revenue, trying to collect $500,000 in back income taxes from Terry Druggan and Frankie Lake of the Cook County beerage; driving to Terry's palatial Sonola Farm, near Lake Zurich, Illinois, to slap a lien on it; learning it was in Terry's mamma's name; that all Terry owned was the cows. "You can have the cows," said Terry, but Mrs. Blacklidge couldn't use the cows. Next move, a lien on the Druggan-Lake brewery, at 1225 South Campbell Avenue—the idea being that the Government could auction it off and net a pretty penny. It auctioned it. Nobody bid. The Government bought it in for $1. Representing Druggan now was William F. Waugh, in 1924 an assistant United States district attorney.

Congressman M. Alfred Michaelson of Chicago, who

votes dry and has Anti-Saloon League support, returning from Cuba with six trunks—all passed at Key West
without customs inspection—one of which springs a
leak and is found to contain thirteen bottles of liquor.

State Street; a mile of bootlegging auxiliaries; the
window displays of its great stores and shops, especially during the holidays, presenting a congeries of
cocktail shakers, silver hip flasks, hollow canes, and
other subterfuge devices, wine sets, decanters, decorative whiskey kegs, home-brew outfits, etc.; a violation
of the spirit of the law as flagrant as if the merchants
sold, say, opium-smoking outfits, but having the sanc-
tion of public opinion—and public demand.

Chicago's high schools, around which speakeasies
thrive. They have been the objects of crusades and
police activities, but they mushroom back again, in their
various guises as sandwich counters, stationery stores,
soda fountains, and tearooms. They cater exclusively to
the students, boys and girls. One investigation uncovered five near Senn High School; six near Hyde Park
High School, and six near Englewood High School. The
three are outstanding as representative institutions of
their kind.

Evanston, birthplace and national headquarters of
the Woman's Christian Temperance Union, and home
of Charles G. Dawes, where gin may be purchased within
five minutes of the campus of Northwestern University
and moon is plentiful; where the hip flask has become
an appurtenance of class proms and fraternity and so-
rority dances and social affairs. Northwestern, situated
on the western shore of Lake Michigan, may be said to
be rimmed, crescent-wise, by booze joints—nests of

roadhouses easily reached on boulevard highways. Out Davis Street, a short ride from the Evanston High School, is a notorious petting farm, so called, patronized largely by the high-school students. A section of the first floor of the ramshackle dwelling has been equipped as a café, with a mechanical piano. Gin is sold. The café is generally empty, the patrons sitting in their cars, there being unlimited parking space in an old orchard.

These things we mention because they serve further to explain Capone, to mitigate him, and to remind many, many estimable citizens who go to church on Sunday, and who are wont to uplift their hands in sanctimonious horror at his name, that much of the phenomenon yclept Capone begins, like charity, at home.

Item: Less than one per cent of a thirtieth of Chicago's population commits its crime and perpetrates its predatory racketeering—with the collusion of crooked politicians. Chicago is a magnificent ship, sailing a steadfast course for its port of destiny—but with a few rats in the hold.

Capone, his sentence commuted to ten months for good behavior, left Eastern Penitentiary, Monday, March 17th, to receive a confidential request from influential Chicago friends to "lay low, and go easy. We're organizing for an important election campaign; we want to get set for World's Fair year."

The Capone picture is never in focus with the realities. They merge into it to lose their factual identities and regularities of form as in a side-show distortion mirror, then to leer back in preposterous travesty, hoaxing

345

reason and mocking the data of common sense. The picture is theatrical. It is Gilbert and Sullivan extravaganza without the music. The prison exit is typical. In some respects it outdoes the Count of Monte Cristo.

Dumas's opulent imagination could do no better for Edmund Dantes in his getaway from the dungeon in the Château d'If than to summon the aid of another felon. Capone, surreptitiously departing from his cell, with its $500 radio, its pair of easy chairs, its reading shelf, table, tufted rug, and other hotel comforts, had the co-operation of a warden, Herbert B. Smith, a governor, John S. Fisher, and the Philadelphia police department. Dantes went out stitched in a sack, Capone tucked in the rear seat of a motor car. Dantes was fleeing further penal servitude, which was logical; Capone was being spared the ordeal of curious stares and reportorial Q. and A., which was Gilbert and Sullivan.

Consider: The established procedure in discharging a convict from a penitentiary is to give him his new suit, and his gratuity—generally $5—swing open the gate and be rid of him. What befalls him then is his own worry. Capone was actually freed from Eastern Penitentiary twenty-four hours before the expiration of his sentence, smuggled out in the warden's automobile Sunday evening, and conveyed to Graters Ford, thirty miles distant, to await 4 o'clock of Monday afternoon.

An elaborate deception was practiced. Squads of city police patrolled the street in front of the prison, roping off a space for a block to keep the crowds back. Motorcycle police were stationed as if in readiness for a convoy. Bulletins were fed at intervals to the hungry and unsuspecting correspondents and newsreel men, telling of Capone's impatience, of the uncertainty as to when the commutation papers would arrive from Harrisburg, the capital—the governor had been late signing them; they had not been put in the mail for Philadelphia until Monday afternoon. As a matter of fact, Warden Smith had driven to Harrisburg and obtained the governor's signature, and the papers were in the hands of the secretary of the pardon and parole board.

The deception was maintained until 8 o'clock Monday night, thus allowing Capone a four-hour start in the game of hare and hounds with the gentlemen of the press, and seriously impairing their professional dignity. Warden Smith, standing beside the prison gate, broke the news in these words:

"We stuck one in your eye that time. The big guy's gone."

Committed as a gun-toting hoodlum, he had been discharged as a prisoner of state.

However much solicitude for Capone the individual may have been indicated in the unprecedented manner of his release, just as much undoubtedly was indicated for Capone the problem. That phase of him becomes increasingly evident—and increasingly embarrassing to the harassed authorities. It was attested in the Chicago welcome program, arranged by Deputy Commissioner Stege. For three days and nights—Tuesday, Wednesday, and Thursday—a detail of twenty-five officers was posted at his home, 7244 Prairie Avenue, in anticipation of his return. Of course he didn't return there. So what the vigil resolved itself into was a seventy-two hour surveillance of two women and a couple of children.

No indictments had been voted against Capone, no charges filed; his status was as it had always been. Stege, on the record in the Chicago and Cook County courts, was without warrant in law for molesting him. He could not have arrested him for disorderly conduct and made it stick. The wise Stege knew that. He did not have to be reminded by Thomas D. Nash of the highest-priced firm of criminal lawyers in town (and there is never an unemployment situation for such when Al's around), "My client has legal rights."

What then?

This: Al was the local bogey man. Somebody had to say boo.

Al was as painfully and resentfully conscious of Capone the problem—"Capone, the Nineteenth Amendment," as an English editor put it—as were the authorities:

"There's a lot of grief attached to this limelight."

The mad welter of circumstances that had combined to hoist him, Humpty Dumpty like, to the top of the bootleg wall, had also, it seemed, enmeshed him in a web of petty annoyances and troubles, from which he was powerless to extricate himself.

Clinging precariously to the wall, which more than five hundred men had tried to climb with fatal consequences, he was defiant:

"I'm not afraid of anybody."

And philosophical:

"I never had a number until they picked me up in Philadelphia for carrying a gun and gave me a year, not for carrying the gun, but because my name's Capone."

After an absence of ten months he was again seated at his mahogany desk in the spacious offices in the Lexington Hotel, 2135 South Michigan Avenue, the G.H.Q. having been moved from the Metropole. At his right was a French 'phone, which rang incessantly. In front of him was a gold-encrusted inkstand and a stack of mail a foot high.

"Letters," he explained. "Bugs and business."

Looking down on the inkstand were the pictures of two prominent wets—George Washington and William Hale Thompson. A beautifully carved Chinese chest stood hard by; above it a clock of intricate mechanism, with a quail to sound the quarter hours, and a cuckoo the hours. Al was in an expansive mood, discussing himself candidly. To quote verbatim:

"All I ever did was to sell beer and whiskey to our best people. All I ever did was to supply a demand that was pretty popular. Why, the very guys that make my trade good are the ones that yell loudest about me. Some of the leading judges use the stuff.

"They talk about me not being on the legitimate. Nobody's on the legit. You know that and so do they. Your brother or your father gets in a jam. What do you do? Do you sit back and let him go over the road, without trying to help him? You'd be a yellow dog if you did. Nobody's really on the legit when it comes down to cases.

"The funny part of the whole thing is that a man in this line of business has so much company. I mean his customers. If people did not want beer and wouldn't drink it, a fellow would be crazy for going around trying to sell it.

"I've seen gambling houses, too, in my travels, you understand, and I never saw anyone point a gun at a man and make him go in.

"I never heard of anyone being forced to go to a place to have some fun. I have read in the newspapers, though, of bank cashiers being put in cars, with pistols stuck in their slats, and taken to the bank, where they had to open the vault for the fellow with the gun.

"It really looks like taking a drink was worse than robbing a bank. Maybe I'm wrong. Maybe it is.

"People come here from out of town, and they expect when they're traveling around, having a good time, that they will take a little drink, or maybe go to a night club. They had better not get caught at it, because if they are—in the jug and see the judge the next morning."

Capone, his whereabouts page-one speculation for four days, had appeared at the detective bureau with his attorney, Mr. Nash, at 1:30 o'clock Friday afternoon, to inquire as to the hue and cry. Stege didn't want him, it seemed, Captain John Egan, chief of detectives, escorted him over to State's Attorney Swanson's office. He didn't want him. Neither did United States District Attorney Johnson. Later, perhaps, but not now.

"It's kind of hard trying to find out who wants me," mildly observed Al, as the afternoon waned.

Nobody wanted him, but the police had said boo.

Al was understanding:

"Egan couldn't help it; Stege couldn't help it. If they had let me come in and go about my business, there would have been plenty of people saying they were afraid of me. I made it easy for them. I was willing to face any charge anyone had to make, and come to find out, there wasn't any."

The bogey-man phase of Capone, largely a post-prison development, cast him in the rôle of archvillain in a miscellany of plots, schemes, and rackets. He was accused of pretty nearly every sinister activity of underworld origin. In all of which there was some truth, some politics, considerable hysteria, and an admission by the authorities of their inability to cope with Capone the problem. A few examples:

1. Capone was effecting a new gang combine. He had made peace with Joseph Aiello, now head of the Unione Sicilione. They were promoting a gambling syndicate of the city's bookmakers—some 5,000—who handle both horse-race and dog-track betting. Complete protection and immunity guaranteed.

2. Capone was maneuvering to establish himself as the Mussolini of organized labor. Already, among others, he dominated the Plumbers' Union, the Street Sweepers' Union, the Newsboys' Union, the City Hall Clerks' Union and the Marble Setters' Union.

3. Capone was ambitious to build a political machine and was seeking to wrest City Hall patronage from aldermen and members of the mayor's cabinet family. He was back of a proposal to appoint his henchman, City Sealer Daniel A. Serritella, city superintendent of streets—thus giving him control of an annual budget of $7,000,000, 3,000 jobs, and the supervision of $5,000,-000 a year in street repair work. He was author of an ordinance to create a plumbers' bureau, which would have put an additional 1,200 jobs at his disposal. Ser-

ritella, in the April primary of 1930 had been reëlected Republican committeeman of the First Ward, and had won the nomination of State senator over Adolph Marks, incumbent. The First, by the way, was the only ward in Chicago that returned a majority for United States Senator Deneen, in his losing contest with Ruth Hanna McCormick. Otherwise, Mrs. McCormick, a dry, was supported in the city and county by the "wetter than the middle of the Atlantic" Thompson-Crowe organization.

4. Easter Sunday three men were shot to death by a lone pistoleer in a speakeasy at 2900 South Wells Street—Walter L. Wakefield and Frank Delre, proprietors, and Joseph Special, waiter. Capone men, said the police; either politics or a labor feud. Wakefield had lined up the vote for Serritella at the primary election; Wakefield also had tried to muscle in on the Pie Wagon Drivers' Union, in accordance with Capone's design to be the big boss of organized labor.

"They've hung everything on me except the Chicago fire," was Al's retort.

The Chicago Crime Commission issued a blast proclaiming him and twenty-seven lesser booze gangsters "public enemies," and demanding that they be "treated accordingly." Tall words, but familiar through much repetition.

Frank Nitti of his executive staff had been indicted for failure to report a net income of $742,887.81 for 1925, 1926, and 1927.

Down in balmy Florida, Governor Doyle E. Carlton had notified each of the sixty-seven sheriffs of the State:

"It is reported that Al Capone is on his way to

Florida. Arrest promptly if he comes your way, and escort him to the State border. He cannot remain in Florida. If you need additional assistance call me."

The spectacle of the sixty-seven embattled sheriffs on guard to protect the playground commonwealth from our fellow townsman is as distinctly Gilbert and Sullivan as Warden Smith's skit at Eastern Penitentiary.

Al again put himself in the hands of his friends, the members of the bar. Attorneys J. F. Cordon and Vincent Giblin of Miami obtained a temporary injunction from Federal Judge Halsted L. Ritter, restraining the sheriffs from "seizing, arresting, kidnaping or abusing the plaintiff, Alphonse Capone," and he was enabled to return to his Palm Island villa. The injunction was eventually made permanent.

His chief gunner's mate, Jack McGurn, of the twenty-two odd notches, had been unceremoniously dragged off a Miami golf links by the police and jailed. They evidently were prejudiced by an incident that had occurred some weeks previously. Ernest Byfield, the hotel man, revealed it to Ashton Stevens, the dramatic critic and columnist, and Stevens labeled it, "the best Al Capone story of the season." To quote:

"Ernest Byfield is back from Miami. . . . Mr. Byfield and Mr. Capone occupy adjacent islands near Miami Beach, the hotel baron's Florida home being the isle called Hibiscus and the estate of the Chicago underworld overlord being on an isle named Palm.

"Well, workmen employed on Hibiscus recently ran with blanched faces to the contractor who employed them, and who is Mr. Byfield's next-door neighbor, ávowing that they were being peppered with bullets by invisible marksmen.

" 'Nonsense,' said the contractor—till they showed him the bullets. Then he got out his field glasses and . . . a merry band of machine gunners on Palm Island [were] shooting from the Capone place at empty pop bottles floating in the water. They were practicing in Florida the pastime that has done its bit to make Cook County famous.

"The contractor hastily informed the Miami Beach police that the Capone gang were shooting up the land and seascape with machine guns. The police department went into a clinch with itself. The outcome was that its chief telephoned the machine gunners and asked them—very politely—if they would not please find another direction and range."

McGurn's presence at their favorite spa outraged the civic patriotism of three distinguished and eminently broad-minded Chicagoans—Albert D. Lasker, former chairman of the United States Shipping Board, John D. Hertz, founder of the Yellow Cab Company, and Charles A. McCullough, president of the Parmelee Transfer Company. Deputy Commissioner Stege received peremptory notification via telegraph that it was their wish that McGurn be kept at home. Stege immediately sent Detectives John Howe and William Drury down to bring him back.

The stern city fathers of Miami had solemnly decreed, in effect:

"Here's your hat, Al; don't slam the door."

Tourists were getting timorous. Business men were

kicking at Miami's reputation as "the Cicero of the East Coast."

"And all I've ever done in Miami," said Capone, "was to spend my money there."

So did an ungrateful public bite the hand that fed it.

Poor little rich boy—the Horatio Alger lad of prohibition—the gamin from the sidewalks of New York, who made good in a Big Shot way in Chicago—General Al the Scarface, who won the war to make the world safe for public demand—Volstead's King for a Day—creature of the strangest, craziest fate, in the strangest, craziest era of American history.

The story ends—unfinished, like his life—the red thread still unspun by the gods amuck.

". . . you never know when the light's going suddenly out. . . ."

The story ends—and there he stands—waiting, watching, wondering . . .

The moving trigger-finger writes . . .